BEYOND REASON

MW00559138

THE LITTMAN LIBRARY OF
JEWISH CIVILIZATION

MANAGING EDITOR
Connie Webber

Dedicated to the memory of
LOUIS THOMAS SIDNEY LITTMAN
*who founded the Littman Library
for the love of God
and in memory of his father*
JOSEPH AARON LITTMAN
יהא זכרם ברוך

'*Get wisdom, get understanding:
Forsake her not and she shall preserve thee*'
PROV. 4: 5

*The Littman Library of Jewish Civilization is a registered UK charity
Registered charity no.* 1000784

BEYOND REASONABLE DOUBT

◆

LOUIS JACOBS

Oxford · Portland, Oregon
The Littman Library of Jewish Civilization

The Littman Library of Jewish Civilization
Chief Executive Officer: Ludo Craddock

PO Box 645, Oxford OX2 OUJ, UK

———

Published in the United States and Canada by
The Littman Library of Jewish Civilization
c/o ISBS, 920 N.E. 58th Avenue, Suite 300
Portland, Oregon 97213-3786

First published 1999
First issued in paperback 2004

© Louis Jacobs 1999, 2004

All rights reserved.
No part of this publication may be reproduced,
stored in a retrieval system, or transmitted, in any form or by
any means, without the prior permission in writing of
The Littman Library of Jewish Civilization

This book is sold subject to the condition that it shall not,
by way of trade or otherwise, be lent, re-sold, hired out or
otherwise circulated without the publisher's prior consent in any
form of binding or cover other than that in which it is published
and without a similar condition including this condition
being imposed on the subsequent purchaser

A catalogue record for this book is available from the British Library
The Library of Congress catalogued the hardback edition as follows:
Jacobs, Louis.
Beyond reasonable doubt / Louis Jacobs.
p.   cm.
Includes bibliographical references and index.
1. Judaism—Doctrines. 2. Judaism—20th century. I. Title.
BM601.J25 1999   296.3—dc21   99-10682 CIP
ISBN 1-904113-11-7

Publishing co-ordinator: Janet Moth
Design: Pete Russell, Faringdon, Oxon.
Copy-editing: Lindsey Taylor-Guthartz
Index: Bonnie Blackburn
Production manager: John Saunders
Typeset by Footnote Graphics, Warminster, Wilts.
Printed in Great Britain on acid-free paper by
MPG Books Ltd, Bodmin, Cornwall

To my children
IVOR, NAOMI, *and* DAVID

who steadfastly remained on their father's side
from their childhood, when it was comparatively easy,
through to adulthood, when it was rather more difficult.
It is good to know that they enjoy *naches* from their
children as I have from them.

Acknowledgements

Colette Littman, Director of the Littman Library founded by her husband Louis, with whom I was privileged to work from the day the Library was established, has been a constant source of encouragement. Colette persuaded me to write this book as an addition to the other books of mine published by the Littman Library. Connie Webber and Janet Moth have seen the book through to press with their customary skill and expertise. Lindsey Taylor-Guthartz not only did an excellent job of copy-editing but made many helpful suggestions for the improvement of the book. I am grateful to all of these friends.

Contents

ONE

INTRODUCTION
THE 'JACOBS AFFAIR'

IT IS NOW WELL OVER FORTY YEARS since my book *We Have Reason to Believe* was published, during which time the views on the nature of revelation expressed there have been criticized again and again; by the right for alleged heresy and by the left for failing to go far enough in the direction of liberalism. My aim in writing yet another book on the subject is to try to meet the arguments against a position I still maintain after all these years and which I now seek to defend in a systematic manner. It is for readers of this book to decide whether I have presented a case 'beyond reasonable doubt'.

The central thesis of this book is that traditional Judaism can be interpreted so as to render it compatible with the findings of modern research on how the Jewish religion has come to be. The application, by a host of scholars, Jewish as well as non-Jewish, of the historical critical methodology to the classical sources of traditional Judaism (particularly the Bible and the rabbinic literature) has demonstrated to the satisfaction of many believers that the Torah did not simply drop down, ready packaged, so to speak, from Heaven but has evolved over the ages, partly, at least, in response to, and influenced by, external conditions. Many religious Jews still hold fast to belief in the Torah as the word of God but have come to realize that the whole idea of divine revelation must be understood to mean, in the light of our present knowledge, that, while there is a divine element in the Torah, there is also a human element, in that God gives the Torah, as it has often been put, not only *to* the Jewish people but *through* the Jewish people. As I once formulated it, it is still possible to accept the dogma 'The Torah is from Heaven' provided one understands the meaning of 'from' in a more sophisticated manner than is commonly done.

The above brief statement hardly does justice to a very complex religious position, one which demands the more thorough investigation upon which this book embarks with trepidation. I believe that theology can and should be examined in a detached manner, but critics of my theological writings have argued that too impersonal statements in this area tend to give an impression of lack of concern. A committed Jew, so the argument runs, should not give expression to his beliefs as if he himself were not affected by them, as if he were talking about Chinese metaphysics or describing mathematical formulae. Now, for my sins and as will appear, I have been personally affected and intimately involved with this issue for over forty years, from the publication of my book *We Have Reason to Believe* and the trouble it caused that led to the so-called 'Jacobs Affair'. For me to treat the subject in an entirely dispassionate manner would be sheer pretence. I bow, therefore, to the criticism and first tell my own story in so far as it is relevant to the major theme of the book.

A speedy glance at the religious history of British Jewry (Anglo-Jewry as it is commonly called) is necessary in order to set the scene. By the start of the twentieth century, Jews were divided on religious lines into Orthodoxy and Reform (with Liberal Judaism emerging later as a left-wing offshoot of Reform). Orthodox, and a few Reform, congregations had been established in London and the provinces. With the influx of east European, and later German and Hungarian Jews, synagogues were founded to cater to their particular spiritual needs. Some of the small Russian, Polish, and Lithuanian congregations in London became organized as the Federation of Synagogues. To the right of the Federation in London were the Adas Israel congregations, established by Orthodox German Jews with a German background. There were also a small number of hasidic *shtiebels*. The oldest of the religious bodies in England was the Sephardi community, with its own traditions, under the religious leadership of a Haham. The major Orthodox institution was the United Synagogue, with the chief rabbi as its sole religious authority, established by Act of Parliament in 1870 but with its origins in Orthodox synagogues which had previously been independent. The office of chief rabbi originated in the rabbinate of the Great Synagogue in London, where Rabbi Salomon Hirschell was rabbi from 1801 until 1842. Hirschell, an imposing figure by all accounts, though born in England, was taken as a child to Germany. He was, by education and training, basically a rabbi of the old school, Yiddish-speaking and using only broken English to his dying day. Nevertheless, he was often referred to in the general press as 'the High Priest of the Jews', a foretaste of things to come.

It was Hirschell's successor, Nathan Marcus Adler (chief rabbi, 1845–90) and his son and successor Hermann Adler (chief rabbi, 1891–1911), who established the chief rabbinate in its peculiarly English form, fairly obviously modelled on the position of archbishop in the Anglican Church. It is rumoured that, at one time, Hermann Adler wore gaiters! One should not be too scathing about such conscious assimilation to the Christian pattern. Jews, prominent by this time in English political and social life, had a need to show non-Jews that they were respectably English. In any event, there was only adaptation in external matters, never, of course, in matters of Jewish dogma. Adler was succeeded by Joseph Herman Hertz (chief rabbi, 1913–46), Hertz by Israel Brodie (chief rabbi, 1948–65), and Brodie by Immanuel Jakobovits (chief rabbi, 1967–91). The present chief rabbi is Jonathan Sacks.

The right wing of Orthodox Jewry, strong in its piety, learning, and convictions but originally viewing the United Synagogue and the chief rabbinate with suspicion, began, not necessarily consciously, to influence these institutions and, eventually, to transform them. Sir Isaac Wolfson, president of the United Synagogue at the time of the 'Jacobs Affair', was a fully observant Jew, unlike his predecessors in that office, Sir Robert Waley-Cohen and the Hon. Ewen Montagu, who, though strong on traditionalism and giving yeoman service to the United Synagogue, were Orthodox in name only. In the first half of the twentieth century, each provincial synagogue had, in addition to the more 'foreign' type of congregations, its 'English shul' such as the Princes Road Synagogue in Liverpool, the Singers Hill Synagogue in Birmingham, and the Great Synagogue in Manchester, where my parents were married by Dr Salomon, a graduate of the Orthodox but Western-oriented Seminary in Berlin. Although nominally the chief rabbi was only, to give him his full title, 'chief rabbi of the United Hebrew Congregations of the British Empire' (later, 'the British Commonwealth'—here, again, the Anglican influence), in practice he was recognized by all the Orthodox congregations as their spiritual head. Even the Reform and Liberal congregations acknowledged the chief rabbi as their representative in religious matters to the outside world. At the time of writing, the non-Orthodox communities are attempting to distance themselves from the chief rabbinate. Whether they will succeed is anyone's guess. The point here, however, is that the chief rabbi's authority does not extend to the non-Orthodox who, for example, can appoint any rabbi they want without having to obtain the permission of the chief rabbi and who, in fact, never consult him for this purpose. How could they? In the chief rabbi's official eyes the Reform movement has no standing, and he can as little recognize Reform rabbis as rabbis as the pope can recognize Protestant clergymen as priests.

We Have Reason to Believe

To turn now to *We Have Reason to Believe*. The book, first published in 1957, had its origin in the study group I conducted for the young men and women of the New West End Synagogue, a member of the United Synagogue, where I had been appointed minister–preacher in 1954. At first, the title minister–preacher, in contradistinction to the minister–reader, the *ḥazan*, was a little disconcerting. As a former rabbi I asked myself whether the title minister did not belong to the clergy of the Methodist Church? But I soon came to appreciate that this Victorian arrangement, peculiar to Anglo-Jewry, was based on the notion that the United Synagogue only acknowledges a single spiritual head, the chief rabbi. The fiction was maintained that there were, in fact, no other rabbis, whether or not they had been ordained as such, than the chief rabbi, whose subordinates functioned as ministers, and I quickly adjusted myself to the odd situation, one advantage of which—if it is an advantage—was that I was relieved of the responsibility of coping with difficult problems and was able, like my fellow-ministers, to pass the buck to the chief rabbi. This whole system often came under fire from United Synagogue ministers since it tended to turn them into mere functionaries. For all that, the terms of employment were fairly satisfactory. The ministerial contract was not with the local congregation but with the United Synagogue. A minister had tenure, and provided he was not guilty of gross misconduct he could not be given the sack. Moreover, although his salary was far from princely, he was provided with adequate accommodation by the United Synagogue, on which alone, and not on the local honorary officers, he was dependent.

My colleague, the minister–reader the Reverend Raphael Levy, had an MA degree from Manchester University and was very erudite in purely Jewish subjects as well. While I, musically challenged, to use the current politically correct jargon, could never have functioned as a *ḥazan*, Raphael Levy was easily capable of donning the preacher's garb. While this set-up might conceivably have led to friction, as it did in some United Synagogue congregations, the relationship between us was, in fact, harmonious and it all worked well. Raphael never wished to occupy the pulpit, though he was capable of it, while I never aspired to the role of *ḥazan*, which was beyond me in any event. Raphael Levy, it should be said, was thoroughly at home with the musical and other traditions of the United Synagogue. When a young boy he was a chorister of the Great Synagogue in Duke's Place, the 'Cathedral' synagogue, as it was quaintly and popularly called, being the seat of the chief rabbi. It is interesting that Raphael Levy's son, Elkan, is at the time of writing president of the United Synagogue, making a brave attempt at preserving its mode of worship in the face of those of its members who prefer the informality and allegedly warmer atmosphere of the *shtiebel*. The middle way is fast disappearing. A good thing, some say, while others deplore the threatened disappearance of an elegance typical of a more refined and less clap-happy age.

Although the majority of congregations in the provinces also accepted the authority of the chief rabbi, it was an authority that sat lightly upon them, whereas in the United Synagogue, comprising some sixty congregations in London and Greater London, he was not only the chief rabbi but the only rabbi. This would have been of little moment, since the chief rabbi at the time of my appointment, Israel (later Sir Israel) Brodie was, in himself, far too liberal-minded and tolerant a man to wish to lord it over those he thought of as his colleagues rather than his subordinates. The trouble was that Chief Rabbi Brodie came increasingly under pressure from the *dayanim* of the London Beth Din, known in English as the 'Court of the Chief Rabbi'. Essentially, for a man to be appointed to the office of *dayan*, he was required to be competent in deciding matters of Jewish law. Traditionally, a *dayan* is a rabbi's assistant. Only in Anglo-Jewry, especially in the United Synagogue, did the title *dayan* come to be treated as superior to that of other rabbis except to that of chief rabbi. Learned judges though the *dayanim* of the London Beth Din undoubtedly were, they had neither the right, on paper at least, nor the ability to make pronouncements on matters of communal policy or religious dogma. Yet Chief Rabbi Brodie's deference to his right-wing *dayanim* often meant that it was their voice that was heard when the chief rabbi spoke on these matters. Chief Rabbi Brodie was a mild-mannered man too ready to yield to right-wing pressure. But even his predecessor, Dr Hertz, a fiery personality, of whom it was said that he preferred the way of peace if there was no alternative, had trouble from Dayan Yehezkel Abramsky, an equally spirited personality. It is rumoured that Dr Hertz once protested to the learned *dayan*: 'Rabbi Abramsky, you know more Talmud than I shall ever know. But please do not forget that I know many things you will never know.'

The religious complexion of the United Synagogue, nowadays, is of an Orthodoxy that borders on uncompromising and unquestioning ultra-Orthodoxy. But at the time of my induction as a minister of the New West End, though signs of the swing to the right could already be detected, it was of a far more tepid variety. For example, the New West End and other Anglicized synagogues had a mixed choir; there was mixed seating for weddings, though not for standard services, and, also at weddings only, an organ was played; the *ḥazan* recited only part of the Musaf service in order to avoid praying aloud for the actual restoration of sacrifices; the ministers sported clerical collars and wore canonicals for the services; and they rarely wore *yarmulkes* except for prayer and study—all practices which were anathema to the strictly Orthodox and most of which the United Synagogue has now abandoned. Fraternization with Reform rabbis was tolerated. There even existed an Association of Anglo-Jewish Preachers with both Orthodox and Reform members, who met regularly to exchange ideas for sermons and discuss general matters of communal concern.

Apart from the less rigid position of the United Synagogue as a whole at the time, the pulpit of the New West End had enjoyed much freedom under my predecessors, Simeon Singer of prayerbook fame, Joseph Hochman, and Ephraim Levine, none of whom would be classed as Orthodox in the present climate. Singer had studied for a time in Vienna with I. H. Weiss, a pioneer in the application of scholarly method to talmudic literature. Singer had obtained his *semikhah* ('ordination') from Weiss, though he was never allowed by Chief Rabbi Hermann Adler to call himself rabbi.

The Reverend Ephraim Levine, in his short booklet published on the fiftieth anniversary of the New West End Synagogue in 1929, gave this brief sketch of Singer, the first minister of the congregation:

Simeon Singer is still regarded as the ideal of an Anglo-Jewish Minister. His scholarship, both Jewish and secular, was of a high order. He had a very wide and penetrating knowledge of English and Foreign literature; he was a great and keen reader, gifted with a very retentive memory, able to draw upon his large storehouse of learning both for homiletic and for teaching purposes.

Speaking of Singer's religious attitude, Levine remarks:

His religious standpoint was conservative and progressive at the same time. By training and by practice he was conservative: he loved to maintain traditional Jewish custom: his intimate knowledge of the liturgy and its history served to keep alive his natural love for the old form of service and the traditional Prayer Book. He was progressive too, in that he recognized the ever-changing needs of the rising generation, and all his efforts were directed to fostering the love of the Synagogue in the hearts of the young. At the same time he never allowed them to lose sight of the fact that a healthy Jewish religious life must have its roots deep in tradition. He welcomed change where signs of life were evident: he espoused any cause that promised to strengthen Jewish allegiance: he even ran the risk of being misunderstood if he believed in a cause and its ultimate Jewish possibilities. His was a broad and catholic Judaism which won adherents from representatives of all shades of opinion. The man himself was true, and men put their trust in him.

This attitude prevailed at the New West End and was that of Ephraim Levine himself.

Not surprisingly, the New West End's traditional stance met with opposition from time to time on the part of the more progressive members of the congregation. In 1892 there took place the 'Battle of the Ritual'. The wardens at the time were Isidore Spielmann and Arthur Franklin, and the Board of Management, elected the previous year, contained some men who were known to favour religious progress. Ephraim Levine records in his booklet that a packed meeting fought out the question of alterations to the traditional service. The opposition on the part of the traditionalists was led by Samuel Montagu (later the first Lord Swaythling). Levine explains the issues involved:

The general plea was for the introduction of some English prayers, for the omission of one or two alleged obsolete passages from the liturgy, and, in the case of a small minority, for the use of an organ in the Synagogue. The last-named idea was not persisted in. But strictures were passed on the Kol Nidrei passage, on the retention of some phrases in the Kethubah, or marriage contract. Some of the suggestions were approved, and subsequently adopted. The result was, however, satisfactory. No bitterness remained to disturb the harmony of the Congregation, and all parties were united in the common endeavour to promote the best interests of the Synagogue.

I have in my possession a rare pamphlet published in 1892 (only one hundred copies were printed for private circulation) by Namport Key (a pen-name for a writer for the magazine *Punch*) entitled 'A Lay of the Battle of New West End', referring to this debate, from which I cannot help quoting the opening stanzas in order to convey the particular genial quality of religious debate in the late nineteenth century:

> Come, people all, both old and young
>   And hearken to my lay:
> And give you ear while I give tongue,
> And sing a song that ought to be sung,
>   And say my soulful say.
> I sing a Board of Management—
>   A trusty righteous Board—
> 'Gainst which none in disparagement
>   Can say a single word.—
> Save some, 'tis true, who have ignored
> The positive fact that we cannot afford
> To use coercion as a cord
>   To bind those Jews
>   Who do not choose
> To see in worn-out customs quaint
> The makings of a modern saint
>   A brave, enlightened, trusty Board—
>   More power to its thews!

The other great discussion on ritual reforms took place in 1912 when Dr Hochman was minister of the New West End. It has become the universal custom to follow the Babylonian practice of reading the Torah in an annual cycle, the completion of the reading to take place each year on Simhat Torah. But the ancient Palestinian custom was to read smaller portions each week, the cycle of readings taking three years instead of the Babylonian year-long reading. At a meeting of the seatholders of the New West End held on 19 May 1912 the following resolution was passed: 'That a committee be appointed to consider the possibility and desirability of introducing the Reading of the Scriptures in the Synagogue in a Triennial Cycle, and to report thereon'. The report of the special committee was published in 1913 as the *Report on the Sabbath Reading of the Scriptures in a Triennial Cycle*. Various authorities were consulted regarding the desirability and practicality of the proposal and different replies were given. Dr Elbogen of Berlin, probably the foremost authority on the liturgy, wrote to the committee, 'Personally I regard the introduction of the Triennial Cycle as a return to a healthy order of things founded on an old tradition.' But Dr Buchler, a great talmudist and rabbinic scholar, replied, 'If you ask me about the Din, I have to answer that it is against our codified law from the 12th century onwards, and even much earlier in Babylon whence our law proceeded. If you introduce the triennial cycle, you separate yourself from the main body of Judaism.'

The report concludes:

To break in any respect from the established ritual is to break with the United Synagogue and indeed from orthodoxy. In this instance the introduction of a desirable reform is rendered impossible by the fetters imposed at present by the provisions of the United Synagogue Act and the veto possessed by the ecclesiastical authorities. We are, therefore, of opinion that the Seatholders should earnestly consider whether the time has not arrived to take steps to modify the inelasticity caused by these barriers, so as to admit of a degree of local option under which certain modifications of the ritual would be permissible.

Nothing came, in fact, of this suggestion and the annual cycle of readings was retained.

I refer to the above only to demonstrate the kind of Orthodoxy, and strong dissatisfaction with it on the part of many, that prevailed at the New West End Synagogue when I was elected to be the minister–preacher of the congregation—indeed before I was even born. I knew perfectly well that, by occupying the pulpit of the New West End Synagogue I was throwing in my lot with an 'Orthodoxy' of a peculiar kind—very traditional with regard to the liturgy and such matters but with a degree of flexibility unthinkable in the United Synagogue today. In point of fact, the emphasis on the liturgy was only intelligible against the background of the strongly synagogue-orientated pattern of Anglo-Jewry at that time. Wider questions such as the nature of revelation, though no doubt discussed in private, were, so far as I know, never debated in public. The mood which prevailed was one of freedom in thought, though, it was implied, you do not think about theological questions which are irrelevant to practice. I recall that when I paid a courtesy visit to Ephraim Levine after my election, he quite casually offered to give me his set of the International Critical Commentaries, a series based entirely on biblical criticism in the modern vein, to help in the preparation of my sermons. It was taken for granted by my predecessor that I would find nothing shocking in this, as, by this time, indeed I did not.

All this historical background is relevant, I believe, to the 'Jacobs Affair'. If I had given expression to my views in what now passes for Orthodoxy in Anglo-Jewry, even in the New West End Synagogue, it would have been thoroughly dishonest. It was neither deceitful nor disloyal to what passed for Orthodoxy in this unique synagogue.

Chief Rabbi Brodie, resplendent in the special 'priestly garments' he wore like his predecessors in office (modelled it would seem, as were the vestments of Anglican bishops, on the accoutrements of the high priest in Temple times), consisting of a dark blue octagonal hat (the hats of his ministers were black), a long blue robe, and girdle (he used to joke that the latter, reminiscent of the *gartel* worn by hasidim as a physical separation between the brain and heart and the lower body, was the only Jewish thing about them), inducted me into office. He also addressed my son Ivor on his bar mitzvah. On both these occasions there was a mixed choir in the synagogue at which the chief rabbi grumbled, referring to the ladies of the choir as *bleckitchers* ('screechers') but going along with it nonetheless. Nor did he protest at the tacit omission of prayers for the restoration of sacrifices. During his interview with me before I was accepted as minister of the New West End, the chief rabbi told me that in the matter of mixed choirs he relied on a ruling by Chief Rabbi Adler that the prohibition on listening to a woman's voice while reciting the prayers (*kol be'ishah ervah*) only applies if the woman is singing something other than the words of the prayer, not when women join in the singing of the prayers themselves. Even today, when mixed choirs are taboo, no one seems to object to ladies of the congregation in their ladies' gallery joining in the singing.

Against this background, my pulpit was unfettered and my study group able to proceed tranquilly in the spirit of a tolerant traditionalism without interference from above. Neither the members of the study group nor I myself were in any way bent on being iconoclastic. Most of the members of the group attended the synagogue regularly. Some were *frum* in an Anglo-Jewish sort of way but none *meshugga frum*, as they used to call extreme pietists in those days. Others were rather less observant. What they all had in common was a keen interest in exploring how traditional Judaism can face the challenge of modernity. We met in private houses in a congenial atmosphere in which views could be exchanged without rancour. When the members of the group urged me to publish in book form some of our explorations, I presented these to Messrs Vallentine Mitchell, who published them under the title *We Have Reason to Believe* in 1957.

I gave the book to Chief Rabbi Brodie, but he offered no criticism at all, either because he had not bothered to read it (why should he have?) or had read it without discovering in it any of the heretical ideas he was later to find when these were brought to his attention. It is also possible that he was not troubled by heresies emanating from the New West End, progressive as it had always been in its thinking. Perhaps he also thought that I, with my yeshiva background, should have known better. The book created no stir until, after I had served six years at the New West End, the honorary officers of Jews' College, the training college for Modern Orthodox ministers, invited me to become Moral Tutor and Lecturer in Pastoral Theology to the College, giving me an assurance that on the forthcoming retirement of Dr Epstein, a great scholar and the editor of the famed Soncino translation of the Talmud, I would succeed him as principal. The chief rabbi, president of Jews' College, had to approve the appointment of a principal, but the honorary officers, convinced that the chief rabbi would eventually give his approval, urged me not to stir the pot, rumoured then to be on the boil, by pressing for my appointment, because, after reading *We Have Reason to Believe*, the chief rabbi had detected in it a departure from the Orthodox position. It was all cloak-and-dagger stuff. On the surface I had simply exchanged a pulpit for an academic position, the scope of which remained intentionally vague and undefined, since everyone was supposed to know that it was only a stepping stone to the principalship; everyone, that is, except the chief rabbi, who kept quiet about it and even canvassed for scholars he thought more suitable to fill the post. To cut a long story short, the chief rabbi eventually refused to allow me even to be considered for the position of principal of the College when Dr Epstein retired. Becoming convinced that I would never have the chief rabbi's approval, I resigned from the position I held at the College and the honorary officers of the College resigned with me in frustration, leaving me in limbo until a number of my supporters created the Society for the Study of Jewish Theology with me as its director.[1]

[1] A more detailed account of the 'Jacobs Affair' appears in my autobiography, *Helping with Inquiries* (London, 1989).

In the meantime, Rabbi Chaim Pearl, my successor in the pulpit of the New West End, had left the synagogue to become rabbi of Riverside Drive Synagogue, a prominent Conservative congregation in New York, upon which the honorary officers and members of the New West End invited me to return to my former position. After much coming and going it was decided by the honorary officers of the United Synagogue that the chief rabbi had the power, which he exercised, to veto this appointment as well. Eventually, in 1964, my supporters at the New West End, chafing at this restriction on their freedom of choice, formed an independent congregation, the New London Synagogue, with me as its rabbi, a position I still occupy at the time of writing.

What was all the fuss really about? The subtitle of *We Have Reason to Believe* was *Some Aspects of Jewish Theology Examined in the Light of Modern Thought*. As mentioned above, this was the theme of the discussion group at the New West End in which the book originated. The parts of the book dealing with belief in God, the meaning of religious language, the Freudian critique of religious faith as an illusion, the problem of pain, miracles, the afterlife, and the Chosen People idea seem not to have disturbed the faith of the most Orthodox. Judging by the reaction, the ideas in this section of the book were, if not entirely innocuous, at least not such as to appear contrary to the Orthodox system of belief as formulated eight hundred years ago by Maimonides in his thirteen principles of faith. In this section of the book, I argued, as so many Jewish theologians have done, that there is nothing in modern thought to warrant any departure from the traditional theistic view, according to which God is not merely the 'force that makes for righteousness' but ultimate Being; in Pascal's famous affirmation 'not the God of the philosophers but the God of Abraham, Isaac, and Jacob'. I also argued for a reaffirmation of the belief in what the ancient rabbis called 'the world to come'; that, however much we reinterpret the concept, it denotes that the death of the body is not the final end of the individual soul. Taking up the cudgels against Mordecai Kaplan's Reconstructionism, I quoted Bernard J. Heller, an American Reform rabbi, who wrote 'While Classical Reform was eating *terefah* and thinking *kasher*, Reconstructionists eat *kasher* and think *terefah*.' I believed then, and still believe now, that it is possible and highly desirable both to eat and think *kasher*, provided that thinking *kasher* does not include the fundamentalist notion on how the Torah came to be. In other words, as I said at the beginning of this introduction, to believe that God has revealed His will to His people, and through them to all mankind, need not imply that He revealed it in the form of direct divine communication. In later writings I have described this position as 'liberal supernaturalism'; 'supernaturalism' in that it affirms God as transcendent and 'personal', wholly Other and yet in control of the universe He has created; 'liberal' in that it accepts the findings of modern scholarship, resulting in a non-fundamentalistic understanding of how ancient traditions, ideas, and practices were combined, over many centuries and through human trial and error, to form the Torah. I shall try to formulate this position in detail in the next chapter. For the moment, I refer to it in the context of my struggle with the Anglo-Jewish establishment.

The charge of 'heresy' was brought against me on the strength of what I had written in *We Have Reason to Believe* on the doctrine of revelation. The view I put forward on this theme, that we can and should keep the *mitsvot* while keeping an open mind on their origin, was hardly original. I tried to show in *We Have Reason to Believe* that even in the Middle Ages the human element in the Torah was not entirely unacknowledged. In modern times this attitude was held by Zechariah Frankel (1801–73) and the Breslau school which he founded, and later became the basic philosophy of the Conservative movement in the USA, strongly influenced by Frankel, Solomon Schechter, Louis Ginzberg, Louis Finkelstein, and many others. In more recent years, in the Masorti movement in Israel, this philosophy of the *mitsvot* was given expression with the special needs of Israel in mind. In the UK the Masorti movement was later established with the similar aim of creating a mood suitable for the highly traditional atmosphere of Anglo-Jewry. Already in *We Have Reason to Believe* I had quoted Will Herberg, J. Abelson, and Hayyim Hirschenson, who had grappled with the problem. Herbert Loewe's acute observations in his debate with C. G. Montefiore, *A Rabbinic Anthology*, show how biblical criticism, both higher and textual, is compatible with a refined interpretation of Orthodoxy, but, as his son Raphael Loewe noted in his introduction to the new edition of the book, the licence given to a distinguished academic in the days of Chief Rabbi Hertz could evidently not have been granted to a man who claimed to be an Orthodox rabbi under the jurisdiction of Chief Rabbi Brodie. This latter is precisely the point: was I not being naïvely trusting and optimistic in believing that I could be a 'modernist' within the

Orthodox camp? In the present climate of opinion, it would indeed be ridiculous for someone with my views to lay claim to Orthodoxy, which is why I do not now make any such claim. But at the time of the controversy there had long been a tolerant, rather bemused acceptance of unconventional views within Anglo-Jewry. At that time, it was not completely hypocritical for me to label myself as Orthodox, meaning, at the time, simply kosher, in the sense of observant of the precepts, and yet wish to be the head of a traditional institution like Jews' College. This was not to be, however, and, though labels are often restrictive and misleading, honesty now compels me, in order to avoid confusion, to describe my position not as Orthodox but as Masorti.

On the term 'fundamentalism', used frequently in this book and in my earlier works, I have to say that I do not use it pejoratively as a synonym for fanaticism or religious extremism, and certainly not to denote, on the Jewish side, anything like Hamas suicide bombers or the Bible-thumpers of right-wing American evangelism, but in its original connotation (in the second decade of the twentieth century in the USA) of one who believes that to take Sacred Scripture as divinely inspired in a direct manner and hence as an infallible source of knowledge on all matters on which it pronounces, is so *fundamental* to religious faith that without it one might as well be an unbeliever. I shall elaborate on this point later on in the book, but I have to say right away that while it is possible and, I believe, desirable to contest the Jewish fundamentalist position, it is unfair to characterize those who hold it as insincere or dishonest.

While the problem of 'fundamentalism' versus criticism has long been an issue for thinking Jews world-wide from the middle of the nineteenth century onwards, there were features peculiar to the social and religious life of Anglo-Jewry which produced the controversy in which I was involved. The extraordinary powers vested in the office of chief rabbi have already been noted. The lay leaders of Anglo-Jewry, most of whom were only nominally Orthodox, still expected their rabbinic leaders to uphold traditional values and observances but, as in many other Jewish communities, the real power was vested in them. It was no accident, therefore, that when the 'Affair' erupted, it was not only the chief rabbi, under pressure from his Beth Din, who barred me from officiating as a minister of the United Synagogue but also, and particularly, the president of the United Synagogue, Sir Isaac Wolfson. Sir Isaac himself seemed to have been on my side in the dispute but felt obliged, as president of the United Synagogue, to uphold its constitution. As a matter of fact, the *dayanim* of the London Beth Din actually urged Rabbi Brodie to allow my return to the pulpit of the New West End, where, they argued, my isolation in an old-time Anglo-Jewish congregation would effectively prevent my heresies spreading to harm the poor innocents in the community as a whole. But Rabbi Brodie dug in his heels and I was barred. My attempt to return to the New West End was thus prevented largely on political rather than theological grounds. It was in the previous episode of my appointment to the principalship of Jews' College that the theological aspect loomed large.

Jews' College, founded in 1856 as an institution for training ministers and teachers, placed the emphasis on providing its students with the skills they would need on graduation, without bothering over-much with theological niceties. It was a case of English practical muddling through at its best, or worst, depending on how one looks at it. No clear statements regarding Orthodox beliefs were made and some of the graduates, like Bernard Hooker and Allan Miller, became Reform rabbis. These latter, on the continental pattern, preferred the title rabbi to that of minister. At one stage in the history of the College, C. G. Montefiore, the founder of the Liberal movement, served in an advisory capacity as a member of the College Council. In a typical example of the general broad approach that prevailed in Anglo-Jewry, Montefiore also collaborated with Simeon Singer in the compilation of the latter's 'Authorised Daily Prayer Book', 'Authorised', that is, by the chief rabbi, an ironic illustration of the influence of the Anglican Church on the very prayerbook used by the Orthodox. Incidentally, Singer, in the earlier editions of the prayerbook, acknowledged his indebtedness to Montefiore but, indicative of the swing to the right, Montefiore's name was omitted from later editions.

On the question of biblical criticism, the faculty of the College generally had an equivocal attitude. Dr M. Friedlander, principal of the College from 1865 to 1907 and a distinguished scholar, famed as the author of the first English translation of Maimonides' *Guide of the Perplexed*, did attack the critics in his book *The Jewish Religion*. He defended traditional views on the authorship of the biblical books on dogmatic rather than scholarly grounds but, while stating that we generally speak of the Psalms of David, noted that 'only a portion of them was composed by David' and that some 'seem to belong to a later period'. Purely objective scholarship came into its own at the College when its faculty was composed of world-renowned scholars, whose research was pursued using the most rigorous scholarly standards. Yet the teaching and researches of these outstandingly competent scholars were confined largely to Jewish history and grammar, the Talmud and the Codes, medieval philosophy and poetry, touching only obliquely on questions of biblical criticism. More to the point, the College was affiliated to London University, which awarded an honours degree in Semitics, towards the obtaining of which the students were trained, side by side with their studies for the Minister's Diploma. In order to qualify for this degree the students were required to master the application of modern historical critical methods to the Hebrew Bible. They were taught, among other subjects, biblical criticism, both higher and lower, the background to the Bible uncovered by archaeology, and the ancient Semitic languages, and were expected to be familiar with the whole critical position. For instance, in one of the papers set for the degree by Herbert Danby, the non-Jewish translator of the Mishnah into English, and Dr Epstein, the principal of the College, the student was expected to discuss whether the Patriarchs Abraham, Isaac, and Jacob were historical figures, a discussion only possible for a candidate who was familiar with the verdict of some scholars that the patriarchal narratives in the book of Genesis reflect tribal movements and belong to myth rather than to sober history. It is not clear how the College managed to cope with the trauma that this two-sided scheme of studies produced in the students. On the one hand, the students were expected, if they were to obtain a good degree in Semitics, to be thoroughly at home in biblical scholarship; on the other hand, in their practice and later preaching, they had to accept the fundamentalist view on which these appear to be based. For some students this dichotomy turned them against Orthodoxy entirely. For others it resulted in a kind of 'two truths' attitude— biblical studies in the modern vein were fine in theory and for recognition by the university, while in practice it was to be avoided as un-Jewish heresy.

Jews' College was thus, at one and the same time, a modern scholarly institution in the best university tradition, and a kind of modern yeshiva, in which the subjects were taught in English rather than in Yiddish. But in the traditional yeshiva modern scholarship was not so much rejected as completely ignored. If anyone had dared to set a paper for a yeshiva student asking him to discuss whether the Patriarchs were historical figures, the only possible answer would have been to deny the relevance of the question. Of course, he would have vehemently retorted, the Patriarchs were real, historical figures since they are so described in the Bible which is the direct, infallible word of God and upon which all our Jewish practices, ideas, and beliefs are based. What I had fondly hoped to promote, had I been appointed principal of the College, within the circumscribed area of an Anglo-Jewish type of piety, was an atmosphere in which the students of the College were encouraged to face the problem courageously and try to deal with it honestly and constructively, out of the conviction that Judaism can meet the challenge of critical scholarship as it met the different challenge of Greek philosophy in the medieval period. Naturally this was far from implying that the challenge was not being met adequately in the larger Jewish world, only that Jews' College, in its traditions of openness to the new learning, could provide special opportunities at the time.

Through the repercussions of the controversy, *We Have Reason to Believe* was published in four separate editions. In the third and fourth editions I added my replies to critics, and I have taken up the issue in other of my theological works. In this book I undertake not a rehash of views I have already dealt with, *ad nauseam* some will say, but a fresh examination of the whole question as well as my replies to objections raised over the years. The four editions of *We Have Reason to Believe* were all published by Vallentine Mitchell, a subsidiary of the firm Frank Cass. It was Frank Cass who invited me to publish the fourth edition when my views again came under fire from Chief Rabbi Jonathan Sacks. Frank Cass also published my autobiography, *Helping with Inquiries*. In the latter work I have surveyed the 'Jacobs Affair' from a personal, not to say biased, angle. In the present book, except in this introduction, I have tried to look at the whole issue as objectively as is possible for an author as involved in it as I have been. Yet it is still my own view I am trying to delineate, at least within the confines of Anglo-Jewry. My colleagues in the Masorti rabbinate have their own views and may not agree with some of what I say. The Masorti in the UK is at present the smallest of the Jewish religious movements in this country, but it does comprise several congregations with a total membership of some three thousand and is growing rapidly. As stated, similar views are held not only among the Conservatives in the USA and Masorti here and in Israel but also among some Reform rabbis and even, dare I suggest, among some Orthodox rabbis, though, for obvious reasons, the latter prefer silence to a controversy that might bring them nothing but heartache. For all that, it would be cumbersome always to compare this view to what others in the Jewish world have been saying; so, for better or for worse, I shall call it my view in this book, without claiming too much originality for it.

On Reason and Belief

It is impossible, nowadays, to discuss the role of reason in matters of religion without referring to Maimonides, or Rambam (*Rabbi Moshe ben Maimon*), as he is called by Orthodox Jews, since reason was such an important element in his life and thought, and he is so often mentioned whenever the possibility of a rational approach to religion is considered.

We have very few details about Maimonides as a person. We know that he was born in Cordova in 1138, lived and worked in Egypt for the greater part of his life, and died in 1204. The frequently reproduced portrait said to be of him—with a trimmed beard, a turban, and more or less nondescript features—is not authentic. Students of his writings cannot imagine the austere figure that emerges from them actually sitting for a portrait. One can hardly imagine any of the great rabbinic figures allowing themselves such an indulgence in self-glorification. Nor do we know much about his family life. He was married, no doubt happily, but we have no information about his wife, not even her name. His son, Abraham, followed in his father's footsteps to a large extent, and we know that the Rambam's father, Maimon, was a *dayan* in Spain and was descended from a long line of *dayanim*. A *dayan*, in those days, was a scholar who voluntarily undertook to render decisions in Jewish law. Maimonides himself, like many other medieval teachers, held that it was wrong to accept payment for teaching the Torah (the professional rabbi did not emerge in Judaism until some time after his day). He earned his living as a physician. In addition, he served as the leader of the Egyptian Jewish community. At one period he was so busy with his medical and communal activities that he wrote to advise a favourite pupil not to visit him. The visit would be futile, he wrote, since there would be no time for the two to have a worthwhile meeting. Beyond these and a few other details that can be culled from his writings (especially from his letters), it is the thought of the man rather than the events of his life that has grasped the imagination of successive generations of thinking Jews.

Was Maimonides a rationalist? Ahad Ha'am, in a famous essay (with the revealing title *Shilton hasekhel*, 'The Supremacy of Reason'), argued that Maimonides was the supreme rationalist, a religious teacher for whom reason was all.[2] This view is as one-sided as that which turns him into a crypto-kabbalist. (There is an old legend that towards the end of his life Maimonides was convinced by a kabbalist of the error of his ways, or rather his thoughts, and that he was 'converted' to kabbalism.) The truth lies somewhere in between. He believed in reason but seemingly held that it was unreasonable to be too reasonable, so that there is more than a touch of mysticism in his writings. Since this book is concerned with some aspects of the relationship between faith and reason and since, at least in former times, Maimonides was always hailed as the leading figure in the consideration of the question, one or two illustrations should be given both of his use of reason and of the areas where reason fails him, compelling him to fall back on belief.

Maimonides' struggle for a rational approach to Judaism is evident on practically every page of his writings.[3] It was this that led him to try to discover the reasons behind the apparent unreasonableness of some of the precepts of the Torah. Maimonides could not imagine God ordering humans to carry out meaningless acts simply as a demonstration of obedience to Him. Some of his reasoning was exceedingly bold for his day, as when he suggests that the sacrificial system was introduced not because it has intrinsic value but only as a means of weaning people away from idolatry. Moreover, unlike the medieval kabbalists, who found mystical reasons for every detail of the precepts, Maimonides argues that if you are to have a law and discipline in the religious life you have to have order, such order being prompted by the details of the law. For instance, to drive on the left in England has no advantage in itself over driving on the right. It is simply that for chaos to be avoided everyone

[2] *Ahad Ha'am: Essays, Letters, Memoirs*, trans. and ed. L. Simon (Oxford, 1946), 138–82.

[3] There is a wealth of material on Maimonides and reason, but for the purpose of this chapter, see especially A. Cohen, *The Teachings of Maimonides* (London, 1947); Leon Roth, *The Guide for the Perplexed: Moses Maimonides* (London, 1948); David Yellin and Israel Abrahams, *Maimonides* (London, 1935); and Joseph Sarachek, *Faith and Reason: The Conflict over the Rationalism of Maimonides* (New York, 1935).

must drive on the same side, in England on the left, in most other countries on the right. By the same token, according to Maimonides, tsitsit have to be four in number and the tefillin have to have four sections, not because there is any particular significance to the number four (as the kabbalists would aver). The number is, in a sense, quite arbitrary, but is important for the sake of order. It could have been three or five to achieve the same effect, and it would have been as meaningless to ask why these numbers were selected as to ask why four should be.

Another example of Maimonides' strict adherence to the way of reason is his determined opposition to magic and superstition. He is incensed by people who write the names of angels in the *mezuzah* for protection, or who write the *mezuzah* so that its words taper to a point. These people, he protests, convert the *mezuzah*, the sublime attestation of the divine unity, into a talisman for their own self-serving and selfish use. Maimonides also rejects belief in demons and, although he does believe in angels, mentioned frequently in the Bible, he thinks of these as purely spiritual forces, arguing that all the scriptural references to angels appearing in human form are to angels seen in a dream. It is not that angels actually appear or can appear in human guise like men with wings, but that the prophet or whoever else perceives them in this way does so while he dreams, with his imaginative faculty strongly at work. When Maimonides was asked how he could reject astrology since the talmudic rabbis did believe it (throughout he displays the greatest reverence for the talmudic sages), he replied: 'Man has been created with his eyes in the front and not in the back of his head.' In a remarkable passage in his *Guide*, he says that if he had been convinced by reason that Aristotle was correct in holding matter to be eternal, he would have accepted this view and interpreted the creation narrative in Genesis in accordance with it. In fact, he goes on to say, his *reason* does not allow him to follow Aristotle here, and that is why he prefers to hold fast to the Jewish tradition, according to which the material universe has been created and was not always there.

For all that, it would be a gross error to see Maimonides as an all-out rationalist. He is too good a religious thinker to hold that the human mind can grasp the Mind of God. Dealing with the purpose of creation, he believes that we must ultimately postulate that it lies in the inscrutable will of God. Similarly, when faced with the old conundrum as to how man can be free to choose, since God has foreknowledge and therefore knows how he will choose, Maimonides declares that we must hold both beliefs, that man is free and that God has foreknowledge, without trying to resolve the contradiction. God's knowledge is not something added to His Being but is God Himself, so how can finite human beings hope to understand?

Nor is a mystical element lacking in the outlook of the great medieval sage. It was no cold rationalist who described (and in his Code at that) the man who reflects on the divine majesty as revealed in the universe as becoming love-sick for God; and who interpreted the Song of Songs as a dialogue between the soul and her Maker. Nor would a cold rationalist have ever thought of saying, as Maimonides does in his *Guide*, that the ideal, extremely difficult to attain, is for God to be in the mind at all times, and that those few who can approximate to this ideal can walk unharmed through fire because they are immune to all natural hazards.

It has to be appreciated that, for all Maimonides' originality and breadth of vision and for all the fact that no one can dare ignore him when discussing the relationship between faith and reason, or, for that matter, when discussing any other aspect of Judaism, the great teacher was a child of his age, believing, for example, that the sun, moon, and stars are affixed to revolving, transparent spheres, which are intelligent beings singing God's praises as they move in accordance with His will. This idea of the 'music of the spheres' still persisted in Shakespeare's day:

> There's not the smallest orb which thou behold'st
> But in his motion like an angel sings
> Still quiring to the young-eyed cherubins;
> Such harmony is in immortal souls;
> But, while this muddy vesture of decay
> Doth grossly close it in, we cannot hear it.

Shakespeare and his contemporaries had the same world-view as Maimonides. Newton, to say nothing of Einstein, had yet to be born. To come to the theme of this book, nor could Maimonides have known anything of biblical criticism, for example, when he formulated the eighth of his thirteen principles of the faith: that it is essential to believe that every single word of the Torah was communicated in a single period by God to Moses. Maimonides had what this book calls a fundamentalist view, though, since that particular challenge could not have been presented to him, he was no fundamentalist. We can be confident that if he were alive today, he would face this challenge with integrity and the spirit of intellectual honesty he exhibited when facing the challenge presented by Aristotelian philosophy, which meant so much in his day but which means nothing, for religious life, to us today.

It is a common error to quote Maimonides' formulation of faith as if there has been no progress in the world of thought. What was a perfectly respectable position in the twelfth century is not necessarily a respectable position for us to hold today, any more than our present-day knowledge of the universe will be true for all time without revision. But, as this book seeks to show, there can be no going back to Maimonides' formulation. The modern view is based on empirical investigation, which no one thought of undertaking in the Middle Ages. Where, in many instances, Jewish law follows the rulings of Maimonides, it is proper to ask what Maimonides actually said and follow the rulings he gave. In matters of faith, the more correct approach is not to ask what Maimonides said eight hundred years ago, but what a teacher with his intellectual integrity would say if he were alive today.

Levi ben Gershon, also known as Gersonides (1288–1344), outshines Maimonides in his rationalist approach.[4] For Gersonides, God did not create the world out of nothing, but imposed form on a kind of formless matter which was always there. Faced with the problem of God's foreknowledge and human free will, Gersonides holds that God knows all the choices open to an individual, but does not know beforehand which choice that individual will actually make. Although Gersonides does believe that the biblical miracles really happened, he is at pains to explain them, wherever possible, in a naturalistic way. The walls of Jericho fell (Josh. 6) because the processions around the city and the loud trumpeting caused the ground on which they stood to be incapable of holding them upright. The sun did not really stop for Joshua (Josh. 10: 12–14), but only appeared to do so because he was successful in bringing the battle to a swift conclusion. It was only the shadow on the sundial that moved because of the clouds in the incident of Hezekiah (2 Kgs. 20: 8–9), not that the sun could really move forwards or backwards. It is true that opponents of Gersonides' extreme rationalism said that his *magnum opus, The Wars of the Lord*, should have been called *The Wars against the Lord*, yet his work became acceptable to Orthodox Jews at

---

[4] On Gersonides, see I. Husik, *A History of Mediaeval Jewish Philosophy* (Philadelphia, Pa., 1958), 228–361.

least as an illustration of how far reason is allowed to have a speculative say. It is also possible that Gersonides' fame as a talmudist and moralist saved his work as a whole from being treated as heretical.

Yet there have been a number of anti-rationalists in Judaism, as I have tried to show in my book *Faith*.[5] Dr I. Epstein writes:

Applied to the doctrines of Judaism, we can see that though they are not all in accord with understanding they are all in accord alike with reason and the established truths of scientific teaching. Contrast this with the Tertullian dicta: '*Credo quia absurdum*', '*Credibile quia ineptum*', '*Certum est quia impossibile est*' ('I believe because it is absurd', 'To be believed because it is foolish', 'It is certain because it is impossible'), making incredibility the test of credibility . . . Judaism, on the other hand, whilst having too much respect for human intelligence to subscribe to any proposition involving the total surrender of human reason, nevertheless rightly recognises the limitations of the human faculties and senses and may well proclaim as an act of revealed faith '*Credibile quia non intellectum est*' ('To be believed because it is beyond the understanding')— quite a tenable and rational proposition which would be unscientific to assail or deny *a priori*.[6]

Similarly, Milton Steinberg remarks, 'No Jewish thinker is on record as advancing Kierkegaard's contention of the radical incompatibility of religious truth and reason.'[7]

Both Epstein and Steinberg are far too sweeping. There have been a few thinkers in the history of Jewish thought who have decried the use of reason entirely in matters of belief, thinkers who quote the verse: 'The simpleton believeth every word' (Ps. 14: 15) to yield the thought that faith is 'higher' than knowledge and comprehension. The hasidic master Nahman of Bratslav (1772–1811) develops the idea that since, according to Kabbalah, the world only came into being by a withdrawal of God's light to leave a space void of Him into which the finite world could emerge, it follows that for man to seek God through his reason is bound to be futile. Such a man seeks God in the void left after the divine withdrawal where He cannot be found. It is by pure faith alone that man can reach out to God. While Hume and Kant argue, on philosophical grounds, that you cannot extrapolate God from the universe, Nahman arrives at the same conclusion on theological grounds. Nahman goes so

[5] (London, 1968), appendix II: 'Jewish Parallels to the Tertullian Paradox', 201–9.
[6] Isadore Epstein, *The Faith of Judaism* (London, 1956), 117.
[7] *Anatomy of Faith* (New York, 1980), 146.

far as to argue that man is bound to have problems of faith and bound to
have religious doubts, putting it as follows: 'It is entirely proper that
objections can be found to God. It is right and suitable that this should
be so because of God's greatness and exaltedness. Since in His exaltedness He is so far above our minds there are bound to be objections to
Him.'[8] For Nahman and religious thinkers like him, a God who raises
no problems for human thought would not be God for the very reason
that the Infinite is bound to offend the finite mind. Since God cannot be
grasped by the human mind, human reason in itself must not only fail to
bring man to God but must be in contradiction to God. A disciple of
Nahman reported that Nahman took strong issue with the medieval
Jewish philosophers who argued that, while God can do that which
seems impossible to us, even God cannot do the absolutely impossible,
to make a square triangle, for instance. Nahman's disciple remarks:
'They [the philosophers] write in their books: Is it possible for God to
make a triangle into a square? But our master [Nahman] said: I believe
that God can make a square triangle. For God's ways are concealed from
us. He is omnipotent and nothing is impossible for Him.'[9] Nahman is,
of course, being illogical here. If reason is powerless in matters of religious faith how can such a view be argued, since all argument is an
application of the reasoning mind? Moreover, we would say today that,
by definition, a triangle cannot be a square or a square a triangle, so that
to talk of a 'square triangle' is to talk nonsense. What Nahman's hyperbole is presumably intended to convey is the impotence of human
reasoning about God.

I have dealt with this general question of reason in relation to faith in
my other books on theology, of which I have given a brief summary in
the previous paragraphs for one purpose only: to show that the whole
medieval discussion and the denial by thinkers like Nahman of Bratslav
that human reasoning can bring man to God has little to do with the
question discussed in this book and in *We Have Reason to Believe*—that
of the challenge presented to tradition by the comparatively new
discipline in which the facts of the past are uncovered by historical critical

---

[8] *Likutei moharan* (Warsaw, 1808–11), second series, no. 52.

[9] This report was quoted by J. G. Weiss from a pamphlet entitled *Kunteros yemei
tela'ot*, published in Jerusalem in 1933. Weiss does not mention the author's name. See
J. G. Weiss, 'The Question of Religious Problems in the Doctrine of R. Nahman of
Bratslav' (Heb.), in the Schocken Festschrift, *Alei ayin: Minḥat devarim leshelomo
salman shoken* (Jerusalem, 1948–52), 245–91.

methodology. When Gersonides preferred to interpret biblical passages in such a manner as to make them conform with reason, and when others disagreed with his rationalistic approach, the thinkers on both sides treated the biblical record as a given, that is, they believed that what Scripture tells us happened really did happen. The new challenge, as I shall discuss it in the following chapters, is presented by the modern use of the historical critical methodology to show that to say that the miracles really happened is to prejudge the verdict of history. Neither Maimonides nor Gersonides nor Nahman of Bratslav ever thought of questioning whether the events related in Scripture really happened or whether the Bible was really a divine communication. If, in this book, we take further the view stated in *We Have Reason to Believe*, that history now has a voice to be heard, the term 'reason' will not be used to refer primarily to abstract reasoning about God, but to the reasonable conclusions that result from 'scientific' investigation into the origins of the Bible and of Judaism itself. Reason in this sense has compelled many thinking Jews to reject the fundamentalist view according to which every single word of the Torah was conveyed directly by God to Moses and that the rest of the Bible has also come from God, albeit in a less direct fashion, and is an infallible document.

Comparisons have been made over the years of my views in this matter to those of Christians who challenged the truth of their traditions in the nineteenth and early twentieth centuries. But, at the time of the 'Jacobs Affair', Christopher Driver wrote the following perceptive piece in the *Guardian* (18 April 1964):

The points of similarity with the 'Honest to God' row should not be overworked, for this is a debate about Biblical Criticism rather than about our image of God—that is, a debate which in the Church of England was fought a century ago. The true counterpart to Dr Jacobs is perhaps Bishop Colenso or Robertson Smith rather than the Bishop of Woolwich. If Dr Jacobs were a Liberal or Reform Jew, his views would have aroused no controversy, and some of his critics have suggested that he ought in logic and honesty to make the transition. But Dr Jacobs is Orthodox. He remains convinced that the traditional Jewish observances have a religious value in themselves—'there are depths in the human soul which only ritual can reach'—but wants to maintain a critical attitude towards the Scriptures which lay down the observances.

I could not have put it better myself, except that Jewish observances—and this is the heart of the matter—do not stem solely, or even primarily, from 'the Scriptures' but from the interpretation of these found in the rabbinic tradition. But I had no objection then and have none now to Christopher Driver comparing me to a Colenso or a Robertson Smith, in the sense that these men were exploring for their faith that which I, and numerous others, have been exploring for mine. I was not and am not now a Jewish Bishop of Woolwich. I do not hold and never have held that belief in God should be reinterpreted in non-personal terms nor do I hold any kind of 'Death of God' philosophy, which is now itself dead and buried, although resurrected from time to time. Belief in a personal God, the God of the Jewish tradition, in no way offends anyone's reason. On the contrary, it is this belief that 'makes sense' of human life in general and Jewish life in particular. But a belief contrary to the known facts, say, that the world is under six thousand years old, does offend reason, as does any invocation of faith in order to defend untenable theories. With regard to belief in God, even if the traditional 'proofs' for God's existence are now seen as less than knock-down arguments, no believer will say that his belief in God is irrational. Few believers have arrived at belief in God by starting from the beginning to work it all out by reasoned argument. Most people are faced with a traditional belief in God which, when they examine it, seems cogent. It is quite otherwise, if someone says, 'no matter what the established facts my belief compels me to reject them'. He is indeed irrational.

No one admits to being irrational. The usual reply to views such as mine is that the facts are not as I state them: that, for example, the evidence of geology for the vast age of the earth, or of biblical criticism that the Pentateuch is a composite work, is heavily flawed. In the following chapters I shall try to defend my position, which affirms both belief in God and a rejection of fundamentalism. In Chapter 2 I try to develop this position, which I describe as 'liberal supernaturalism'. In the following chapters I defend my view against the charge that it is untraditional or unscientific or otherwise unreasonable, and go on to see how and why I differ from what is now Orthodoxy and from Reform, noting on the way my rejection of secular Judaism and my flirtation with kabbalah, mysticism, and hasidism.

I have left out of the story most of the political aspects—the attacks on the Masorti movement and the repeated but unsuccessful attempts to declare marriages conducted by Masorti rabbis invalid on the grounds that we do not believe in the doctrine of *Torah min hashamayim* ('the Torah is from Heaven'). These have been given many an airing in the Jewish and general press and in the many Masorti publications. But I cannot resist the temptation to conclude this introduction with an account of a curious document sent to me at the end of December 1995 by 'the United Assemblies of Erets Yisrael and *ḥuts la'arets* [the Diaspora]'. This body stated that the document had been 'publicly distributed to *ḥaredim* in Jerusalem'. The actual document bears the letter head of the 'Beth Din Zedek of the Edah Haredit' and is dated the fourth day of Hanukah, 5756 (= 21 December 1995). At the top of the document is the verse (1 Chr. 15: 22) 'and do my prophets no harm'. The document reads (in my translation):

Since it is already well known and is renowned that the 'Dr' called RABBI DOCTOR LOUIS JACOBS (Cheif [*sic*] Rabbi of 'Masorti') does not believe in our Holy Torah which Moses received from Sinai and delivered to Joshua etc., and the Rabbi, the Gaon, Head of all the Sons of the Exile, Rabbi Yehezkel Abramsky, the memory of the *tsadik* and Holy Man is for a blessing for the life of the World to Come, has already testified that he 'completely denies Judaism', behold we all protest against him with all our might and strength.

Let our eyes run with tears and our eyelids drop water over the *ḥilul hashem* [desecration of God's name]. With pride as a chain around his neck [Ps. 73: 6] he has brazenly insulted the Torah of Hashem and the *dayanim* of the Beth Din of London, the metropolis. Whom hast thou taunted and blasphemed? And against whom hast thou exalted thy voice? Yea, thou hast lifted up thine eyes on high, even against the Holy One of Israel [2 Kgs. 19: 22]. Be astonished, O ye heavens, at this [Jer. 2: 12]. Be girded with sackcloth, lament and wail [Jer. 4: 8] over the great catastrophe that has befallen us. Therefore, we come, under the obligation that devolves on all those who sit in judgement wherever they may be, to proceed to utter grievous protests against your whole theory. In our opinion, the opinion of our Holy Torah, 'Dr' LOUIS JACOBS is like all the demolitionists and destroyers who rose up to uproot the boundaries and against whom our holy forefathers and teachers so selflessly battled. No guidance may be obtained from him. His sermons are sermons of utter heresy. And it is forbidden to read any printed work produced by this person since these constitute demolitions of the young which overturn eternal boundaries.

And with these words we have fulfilled our obligation so that they should not say the rabbis have remained silent. However, from now on the words of Solomon, on whom be peace, will be a lamp to our feet and light to our path [Ps. 119: 105]: 'Answer not a fool according to his folly' [Prov. 26: 4]. Our soul waits for the Lord [Ps. 33: 20], our help and our shield, that, in the merit of the *tsadikim*, whose honour we seek and whose Torah is a heritage for us, He will help, shield, and save in order to set the religion on its hill and to strengthen our firm stand against the severe tests that continually pass over us until the earth will be full of knowledge [Isa. 11: 9] and they that err will be taught understanding [based on Isa. 29: 4].

Signed in great distress for the sake of uplifting the horn of the true Torah and Israel, on the fourth day of Hanukah, 5756.

Appended to the document are signatures of the following (the titles are as given):

Harav Hagaon R. Shmuel Wosner
The Gaon, Head of the Beth Din of Jerusalem in the name of all Jerusalem rabbis
The Head of the London Beth Din in the name of all London rabbis
The Head of Gateshead Beth Din in the name of all Gateshead rabbis
The Head of the Manchester Beth Din in the name of all Manchester rabbis
The Head of the Belgium Beth Din
The Gaon R. Eliezer Menahem Shakh, *rosh yeshivah* of Ponevezh
The Gaon R. Nissim Karelitz
The Gaon R. Shaul Eliashav
The *rosh yeshivah* of Torah Or
The *rosh yeshivah* of Tchorkova, Righteous Teacher of the Edah Haharedit
The Holy Admor of Belz
The Holy Admor of Vishnitz

To the original document the following is inserted in English before the signatures, so as to appear as part of the original. This insertion is addressed to me personally.

We the undersigned Rabbonim announce a public *meḥa'ah* [protest] in demonstration against all the untrue and unfounded biblical statements that openly display inaccuracies in the traditional and correctly accepted Jewish beliefs, made by Rabbi Dr Louis Jacobs of the Masorti congregation. We therefore openly publicize that 'MASORTI' is not a jewish [*sic*] society and is a danger to the public. With this united disagreement [*sic*] we wish to denounce the MASORTI as a founded [*sic*] part of Judaism, and we at least fulfil the words of the Talmud: 'If one sees something improper in his friend he must rebuke him' (*Berakhot* 31a). Thus we make clear our opinion in the hope that you will cease from inexplicable behaviour and revert to the way [the following is in

Hebrew] of Israel Saba [the Patriarch Jacob], the ways of our forefathers and the teachers of our ways, speedily and in our days, Amen.

The whole thing appeared suspect to me from the outset. I was absolutely sure that the famous Israeli rabbis, such as the Belzer Rebbe or the Vishnitzer Rebbe, had never even heard of me, and even if they had it was inconceivable that they should bother to issue a protest against my 'heresies'. Moreover, for broadsheets of this type the document is rather mild. There are hardly any diatribes against me as a person and, while 'Dr' is in inverted commas, rabbi is left without them. The Hebrew quote from the Talmud in the English insertion implies that I am a *ḥaver*, which, at the very least, means that I am a 'neighbour' if not a 'friend', and the whole of this insertion is very conciliatory, gently chiding me to desist and finding my behaviour 'inexplicable'. A covering note, sent to me in the same envelope, reads:

The following *meḥa'ah* has been publicly distributed to *ḥaredim* in Jerusalem and has the signatures of the London, Gateshead, Manchester and Jerusalem Botei Din. It will no doubt be of interest to you. Thus we the Botei Din feel you should see it before publication in Europe.

The United Assemblies of Rabbis of Erets Yisrael and *ḥuts la'arets*.

On receiving the document I telephoned my Israeli son-in-law, asking him to see if the protest had appeared on the walls of Me'ah She'arim, ever ready to receive protests of this kind. He reported back that there was no whiff of anything like it anywhere in Jerusalem. From an examination of the document, and from a denial by a prominent *ḥaredi* rabbi who appears as one of the signatories that he had ever seen it, it became clear that the whole thing was a forgery. But what was the purpose? I suspect that the whole document was concocted by erstwhile friends, perhaps from yeshiva days, who wished to have me on their side again after so many years. I remain puzzled.

The document was leaked to the *Manchester Jewish Telegraph*, no friend of mine nor of the Masorti movement. The *Telegraph* (1 January 1996) had the lurid headline 'Louis Jacobs "a danger to the public" say rabbis'. The paper wrote: 'Masorti leader Rabbi Dr Louis Jacobs has been deemed a "danger to the public" by 13 Jerusalem Rabbis.' When it became known that there was no truth at all in the claim, some of my friends thought I ought to issue a writ against the paper, but I felt it not worth bothering about. And I am still intrigued about what was behind it all. I would not have mentioned this here were it not that it is evident both that some in the *ḥaredi* community (I am assuming it came from them) still consider me to be one of them at heart and that they still, after all these years, do not grasp what I have been trying to say. I can only hope that the present book will help to make my views a little clearer.

TWO

LIBERAL
SUPERNATURALISM

NAHMAN KROCHMAL (1785–1840), a pioneer of the Wissenschaft des Judentums movement, in which Judaism was studied in terms of its historical development, wrote for this very purpose his *Moreh nevukhei hazeman* ('Guide for the Perplexed of the Time'), which was published in Lemberg in 1851, fifteen years after Krochmal's death, by the great Jewish historian Leopold Zunz (1794–1886), the leading figure in the Wissenschaft des Judentums movement. Krochmal's title, obviously based on Maimonides' *Moreh nevukhim* ('Guide of the Perplexed'), means that the work is directed to contemporaries, to intelligent Jews in the first half of the nineteenth century, who were quite different from the perplexed individuals to whom Maimonides offered his guidance. The latter were puzzled by the apparent contradictions between Jewish thought and Aristotelian physics and metaphysics. In the Middle Ages philosophical postulates were treated as if they were timeless, as if they belonged in a metahistorical universe of discourse, which is why Maimonides, for example, saw no incongruity in reading Greek ideas into the ancient biblical texts. Krochmal, on the other hand, was offering guidance to Jews with the particular problem of their *time*, of the modern age. These men, through their study of Western thought, had come to realize that Judaism, like all other religions, is not static but dynamic, with the implication that ideas suitable to one age were not necessarily to be accepted in the same way or at all in a different age. As Zunz once put it, the Jewish Middle Ages only came to an end at the time of the French Revolution, Jews having been precipitated into modernity to face problems with which Western thinkers had been grappling for centuries. Krochmal's is probably the most acute philosophical treatment of this basically new approach, although both Krochmal and Zunz acknowledged that the historical critical school owed much to the Italian scholar Azariah dei Rossi (*c.*1511–*c.*1578), the trailblazer in the attempt to discover what actually happened in the past, even if the discoveries ran counter to passages in the Talmud.

Krochmal's introduction, after stating that God in His wisdom has created each age with its own particular way of understanding and interpreting eternal truths, cites Psalm 137 ('By the rivers of Babylon') as an illustration of how this philosophy works. In the rabbinic *midrashim* this psalm is seen as having been composed by King David, to whom the authorship of the whole book of Psalms is attributed. But the anachronism involved in such an interpretation is too glaring to be ignored. How could David, in whose day the Temple had not even been built, write about the events which followed on its destruction over four hundred years later? How could he have known of the Babylonian Empire in an age when people had hardly heard of the existence of Babylon? The traditional reply is that David, in a prophetic vision, did, indeed, see events that were not actually to happen until centuries after his time. But as early as the Middle Ages, a commentator like Abraham Ibn Ezra (1092–1167) could put forward, albeit as only one opinion, the view that nowhere in the Jewish tradition is David regarded as a prophet and that there is, in fact, no attribution of authorship to David in this particular psalm, only in some of the other psalms.

Krochmal observes that the aim of the rabbinic *midrashim* was to awaken the religious emotions of their contemporaries, for whom it was inspiring to think that a man can be so gifted by God with the holy spirit that he can see into the remote future. The ancient rabbis were not historians but religious teachers who catered to the spiritual needs of the people; they were teaching religious and moral, not historical, truths.

The more highly developed sense of history in modern times demands, says Krochmal, a far less fanciful way at looking at the whole question of the attribution of the biblical books to their supposed authors. To attribute Psalm 137 to King David has, nowadays, the opposite effect to that intended by the ancient teachers. It is, nowadays, far less off-putting and far more inspiring to read the psalm as composed by a contemporary Levite, taunted by his Babylonian captors to sing the Lord's song in a foreign land. Such a man must have composed the psalm as a passionate lament. His fiery patriotism provoked him into calling down God's wrath on those who had destroyed the Temple and exiled the Jewish people from its land.

Krochmal has the same approach to the question of a second Isaiah. From chapter 40 onwards the biblical book of Isaiah describes the exiles returning from Babylon, rebuilding the Temple and re-establishing their national life. But the prophet Isaiah, the author of the prophecies in the first part of the book, after whom the book as a whole is named, lived about 150 years before the Return. Here again, the rabbinic tradition understands the prophet Isaiah as seeing in a vision events that were not actually to happen until long after his time. According to this view, he even foresaw the edict of the Persian King Cyrus permitting the Jews to return, since Cyrus is mentioned by name. If a man can be enabled by God to see future events there is no reason why he should not know by name a person who played a significant role in these events. But it is far more plausible, surely, argues Krochmal, to see this whole section of the book as composed, not by the prophet Isaiah, but by a contemporary of the events related, whose 'prophecies' were added to the book at a much later date. Krochmal is fully aware that the attribution of these chapters to the prophet Isaiah belongs to a long-established tradition among the Jews, referred to not only by the rabbis but by Josephus and Ben Sira.[1] Yet he feels obliged to reject even such a long tradition in favour of the suggestion of the biblical critics that there is a Deutero-Isaiah. Here too Krochmal invokes the medieval commentator Ibn Ezra who, though very circumspect, holds that the second part of Isaiah was written much later than the first. Krochmal tries to show that the ancient rabbis also acknowledged, by way of a hint, at least, that these chapters were composed at a later date, which is why, Krochmal suggests, in one talmudic arrangement of the order of the biblical books (*Baba batra* 14*b*) the book of Isaiah is placed after the books of Jeremiah and Ezekiel, even though the prophet Isaiah lived much earlier than these two prophets.

Krochmal's views have been quoted as typical of the Wissenschaft des Judentums school as a whole in the first half of the nineteenth century. In addition to Krochmal in Galicia and Zunz in Germany, the main practitioners of the historical critical methodology, upon which the school is based, were Zechariah Frankel (1801–73) and Abraham Geiger (1810–74) in Germany, Samuel David Luzzatto (1800–65) in Italy, and Solomon Judah Rapoport (1790–1867) in Galicia. Moses Mendelssohn (1729–86) in Berlin and the Haskalah ('Enlightenment') movement

---

[1] Second-century BCE author of Ecclesiasticus (Wisdom of Ben Sira).

which followed him had paved the way for an accommodation of Jewish life and thought to Western culture and the members of the Wissenschaft school were all indebted to the Haskalah. However, the *maskilim* were often so allured by Western culture as to accept it all uncritically. The major contribution of the Wissenschaft school was to approach Judaism with reverence but using the historical critical approach.[2]

In speaking of a school one must not think of a consciously organized movement. What happened was rather that a number of traditionally educated Jews who had become familiar with the languages of Western culture resolved independently, though in close communication with one another, to use these new methods to investigate the classical sources of Judaism and to demonstrate how Jewish religion, literature, and philosophy had developed in response to the different civilizations with which Jews had come into contact through the ages. A primary aim of Wissenschaft des Judentums was to establish correct texts by comparing current texts with those found in libraries open to Jews for the first time. Instead of the piecemeal treatment typical of the older approach, texts were studied as a whole and set in the proper period. According to the traditional view, King David did compose the book of Psalms, but that was taken for granted by the ancient rabbis and was only of concern to them in that it provided a divine guarantee that the text of Psalms was an inspired text which they then proceeded to examine, interpreting the verses and even, in some instances, the very words of the book in isolation. The Wissenschaft school, like the Christian Bible critics of the nineteenth century, began to ask questions such as when the book of Psalms was actually written, what the book meant as a whole into which its various verses fitted, what the relationship of the book to the messages conveyed in the rest of the Bible was, and so forth. For the first time this approach tended to override completely the isolationist approach to the Talmud and Midrash, to the chagrin of the traditionalists for whom talmudic literature was hallowed almost to the same degree as Scripture itself.

The Greek and Latin classics were studied by the Wissenschaft school in order to throw light on the talmudic sources; Arabic and Islamic

[2] For the Wissenschaft des Judentums movement, see Nathan Stern, *The Jewish Historico-Critical School of the Nineteenth Century* (New York, 1910), and, more comprehensively, Benzion Dinur, 'Wissenschaft des Judentums', *Encyclopaedia Judaica* (Jerusalem, 1972), xvi. 570–84.

thought for the better understanding of the medieval Jewish works; the ancient Semitic tongues for a better appreciation of the biblical texts and, above all, world history for the purpose of showing how Jewish history followed universal historical trends.

It cannot be denied that there was a strong apologetic tendency in the Wissenschaft des Judentums movement, its practitioners seeking to demonstrate that Judaism, too, is normal and 'respectable' in having a history, a literature, and a philosophy like other cultures, and that the great men of the Jewish past were not mere ciphers or irrational isolationists but creatures of flesh and blood responsive to the world around them. Yet the scholars of the Wissenschaft movement did strive for objectivity and thus paved the way, in turn, for the employment of the new methodology in higher institutions of Jewish learning and in Jewish learned journals in which articles of impeccable, objective scholarship now appear.

While the Wissenschaft pioneers were prepared, like Krochmal, to accept biblical criticism with regard to some of the biblical books, on which they also advanced critical theories of their own, they were very guarded when it came to applying critical methods to the Pentateuch. While Rapoport, for instance, was prepared to find traces of Maccabean influence in the Psalms and Persian influence in Deutero-Isaiah, he was completely silent on the question of pentateuchal criticism. Samuel David Luzzatto, in his youth, held that the book of Ecclesiastes could not have been written, as the tradition holds, by King Solomon, but with regard to the rest of the Bible he remained firmly within the tradition. Luzzatto defended the unity of the book of Isaiah, and it goes without saying that he would have had no truck with any critical theory that denied the unity and the Mosaic authorship of the Pentateuch. For Luzzatto the whole of the Pentateuch was written down by Moses as God had told him to do.

Although there is no logic in applying criticism to other books of the Bible while stopping short of the Pentateuch—after all the method is exactly the same in both instances—it would be wrong to accuse these early scholars of inconsistency or cowardice. Biblical criticism in their day was still in its infancy. The Documentary Hypothesis had not yet been worked out in any detail. They were brave enough to tackle the problem of critical theory as applied to some of the biblical books. For them, in their day, to have followed the heretic Spinoza in order to deny the tradition, or even to examine it, in connection with the Pentateuch, the Holy of Holies of Judaism, would have been foolhardy in the extreme. Neither they nor their readers were ready for the application of their methodology in the dangerous area of pentateuchal criticism. Zunz was the only Wissenschaft scholar to focus on pentateuchal criticism and then only towards the end of his very long life, when he advanced critical views on the Pentateuch by comparing, for instance, Deuteronomy with Jeremiah and Ezekiel in order to show that this book is late and that Leviticus dates from a later period than that of Deuteronomy. The battles in the Christian world over biblical criticism largely passed by Jewish scholars until modern institutions of Jewish learning were established, by which time critical views were generally accepted as so axiomatic that no need was felt to defend them. There was, and still is, an uneasiness with the Documentary Hypothesis, but on the level of objective scholarship, not of dogma. In contemporary scholarship the division of the Pentateuch into the four sources of J, E, D, and P may be rejected on scholarly grounds, but hardly any biblical scholar today, Jewish or non-Jewish, holds otherwise than that the Pentateuch is a composite work. The note of Richard Elliot Friedman in his book, *Who Wrote the Bible?* is pertinent. 'There are many persons who claim to be biblical scholars. I refer to scholars who have the necessary skills to work on the problem, and who meet, discuss and debate their ideas and researches with other scholars through scholarly journals, conferences, etc.'[3]

A few remarks on the history of biblical criticism as applied to the Pentateuch are in order here. (I have treated this matter much more fully in my book *Principles of the Jewish Faith*.[4]) It is important to note that, although modern biblical criticism was, at first, largely a Christian activity, the real pioneer was the medieval Jewish commentator, Abraham Ibn Ezra. Just as this scholar expressed, in advance of his time, his doubts on whether Psalm 137 could be attributed to King David because of the anachronism involved in such a view, as noted by Krochmal, for the same reason he questioned the Mosaic authorship of *some* pentateuchal verses.

Ibn Ezra, in the twelfth century, had to be careful not to be charged with heresy, hence his cryptic remarks on the subject, interpreted by Spinoza in *Tractatus Theologico-politicus*, published in Hamburg in

[3] (San Francisco, Ca., 1989), 261 n. 2.   [4] New edn. (Northvale, NJ, 1988), ch. 9.

1670. In his commentary on Deuteronomy 1: 2, Ibn Ezra is puzzled by
the verse 'These are the words which Moses spoke unto all Israel *beyond
the Jordan*' (Deut. 1: 1). In Moses' day the Israelites had not yet entered
the Land of Israel and the term 'beyond the Jordan' would not have
been used for the side of the Jordan on which they were encamped.
Furthermore, the verse identifies the places at which Moses spoke to his
people. If Moses was the author of the verse he would have had no need
to identify these places since, when he spoke to them, the people were
actually there. Thus the opening of the book of Deuteronomy gives the
impression that it was composed by another writer than Moses. On this
Ibn Ezra comments: 'If you know the secret of the twelve, and of "And
Moses wrote", and of "And the Canaanite was then in the land", and of
"In the mount where the Lord is seen", and of "Behold his bedstead
was a bedstead of iron", you will discover the truth.'

Spinoza explains this cryptic saying (he was anticipated by the
fourteenth-century Jewish scholar Joseph Bonfils) as follows, and he is
surely right. 'The secret of the twelve' refers to the last twelve verses of
the Pentateuch which, dealing with the death and burial of Moses,
could not have been written by Moses himself. Similarly, the verse 'And
Moses wrote this law [Torah]' (Deut. 31: 9), implies that another author
wrote that Moses wrote 'this Torah'. The verse 'And the Canaanite was
then in the land' (Gen. 12: 6) is hard to explain if this verse were written
by Moses, since in Moses' day the Canaanites were still in the land. 'In
the mount where the Lord is seen' (Gen. 22: 14) is understood as referring to the Temple Mount, though the Temple had not yet been built in
Moses' day. 'Behold his bedstead was a bedstead of iron, is it not in
Rabbath of the children of Ammon?' (Deut. 3: 11) tells of the bedstead of
Og, king of Bashan, who was slain by Moses at the end of Moses' life,
while the verse seems to point to a long-standing exhibit of Og's bedstead or sepulchre in Rabbath of the children of Ammon. Moreover,
Moses had never been in this place to see the bedstead. In a separate
comment on the verse 'And the Canaanite was then in the land', Ibn
Ezra first gives the explanation that 'then' means 'just then', but he goes
on to say, if this explanation does not satisfy, that there is a secret here
which the wise will understand. Already in the Talmud (*Baba batra* 15*a*)
there is an opinion that Joshua wrote the last eight verses of the Torah,
since these deal with Moses' death. But Ibn Ezra goes further to speak
of the last twelve verses, beginning at 'And Moses went up' since, as he

observes 'Once he went up he did not come down again [to write these verses]'. This is Ibn Ezra's 'secret of the twelve'. Spinoza himself believed that the Pentateuch was written down by Ezra after the Return from the Babylonian exile.

A long series of later conjectures on the authorship of the Pentateuch culminated in the Graf–Wellhausen Hypothesis or Documentary Hypothesis. According to this hypothesis, there are four documents or sources in the Pentateuch, each stemming from a different period in the history of Israel. These four are given the symbols J, E, D, P, combined by a Redactor, who is given the symbol R. J represents the source in which the divine name is JHVH (the Tetragrammaton). E is the source which uses the divine name Elohim. D represents the book of Deuteronomy, identified with the Book of the Law found in the time of King Josiah (2 Kgs. 22 and 23). P represents the priestly strand comprising the whole book of Leviticus and some other material in the rest of the Pentateuch. A later theory has it that it is no longer possible to disentangle J and E since, even though traces of each can be distinguished, they cannot be clearly detected as separate sources, hence the later tendency to see only three sources: JE, D, and P. Wellhausen placed P as the latest of the four sources and tried to date them according to an evolutionary pattern. Some of the critical theories might seem preposterous, yet even when the Documentary Hypothesis is rejected by scholars (on scholarly not dogmatic grounds), the verdict of all scholars who have investigated the matter is that the Pentateuch is a composite work. More of this in a later chapter.

Reference must also be made to what is called the lower criticism or textual criticism.[5] It has been noted that while the Masoretic text, the current text handed down from generation to generation, is very reliable, it is impossible to ignore the evidence provided by the Greek version, the Septuagint (for which the symbol is LXX), the Targumim, the Peshitta, and the Samaritan Pentateuch for variant readings. Textual scholars take these into account in their efforts to establish the original text, and modern scholars have often suggested emendations of their own. Here, again, it is not a question of whether this or that emendation is plausible—some are very far-fetched and unlikely—but it is equally implausible to reject all textual emendation as if the Masoretic text were itself the one given to Moses.

[5] A good account of textual criticism is given by J. Weingreen, *Introduction to the Critical Study of the Text of the Hebrew Bible* (Oxford, 1982).

As the twentieth century draws to a close, two different and irreconcilable attitudes prevail among Jews with regard to how Judaism came into being. The first of these could be termed the 'fundamentalist' attitude were it not for the fact, noted in the Introduction to this book, that the term 'fundamentalist' has acquired too pejorative a connotation. Better, then, to use the term 'pre-scientific' for this attitude, while using the term 'scientific' for the opposite attitude. T. H. Huxley's famous description of the scientist is that he sits down before the facts like a little child, without preconceived notions, asking what they tell him. This is hardly accurate. There is also an intuitive element in scientific thinking, though this, too, must be judged by its coherence with the facts. The approach of the Wissenschaft des Judentums school and its successors (and that of modern biblical and rabbinic scholarship) can be and is best described as 'scientific' in that in it the sources of Judaism are studied in a detached and objective manner without imposing on them ideas they do not really contain. With regard to King David and Psalm 137, for instance, the scientific approach rejects the notion that King David was the author of this psalm, not because God cannot endow a man with the power to foretell the future in detail, but rather because an objective study of what the psalm actually says succeeds in convincing the unbiased student that no such claim is actually made in the psalm. In the pre-scientific approach, what the psalm is actually saying is what the tradition or the ancient rabbis hold that the psalm is saying, namely, that the evidence of reason or sheer common sense must be rejected as heretical. Reason can hold no sway where it is contradicted by the tradition. Another feature of the 'scientific' approach is that in it every hypothesis put forward by a scholar is argued for and has to meet the criticism of his peers. The great battle between religion and science in the nineteenth century was not so much about the relationship between faith and reason but about precisely this point: whether faith can be invoked in matters that can adequately be decided through the application of reason. In order to make the difference clear the 'pre-scientific' or traditional picture of Judaism must be stated in broad outline.

The Traditional View

According to the traditional view, Judaism is based on the theophany at Sinai (Exod. 19 and 20) but the scope of revelation is widened to include the whole of the Torah, both the 'Written Torah' and the 'Oral Torah', together conceived as the complete communication of God's will for the people of Israel, the Jews, and, through them, for all mankind. The Written Torah includes the whole of the Hebrew Bible since, although the highest degree of revelation is that of the Pentateuch given to Moses ('the Torah of Moses'), the prophetic books were also compiled by inspired prophets, and the authors of the Hagiographa (the 'Ketuvim') were inspired by the holy spirit, a lesser degree of inspiration. The doctrine of the Oral Torah, in its original form, means that Moses received at Sinai during the forty days and nights he stayed on the Mount (Exod. 24: 15–18), the laws, doctrines, and elaborations of the Written Torah, the laws and teachings contained in the Pentateuch. The Oral Torah was itself later recorded in writing in the talmudic literature, together with the vast corpus of rabbinic teachings, and the whole is now referred to as the Oral Torah. The Torah, in the sense of the Pentateuch, is thought of as embracing not only the laws and commandments but the whole five books, including the narrative portions, which are seen as having been conveyed by God to Moses during the forty-year journey of the Children of Israel through the wilderness. Thus the Pentateuch, the Five Books of Moses, is conceived of as a direct communication by God to Moses (the nature of which, though not the content, is obscure, as it must be since finite man cannot grasp the Infinite). There are two opinions in the Talmud (*Gittin* 60*a*) on whether Moses wrote down each event when it happened and later combined them into a single book at the end of the forty years just before he died, or whether he wrote down the whole of the Torah at the end of the forty years.

The Torah is the very word of God—the teachings, laws, doctrines, and rules for the conduct of life as revealed by the Author of life. To study the Torah is to think God's thoughts after Him. To practise the *mitsvot* ('precepts') of the Torah is to obey God's revealed will. And this Torah has remained unchanged throughout the ages, conveyed, through the chain of tradition, from Moses to Joshua, from Joshua to the elders, from the elders to the prophets, and from the prophets to the Men of the Great Synagogue, as stated in the opening passage of *Pirkei avot* ('Ethics of the Fathers'), and then from teacher to disciple, from parent to child, through three thousand years of Jewish history.

Some of the medieval thinkers seem to have held a less mechanical view of how the Torah was delivered (that, for example, some few verses were added by a later prophet, as Ibn Ezra had said and as is found in the work of Judah Hehasid, to be discussed in the next chapter), but the majority of Orthodox Jews accept, in theory, at least, as the only correct formulation of Orthodox faith, Maimonides' definition of *Torah min hashamayim*, concerning which he writes:

This implies our belief that the whole of this Torah found in our hands this day is the Torah that was handed down to Moses and that it is all of divine origin. By this I mean that the whole of the Torah came unto him [Moses] from before God which is metaphorically called 'speaking', but the real nature of that communication is unknown to everyone except Moses to whom it came . . . The interpretation of traditional law [i.e. the Oral Torah] is in like manner of divine origin. And that which we know today of the nature of sukkah, *lulav, shofar, tsitsit* and tefillin is essentially the same as that which God commanded Moses and which the latter told us.

In such a view of Torah there is no room for any notion of development in the Jewish religion; the Torah is a static body of truth revealed by God and handed down intact from generation to generation. Even the Karaites in the Middle Ages held fast to the doctrine that every word of the Pentateuch was 'dictated' by God. Like the Sadducees in an earlier period, the Karaites only took issue with the doctrine of the Oral Torah, which they held to be a rabbinic invention.

According to this view, the Pentateuch, the source of the all-embracing Torah, is not a human composition at all but a book the real Author of which is God, Moses being responsible only for writing it all down at God's behest. Two things follow from this concept of divine Authorship: (1) that the Pentateuch cannot be subjected to any kind of literary analysis that is applied to works composed by human beings; (2) that it is infallible. It follows from the first point that all biblical criticism, when applied to the Pentateuch, is totally misguided. And it follows from the second that the information conveyed in the Pentateuch regarding human history and the nature of the physical universe is completely accurate and can never be false. It is true that even a divine document needs to be interpreted by humans, but for the interpretation to be valid it must be engaged in by believers in the above propositions. Moreover, the authentic interpreters, except in comparatively minor matters which do not affect Jewish practice, are the talmudic rabbis. Why these in particular? Some reply that their authenticity is guaranteed precisely because that is what the tradition has determined. Maimonides says that the authority of the Babylonian Talmud stems from its acceptance as *the* authority by the community of Israel. But others would go further to hold that the talmudic rabbis were spiritual supermen, inspired by God, so that, in a sense, what the rabbis say is itself inspired and infallible teaching.

The Scientific Picture: What Really Happened

The traditional picture sketched above has been assailed in modern times. As a result of the vast increase of modern knowledge, we now know that, for all the values inherent in this picture, things did not happen that way. Take, first, the whole idea of the Oral Law. This doctrine, too, has had a history, as the massive researches of Zechariah Frankel and his successors have shown. Frankel, a rabbi in Breslau, was appointed principal of the Jewish Theological Seminary in that town in 1854. In 1871 he founded the learned journal *Monatschrift für Geschichte und Wissenschaft des Judentums*, the foremost medium for scholarly discussion of how Jewish thought and practices developed. The very existence of such a journal is indicative of the new approach, in which Jewish institutions are studied not only or primarily *as* they came to be but also and especially *how* they came to be. In Frankel's studies of the Septuagint produced in Alexandria, he showed that the school of Alexandrian exegetes had an approach to the Bible with similarities to but also with differences from that which appears in the rabbinic literature. It was the same Bible that both schools were studying, but one was far more influenced by the Greek philosophical background than the other. Saul Lieberman has called attention to the fact that Socrates, Plato, Aristotle, and the other ancient Greek philosophers are nowhere mentioned by name in the rabbinic literature. Thus, for Frankel, scholarly or 'scientific' investigation is not primarily of what the ancient rabbis said on the surface but of what was behind what they said, of why they said it, and why it was said at that particular time.

A good example of the difference between the 'scientific' and 'prescientific' approach is provided by the revealing debate between Frankel and the founder of neo-Orthodoxy, Samson Raphael Hirsch (1808–88), on the rabbinic idea of a law given to Moses at Sinai.[6] That, for instance,

[6] For the debate between Hirsch and Frankel see Hirsch, *The Collected Writings*, 5 vols. (New York, 1988), v. 209–330.

the tefillin have to have a knot and be black and square, together with other details of their form, although none of this is mentioned anywhere in the Torah itself, is said in one talmudic passage (*Menaḥot* 35a–b) to be 'a law given to Moses at Sinai'. Hirsch believed that this has to be taken literally, that at Sinai Moses was given all the instructions regarding the manufacture of the tefillin. As Maimonides formulated it in the quotation given earlier in this chapter, the tefillin we wear now are exactly the same in form as the tefillin which God instructed Moses the Israelites must wear. Frankel, with a more sophisticated historical sense, found it hard to believe that, for instance, King David wore tefillin no different from the tefillin the rabbis wore or from those worn by devout Jews today. Such an idea, for Frankel, is as anachronistic as the notion of David seeing future events was for Krochmal. Consequently, Frankel holds that what the rabbis were really saying is that the origin of the tefillin and their nature is lost in the mists of time. It is a very ancient practice, for which the rabbis used the term 'it is a law given to Moses at Sinai'. Frankel has no difficulty in showing that the rabbis did on one occasion use the term 'a law given to Moses at Sinai' even for a law obviously of rabbinic origin. But Frankel must have known that this was an exception and that the talmudic rabbis really did believe, as Hirsch argued, in the literal meaning of the term except for that single instance. Frankel seems to be saying that, if in one instance the term can only be understood as a very ancient law, we, with a greater sense of history, are justified in suggesting that the reason why the rabbis called certain rules 'laws given to Moses at Sinai', was that, in their day, everyone believed that there were rules given to Moses at Sinai. Although we now find this anachronistic, we only reject what the rabbis said. We do not reject why they said it, namely, that there are rules, clear, obvious, and ancient, that are binding on us as well.

Behind it all is the contention of Frankel, Zunz, Krochmal, and their co-workers of the Wissenschaft des Judentums school, that when ancient Jewish texts are examined historically a whole new world of ideas is opened up. In this school and its successors the first questions to be asked of a text are: is the text accurate or are there copyist's errors? is the information it conveys accurate? and why was it produced just at that time? Why, to take the doctrine of the Oral Law, was the whole doctrine not accepted by the Sadducees if there really was a living tradition of this Oral Law handed down from generation to generation since the time of

Moses' ascent of the Mount? Here is the place to note that, while Frankel had an open mind on the origin of tefillin, he personally wore black, square-shaped tefillin because scholarly investigation into origins is one thing, living religion another. Frankel wore tefillin because that was the way, developed by the tradition, in which a Jew worships God.

To turn to scholarly investigation of the Torah itself, it can immediately be seen that the two propositions that the Torah was given at one time by God to Moses and that the Torah is infallible even when it speaks of historical events and the nature of the physical world, are simply untenable. It has now been established beyond reasonable doubt that the Pentateuch is a heterogeneous or composite work, even if the Documentary Hypothesis is rejected. There are three law codes, for instance, in the Pentateuch: one in Exodus, another in Leviticus, and another in Deuteronomy. Unless these three stem from different periods in Israel's history and from different backgrounds, it is very hard to see why each should have its own vocabulary and why there are some contradictions in the laws formulated in the three. As for infallibility, we need only point to the advance of science after Galileo to show that the Pentateuch was produced in a pre-scientific age. Geologists have demonstrated, contrary to the plain sense of Scripture, the immense age of the earth; astronomers that the universe is not geocentric; anthropologists that human beings have been on earth far longer by hundreds of thousands of years than Genesis seems to suggest—all making it increasingly difficult to believe that the pentateuchal picture is the result of a direct divine communication and hence an infallible source providing completely accurate information on all the topics with which it deals. For most reasonable people the nineteenth-century battles between science and religion belong to thought patterns of an age that will never return.

A few more details should be given here of how the 'scientific' or scholarly picture differs from what we have called the traditional or pre-scientific one, avoiding as far as possible the resurrection of time-worn controversies.

We read in the book of Deuteronomy (12: 13–14): 'Take heed to thyself that thou offer not thy burnt-offerings in every place that thou seest; but in the place which the Lord thy God shall choose in one of thy tribes, there thou shalt offer thy burnt-offerings, and there thou shalt do all that I command thee', meaning that once the Temple had been built sacrifices were not to be offered at any other site. But in the book of

Kings (ch. 18) the prophet Elijah, in his confrontation with the prophets of Baal, offers a sacrifice on Mount Carmel. In the traditional view, Elijah did commit an act otherwise forbidden but, being a prophet, he knew that he had been granted a dispensation to do so, in order to show the people that Baal worship was false. But, in that case, why is the dispensation not mentioned? The story proceeds as if there was nothing even slightly wrong in Elijah's act. According to the critical view, the book of Deuteronomy, with its prohibition of worship outside the Temple, was not written until the time of King Josiah, so that in Elijah's time there was no prohibition against offering sacrifices outside the Temple. Such a solution is impossible for those who hold the traditional view, since Deuteronomy dates from the time of Moses, who lived before Elijah.

We read in Deuteronomy (14: 21): 'Ye shall not eat of any thing that dieth of itself; thou mayest give it to the stranger that is within thy gates, that he may eat it; or thou mayest sell it unto a foreigner; for thou art a holy people unto the Lord thy God.' But in Leviticus (17: 15) we read: 'And every soul that eateth that which dieth of itself, or that which is torn of beasts, whether he be home-born or a stranger, he shall wash his clothes, and bathe himself in water, and be unclean until the even; then shall he be clean.' The word for 'stranger', *ger*, means a sojourner, a non-Israelite who has come to reside in the Land of Israel, unlike the 'foreigner' in the Deuteronomy verse, who is on an occasional visit to the land. According to the critical view, Leviticus, stemming from a priestly source, forbids even the stranger to eat an animal that has died by itself, while Deuteronomy, a different book, not only permits this to the stranger as well as to the foreigner but advocates that he be given the food forbidden to an Israelite. According to the critical view, there is no need to try to harmonize laws mentioned in two different sources. In the traditional view, however, such harmonization is essential since the whole of the Pentateuch, including both Leviticus and Deuteronomy, was given by God to Moses at the same time, that is, during the forty-year journey through the wilderness. The necessary harmonization is achieved in the rabbinic literature by postulating that there are two types of 'stranger'. The stranger to whom the forbidden animal can or should be given is one who, though allowed to reside in the land, has not been converted to the religion of Israel so that the dietary laws do not apply to him. He is known as a *ger toshav* ('a stranger who resides [in the land]'). The 'stranger' in the Leviticus passage is a proselyte (*ger tsedek*, 'righteous proselyte'), one who has been converted to the Jewish religion and is therefore obliged, like all other Israelites, to keep the dietary laws.

The historical problem here is that in biblical times there was no such thing as a proselyte, since the whole concept of conversion to Judaism only arose at a time when many Jews lived outside the land and were identified as Jews by their religious allegiance. In biblical times, the stranger simply threw in his lot with the people of Israel by coming to live in the land. In the book of Ruth we read that Ruth, who later but not in the book itself becomes the prototype of the righteous proselyte, declares to Naomi, 'Whither thou goest, I will go; and where thou lodgest, I will lodge; thy people shall be my people, and thy God my God' (Ruth 1: 16). 'Thy God' becomes 'my God' as a result of 'thy people shall be my people'. It was only when non-Jews were attracted to the *religion* of Israel even when neither they nor the many Jews with whom they had come into contact lived in the land of Israel that the *ger* became identified with the proselyte.

This is an excellent illustration of the two different approaches. In the traditional approach, the God-given Torah, when it speaks of the *ger* in Leviticus and in other passages in the Torah in which he is treated as an Israelite, really means a proselyte—i.e. there really were proselytes in the time of Moses. In the critical view, while it is obviously true that, at a later stage in history, there were proselytes and conversion procedures to establish their status, the actual meaning of *ger* in the days of Moses or, rather, in the time of the sources which describe the days of Moses, is a resident alien. Only at a later date, when there did exist conversion to Judaism, was the *ger* identified with the proselyte.

A further matter has to be noted. In the Leviticus passage, the animal which dies of itself (*nevelah*) is mentioned together with the animal torn by beasts (*terefah*). In the critical view the verse means literally an animal that has died of its own accord and one that has been torn by wild beasts. But in the traditional view, as stated throughout the Talmud, the *nevelah* is any animal that has not been killed by *sheḥitah*, the traditional method of killing animals for food. This method is said to have been conveyed, like the laws governing the shape and form of the tefillin, to Moses at Sinai. The *terefah* includes, in addition to an animal torn by wild beasts, any animal that suffers from a disease of its vital organs.

There are eighteen such defects, the details of which are also said to have been given to Moses at Sinai. According to the traditional view all the later 'developments' are not developments at all, as they are in the critical view, but belong to the original Torah given by God to Moses.

If a religious Jew finds the critical or scientific view convincing, as many would say he must if reason and probability have a say in the matter and he is concerned to preserve intellectual integrity, he obviously cannot maintain, at the same time, that the Torah is a book of which the author is God in any direct sense. If Leviticus was compiled at a different time from Deuteronomy, and if proselytism only came later into Judaism, and if the original meaning of *nevelah* and *terefah* was extended in the form these assume in the rabbinic literature, then the developments must have been precisely that: extensions of and elaborations on the law through human beings at different times under the influence of the different situations in which they found themselves. But this should not mean that a religious Jew who accepts critical theories should not follow the conversion procedures as laid down by the rabbis or should not keep the dietary laws. For even though it has to be granted that Judaism has developed in response to external considerations, it is still the Judaism the religious Jew wishes to follow. Such is basically the attitude of Frankel, the Breslau school, and Conservative/Masorti Judaism: that origins and historical considerations are matters of scholarship, while religion has to do with what has become the Jewish religion.

In all the above the basic principle involved is that which governed Krochmal in his consideration of whether or not Psalm 137 can be attributed to King David simply because that is what the tradition states or appears to state. The principle is this: if, from the events related in a document, it is clear that the document cannot be dated from a time when these events had not yet taken place but must be dated subsequent to those events, it is totally unreasonable to affirm, even on the grounds of tradition, that the document does predate the events of which it tells. It is just possible that logic is not being defied in a particular instance because the document is a miraculous one and actually foretells the future, but the weight of probability is always against such a possibility; and how could we know that the document is so bizarrely contrary to the normal run of events? This is the principle employed in scholarly investigation everywhere. It is no use arguing that this method cannot be applied to the Torah since it is, indeed, such a miraculous document utterly beyond the kind of investigation suitable for normal human documents, as this is precisely the issue: can the Torah be examined and analysed by the methods of normal scholarly investigation? That the methodology has been applied to the Torah, to the satisfaction of most unbiased students, can only mean that the Torah is, in an important sense, a document produced by humans. Where the traditional view contradicts appearances by introducing the idea of prophetic vision, it begs the question. You cannot argue that the evidence that the Torah is a human document must be rejected because the Torah is not a human document. If God has allowed human beings to investigate by their reasoning powers and come to the unanimous conclusion that the Torah has been produced in the manner the critical theory suggests convincingly on the evidence, how can it be said, at the same time, that, by so doing, He has planted false clues to mislead those who trust in Him? If God-given reason successfully convinces those who examine the question that Psalm 137 was composed by a contemporary of the events which it relates, that is sufficient reason to treat the psalm as such, and it is only confusing the issue to invoke the idea of prophetic vision. One does not necessarily deny the workings of divine providence and divine inspiration in order to reject the irrational attribution of Psalm 137 to David. Moreover, to invoke the idea of prophetic vision with regard to the forecasting of future events in detail has the effect of abolishing human history entirely. The tremendous theological problem of how divine foreknowledge can be compatible with human freedom exercised the minds of most of the great medieval thinkers. Any solution or even glimpse of light is postulated on divine knowledge being different from human knowledge. For instance, one idea put forward is that in the divine mind past, present, and future are all one: God sees in the Eternal Now the future as it takes place *then*. But it is hard to see how the *human* King David could know for certain the events of the Babylonian exile hundreds of years before they happened without these events being predetermined.

Liberal Supernaturalism

At this stage of our investigation it would help to clarify matters if we revert, without intending to be rude but simply as convenient shorthand, to the use of the term 'fundamentalist' for the Jew who persists in maintaining a pre-scientific attitude. In reaction to the historical critical approach there are three different attitudes among religious Jews, that is, Jews who embrace a particular religious philosophy of Judaism. These philosophies can be defined as: fundamentalist supernaturalism, liberal naturalism, and liberal supernaturalism, the latter being the standpoint this book adopts and seeks to defend.

Unconvinced by the arguments advanced by the historical critical school, whether as applied to the Bible or to the rabbinic tradition, the Jewish fundamentalist holds that nothing has changed and that the traditional view still retains its full power. God, for him, is not, as in religious naturalism, the name given to 'the force that makes for righteousness' but is the 'living God' of the tradition, the Creator of the universe and all that is in it. He is the transcendent Author of nature as He is of the Torah: in this philosophy the two ideas are inextricably bound together. If you deny that God is the ultimate Author of the Torah, if you accept the 'scientific' picture of how the Torah came to be, you might as well reject belief in God. If you accept, the fundamentalist argues, that human hands have been at work in the compilation of the Torah, how do you know that there is a God since the existence of God is known through His self-revelation in the Torah? How can it be theologically sound to possess complete certainty with regard to belief in God while having reservations regarding His revelationary activity? Better to be an out-and-out atheist, some fundamentalists would say, than, in Elijah's famous charge, halt between two opinions.

The liberal naturalist agrees with the fundamentalist supernaturalist that one who is prepared to accept the approach of the historical critical school and its implications cannot believe in a personal God. The conclusion he draws from the evidence of human creativity in the Torah is that there is no divine element in it at all. Indeed, he holds that there is nothing divine in any creation of the human spirit. There is no revelation because there is no Revealer. If the word 'God' is still used it is only as a way of seeing cherished values as grounded in the ultimate stuff of the universe. Such a Jew can still be said to be religious because religious emotions are themselves natural to human beings. He may even pray, because this is to call attention to the highest within him and in the universe; he may even keep the *mitsvot*, not because they are commanded by God—his God is not, by definition, a Commander—but because they enrich Jewish life or contribute towards Jewish survival. Neither the fundamentalist supernaturalist nor the liberal naturalist is at all bothered by the problem of how to distinguish between the divine and human elements in the Torah. The former holds that there is no human element and the latter that there is no divine element. The liberal naturalist may well see the Bible as a great book, but not as an inspired book, except in the sense in which we speak of Shakespeare or Mozart or Rembrandt as inspired. For the fundamentalist supernaturalist it is both inaccurate and impious to speak of the Bible as a 'great book'; inaccurate because it is not really a book at all but the very word of God, impious because to describe the Bible as great literature comes perilously close to saying that God has a fine literary style.

The liberal supernaturalist refuses to accept the either/or of the other two. He is liberal in that his reason compels him to adopt the historical critical approach and its implications, even though this involves a degree of rejection of the traditional view. He is a supernaturalist because he sees no reason to deny the supernatural elements of his religion. As for the fundamentalist supernaturalist, God is for him the living God and the precepts of the Torah divine commands, albeit these are conveyed indirectly and with human co-operation. To repeat once again Krochmal's illustration of King David and Psalm 137: a liberal Jew (with a small 'l') cannot bring himself to believe, contrary to all the evidence, that King David composed this psalm. He cannot believe, in this and other similar instances, that God inspires a human being to see into the remote future, not because God cannot do this (nothing is impossible for God), but because all the evidence goes to show that He did not do so. But that does not mean, for the liberal supernaturalist, that there are no inspired men who brought the word of God to the world, no sweet singers whose hymns are sung universally to the God of all, no prophets who still speak to us the everlasting truths that God requires men to be just, merciful, holy, and compassionate. But whether or not King David wrote Psalm 137 is a question of fact and, if the evidence is reliable, which it is, the facts are that the psalm was not written by David. Psalm 137 is given only as an illustration. The liberal supernaturalist cannot, in honesty, stop there, but feels obliged to approach the Pentateuch, the Torah, in the same way. For him, the Pentateuch also contains what we may call both a human and a divine element.

To say that there is both a human and a divine element in the Torah is not to say that one can go through the Pentateuch or the Psalms or the

Mishnah or the Talmud with a pencil ticking the passages which appeal to us as divine and those which do not as human. It is rather that God is behind the whole process, that, from the beginning, there was such a reaching out to God among the people of Israel that it produced over the ages the multi-faceted glory we call the Torah, which, since it was produced by humans and since it is eternity expressing itself in time, contains higher and lower, error as well as truth, the ignoble as well as the noble. We distinguish between the two, first, by our moral sense, itself given by God, and secondly, by what the Jewish tradition itself declares. There are less than worthy passages in the Bible, but the tradition does not demand that we act upon them. In Psalm 137 itself no one with any moral sense will advocate that we dash innocent children against a rock as in the psalmist's curse in the final verse. Krochmal seems to be hinting at this when he explains the imprecation as a bitter cry wrung from a tormented heart.

This is among the gains of the historical approach. We are now able to distinguish between the higher and lower in our traditions because both have been set in their historical context. Instead of seeing God 'dictating' both the higher and the lower, with the implication that, in a sense, God 'wanted' the lower, the whole is now seen as human reflection on the past. The tradition, the Oral Law, is now seen as further reflection, in which the higher becomes mandatory, the lower never to be emulated. The tradition treats the passages about the extermination of the Amalekites, men, women, and children, or the law of the rebellious son who is to be stoned to death (Deut. 21: 18–21) as belonging to the past, while treating, say, the Decalogue as binding for all time.

In speaking of three distinct philosophies among religious Jews it is absurd to suggest that each is held consistently all the time, or even that theological reflections by Jews on why they behave Jewishly is at all the norm. Religious Jews, like all other religious people, conform to the mores of the particular group to which they belong, using the theological aspect as underpinning. Many a devout Jew offers his prayers and keeps the *mitsvot* without bothering whether or how many of these were commanded directly by God. He does these things because that is how Jews worship God. If he were to ask himself why he does them he would no doubt reply 'because God has commanded me so to do', but he would rarely pose the question to himself. He would simply get on with it. Deep down he may not even be a believer all the time, but wishes to

LIBERAL SUPERNATURALISM

LIBERAL SUPERNATURALISM

follow the Orthodox way of life because it is warm and homely and demanding and is followed by people whose company he finds congenial. Conversely, many a liberal naturalist may at times be moved to ponder Browning's 'the great perhaps', to feel that his sense of wonder is inadequately catered to by religious naturalism. It is very important that theological exposition should not ignore the sociological aspects of religion.

And so we come to the question of Jewish practice, of why, granted the approach of the liberal supernaturalist, Jews should keep the *mitsvot*. Why, because the men of the past, as they reached out for God, thought that He had commanded them to keep the precepts, should we keep them now we know that it did not happen quite like that? If, according to the theory, the fundamentalist, traditional view is pre-scientific and to put it bluntly, wrong, why, in practice, should the precepts be kept as if the fundamentalist view is correct and the *mitsvot* were really given by God to Moses?

An oft-quoted observation by Professor Louis Ginzberg, who was a biblical and rabbinic critic and historian as well as an observant Jew, is pertinent. Ginzberg, in his famous essay on Zechariah Frankel and the Breslau school, has this to say:

We may now understand the apparent contradiction between the theory and practice of the positive-historic school. One may, for instance, conceive of the origin and idea of Sabbath rest as the professor of Protestant theology at a German university would conceive it, and yet minutely observe the smallest detail of the Sabbath observances known to strict Orthodoxy. For an adherent of this school the sanctity of the Sabbath reposes not upon the fact that it was proclaimed on Sinai, but on the fact that the Sabbath idea found for thousands of years its expression in Jewish souls. It is the task of the historian to examine the beginnings and developments of the numerous customs and observances of the Jews; practical Judaism on the other hand is not concerned with origins, but regards the institutions as they have come to be. If we are convinced that Judaism is a religion of deed, expressing itself in observances which are designed to achieve the moral elevation of man and give reality to his religious spirit, we have a principle in obedience to which reforms in Judaism are possible. From this point of view the evaluation of a law is independent of its origins, and thus the line of demarcation between biblical and rabbinical law almost disappears.[7]

Ginzberg goes on to see here the basic difference between the approaches of Frankel and Hirsch, to which I have alluded. The famous historian

[7] Louis Ginzberg, *Students, Scholars and Saints* (Philadelphia, Pa., 1928), 195–216.

Graetz, a scholar who pursued the same line as Frankel, on a visit to London, was called on to read the *haftarah* in the Great Synagogue; he read the prophetic passage with his own emendations of the text, yet was observed to wrap his handkerchief round his wrist in order to avoid carrying it in the public domain on the Sabbath.

Ginzberg delivered the lecture upon which his essay is based at the beginning of the twentieth century. Though still serving as an excellent summary of the theological position of the Breslau school, it needs to be examined rather more closely. For one thing, Ginzberg, while speaking of the possibilities of reform, does not pursue this matter further and does not explain why, in his personal life, he was somewhat hostile to the Reform movement and did not personally subscribe to Reform Judaism. Frankel was, in fact, a Reform rabbi, though of a very moderate kind. Nor does Ginzberg give adequate weight to the psychological difference between the approach of the historical critical school and strict Orthodoxy. There have no doubt been, and still are, Jews who conceive of the origins of the sabbath observances exactly as the professor at a German university and yet, at the same time, observe the sabbath exactly like the strictest Orthodox Jews, but is there no psychological difference between them, a difference which is bound to have its effect on their practice? Psychologically, it is undeniable that a clear recognition of the human development of Jewish practice and observance is bound to produce a somewhat weaker sense of allegiance to the minutiae of Jewish law. For the Orthodox Jew, every single detail is a direct expression of the divine will. He will go to the utmost limits, as he must, granted his Orthodox belief, to keep every detail of the dietary laws, for example, since they are part of what God has directly commanded him to do. But the Jew who sees the dietary laws as having *evolved*, although he, too, may acknowledge them, in a sense, to be divinely ordained (through the historical experiences of the Jewish people), will find it more difficult to be so scrupulous. And Ginzberg's statement about the *mitsvot* contributing to moral elevation is fine so far as it goes, but fails to consider those laws (very few in number) in the Torah which have the opposite effect.

So liberal supernaturalism also has its problems, to be considered later on in this book. For the present it suffices to say that this approach is the only one that allows untrammelled freedom to the human mind to explore the facts, while avoiding any negation of the deepest longings of the human soul.

In advocating the adoption of liberal supernaturalism one should not be so liberal as to remove from supernaturalism the belief in the Hereafter. The historical critical school has succeeded in showing that this belief, too, has had a history. Belief in life after death was only developed fully in post-biblical Judaism. But if the tradition as it has developed is to be the guide, if the origins of a doctrine are far less relevant to living Judaism than what the doctrine has come to mean, this belief, for all its numerous interpretations and for all the speculations as to its nature, is now part of Judaism, at least according to the liberal supernaturalist view. In this area we should not be concerned only with the historical facts but with whether belief in the afterlife is true for Jews now. It has to be admitted that even by liberal supernaturalists and, possibly, even by fundamentalist supernaturalists, belief in an afterlife tends to be relegated to the background, possibly because of the severe problems Jews have had to face after the Holocaust and the establishment of the State of Israel, and, possibly, because of the strong influence of American pragmatism on Jewish theologians, the majority of whom are American-educated. Yet what kind of supernaturalism is it that affirms the existence of God while being indifferent to the belief that human beings can enjoy Him for ever?

THREE

IS IT TRADITIONAL?

Torah min hashamayim

THE VIEW DESCRIBED in the previous chapter, that revelation has to be seen in terms of divine co-operation with humans, has often been challenged on the grounds that it is contrary to Jewish tradition, especially to the doctrine *Torah min hashamayim* (the Torah is from Heaven), which objection I have countered by saying: it all depends on what you mean by *from*. This chapter considers in greater detail how the historical critical method sheds light on this 'from' and whether the position I adopt can be considered to be in any way traditional.

What Orthodoxy today seems unanimously to accept is that the doctrine that the Torah is from Heaven means that every word of the Pentateuch, the Five Books of Moses, was communicated directly by God to Moses during the forty years the Children of Israel journeyed through the wilderness, as were the laws given to Moses during his stay, for forty days and nights, on Mount Sinai. Unless this view is accepted, it is argued, traditionally minded Jews are speaking falsehoods when they sing, as the Sefer Torah is raised in the synagogue, 'And this is the Torah which Moses set before the Children of Israel according to the commandment of the Lord by the hand of Moses'.

Three separate questions have to be asked. Is this the traditional view? Even if it is, are there now good reasons to reject it? And does it make sense, for those who reject it for good reasons, to affirm that they still believe in *Torah min hashamayim*?

Honesty compels us to admit that the view expressed above is the traditional one—if traditional means the way in which Maimonides formulated the doctrine, as mentioned in the previous chapter, although it has been noted there that some commentators in the Middle Ages did acknowledge that some verses of the Pentateuch must have been added after Moses. That the congregation sings 'And this is the Torah which Moses set before the Children of Israel according to the commandment of the Lord by the hand of Moses' is not found in all rites, but those who introduced this practice in the late Middle Ages did, undoubtedly, believe in the Maimonidean formulation and so do presumably many, perhaps most, Orthodox Jews when they sing this today.

At this stage, history steps in. It is pertinent to observe that in the whole of the Pentateuch the word *torah* never denotes what is now called 'the Torah', i.e. the Pentateuch, but always means a particular *torah* ('teaching') such as the *torah* of the burnt-offering or the *torah* of the sin-offering. It was only when the Pentateuch had been finally compiled that the whole work was called *the* Torah. When the last of the great literary prophets, Malachi, says 'Remember ye the Torah of Moses My servant, which I commanded unto him in Horeb for all Israel, even statutes and ordinances' (Mal. 3: 22), he, in all probability, does mean the whole of the Torah ('statutes and ordinances') given to Moses, since in his time, after the return from the Babylonian exile, the whole Torah of Moses was certainly known. But it is significant that when the prophet speaks of the Torah of Moses 'commanded unto him at Horeb', meaning Sinai, he cannot be referring to the whole of the Pentateuch we now have, since much of the Pentateuch, referring to events which took place later than the theophany at Sinai, was not given at Sinai. Be that as it may, the verse in Deuteronomy 'And this is the *torah* which Moses set before the Children of Israel' (Deut. 4: 14) cannot possibly have meant the whole of the Pentateuch but only the particular *torah* mentioned in the context of the verse. Moreover, the expression 'according to the commandment of the Lord by the hand of Moses' is not found in this verse at all. This expression does occur in other verses: in Numbers 4: 37 and 45, referring to the numbering of the people 'according to the commandment of the Lord'; in Numbers 9: 23 and 10: 13; and in Joshua 22: 9, referring to the journeys of the people 'according to the command of the Lord', but it was only in the late Middle Ages, by which time, it is true, the doctrine of *Torah min hashamayim* had come to be understood as in Maimonides' formulation, that the two verses were combined to read as if they were a single verse: 'And this is the Torah which Moses set before the Children of Israel according to the commandment of the Lord by the hand of Moses'. Thus the precise theological statement of Maimonides becomes a piece of poetry sung by Jews in the dramatic moment when the Torah is elevated after (in the Ashkenazi rite) the reading of the Torah. Yet an affirmation in poetry and song is at least as significant as one in prose so that, whether or not they knew the history of what they were singing, Jews did, and still do, intend their song to indicate their belief in *Torah min hashamayim* in the way Maimonides understood the doctrine. Jews, when they sing this, are neither historians describing how the doctrine came about nor theologians reflecting on its meaning, but are simply giving expression to their belief that the Torah is true because it was given by God. It is misguided to hurl the combined verses at the historian or theologian in an attempt to prejudge the issue. To do this is to attempt an all too easy conversion by quotation. For all that, the only reply to the question, 'Is the position I adopt traditional?' has to be in the negative. The view put forward in this book is untraditional.

To turn to the second question, granted that the understanding of the doctrine as formulated by Maimonides is the traditional one, are there good reasons to reject it? The answer to this is that there are good reasons for rejecting the traditional view so that, if these reasons are convincing, one cannot and should not still retain the traditional view, unless one sees the tradition itself as a divine communication sufficiently powerful to demolish all conclusions arrived at by the exercise of objective reasoning.

In the previous chapter, we considered some of the evidence to demonstrate that the Pentateuch is a composite work produced at different periods in the history of ancient Israel and later combined, and that it is not infallible, as it would be if it were a direct divine communication. Here some further points should be mentioned.

The Pentateuch itself makes no claim anywhere that every one of its words was communicated by God to Moses, or even that it is a single work produced all at once at a particular time. A reader approaching the text as it stands would hardly conclude that the oft-repeated words 'And the Lord spoke unto Moses saying' were themselves 'spoken' by God to Moses. It is all very well protesting, as Orthodox rabbis are wont to do, that the critical view represents outdated nineteenth-century pseudo-scholarship, but even if it were true, which it is not, that the Documentary Hypothesis had been demolished—it is still the dominant theory, albeit with refinements and adjustments, in modern biblical studies—this cannot mean that we can now ignore all the evidence and safely opt for the 'traditional' view.

The Documentary Hypothesis is precisely that—a hypothesis de-signed to answer the question: since Moses did not write the Pentateuch, who did and when? In reputable colleges and universities throughout the world, including the Hebrew University of Jerusalem, the Hebrew Union College, and the Jewish Theological Seminary, in the new com-mentary of the Jewish Publication Society and in the *Encyclopaedia Judaica*, it is now accepted that, Documentary Hypothesis or no Docu-mentary Hypothesis—that is a matter of scholarship, not of faith—the Pentateuch is a composite work produced at different periods in the history of ancient Israel. Some Orthodox rabbis persist in treating the critical view of the Pentateuch as if it were a matter of dogma, to be set beside the authentic Jewish dogma of *Torah min hashamayim*, to its detriment. But modern scholarship does not operate within the sphere of dogma at all. It presents hypotheses, as in any other scientific investi-gation, for the consideration of scholars, and is ready to abandon theories when these are seen to be untrue to the facts. The scholarly consensus is convincing because it has been arrived at by trial and error. To reject it all as heresy is to convert Orthodoxy into obscurantism.

To repeat: unless one is prepared to say that God has planted false clues, the only way to cope with the overwhelming evidence of com-positeness is to accept that there is a human element in the divine Revelation, that the Torah is not the bare text of the Pentateuch but the sum total of Jewish teachings, in which our ancestors reached out halt-ingly to seek God's will and to be found by Him.

So the third question has to be answered: if one holds such a view, can one be said still to believe in *Torah min hashamayim*? The answer is yes, once it is appreciated that Judaism, including the doctrine of *Torah min hashamayim* itself, has had a history and did not simply drop down, ready-made, from Heaven. The earliest reference to the doctrine is in the Mishnah (*Sanhedrin* 10: 1); it is in his Commentary on this *mishnah* that Maimonides formulates his thirteen principles, placing special em-phasis on the eighth principle that the Torah is from Heaven. The *mishnah* reads: 'And these have no share in the World to Come: he that says that there is no resurrection of the dead, and [he that says that] there is no Torah from Heaven, and an *epikoros*.' In the *mishnah* it is fur-ther stated that Rabbi Akiva added that one who reads external (non-canonical) books or utters charms over a wound has no share in the World to Come, and Abba Saul added, 'One who pronounces the di-vine Name with its proper letters'.

The Mishnah as a whole was compiled around 220 CE, but this statement of the Mishnah seems to predate Rabbi Akiva and Abba Saul and may go back in essence even to Temple times, though this is uncertain. From the use of 'one that says' (*ha'omer*) and from the additions of Rabbi Akiva and Abba Saul it would appear that the mishnaic statement is polemical, directed against sectarians who either 'say', that is, declare, certain things or engage in certain practices which the ancient rabbis believed to be contrary to their view of Judaism. The original meaning of *epikoros* is obviously an Epicurean, one who follows the teachings of the Greek philosopher Epicurus, but in rabbinic times the word had come to denote anyone who entertained grossly heretical opinions; there is much discussion in the later literature on which kinds of opinions.

In this *mishnah* there is no reference to the idea that every word of the Torah was conveyed to Moses by God. In fact, the expression used, 'there is no Torah from Heaven' (*ein torah min hashamayim*), on a plain reading, simply denotes lack of belief that there is Torah from Heaven, i.e. that the true doctrine is that God gave *a* Torah, not *the* Torah. However, a talmudic passage (*Sanhedrin 99a*) elaborates on the mishnaic statement and does speak of *the* Torah. This passage reads:

Because he hath despised the word of the Lord [Num. 15: 31]—This refers to one who says there is no Torah from Heaven. And even if he said that the whole of the Torah is from Heaven, excepting a particular verse, which [he says] was not said by the Holy One, blessed be He, but by Moses of his own accord, he is included in *because he hath despised the word of the Lord*. And even if he said that the whole of the Torah is from Heaven, excepting a single deduction [*dikduk*], a particular argument from minor to major [*kal vahomer*], or a certain similar expression [in the Torah from which a law is derived, *gezerah shavah*], he is still included in *because he hath despised the word of the Lord*.

There is an element of hyperbole in this statement, particularly since, as the commentators note, the *kal vahomer* argument is based entirely on human reasoning and is advanced and often refuted everywhere in the Talmud purely on the basis of human reasoning. How, then, unless we are dealing with hyperbole, can it have been given by God? Perhaps the meaning is that he denies that the verse in the Torah on which the reasoning is based was given by God. Or, possibly, the meaning is that he denies that God established the legitimacy of the argument itself when applied to the Torah. By actually referring to the *kal vahomer*, *gezerah shavah*, and *dikduk*, the author of this passage seems to be thinking primarily of the legal material, yet there is a reference to one denying a single *verse*, which would lead to the conclusion that the author does come close to the same formulation as Maimonides who, in fact, seems to find his support in this very passage. It is possible that a 'verse' in this context also refers to a verse of the Torah which has legal consequences, not to the verses in the narrative portions. For all that, it is almost certainly the standard rabbinic view that 'Torah', in the doctrine of *Torah min hashamayim*, denotes the whole of the Pentateuch.

To be noted especially is the description of the unbeliever as one who admits that the whole Torah was given by God but holds that a single verse was uttered by *Moses of his own accord*, that is, that Moses made up some of it himself. The talmudic rabbis were not primarily concerned with the question raised in modern scholarship as to whether Moses wrote the Pentateuch. The Mosaic authorship of the Pentateuch had long been taken for granted and was held to be true by believer and unbeliever alike—that was the opinion of everyone in rabbinic times and earlier. But, the unbeliever maintained, Moses did not receive the whole of the Torah from God but made it all up out of his own head.

Religious modernists, those we have called 'liberal supernaturalists', do not say that Moses invented the Pentateuch; they accept that much of it is post-Mosaic. But they still believe that the actual authors, compilers, and redactors were divinely inspired, though, as human beings, they were prone to error as well as proclaimers of truth. A good illustration is provided by the rabbinic discussion (*Megillah 7a*) on whether the book of Ecclesiastes was written by Solomon under the guidance of the holy spirit or whether the book simply contains Solomon's human wisdom. Most modern scholars hold that Ecclesiastes was not written by Solomon at all, but is a much later work in which there are traces of Greek influence. Yet, they, too, can believe that the work was inspired by the holy spirit. Or perhaps it is better to put it this way, that those eventually responsible for admitting the book into the canon of Scripture were inspired so to do. And of the Pentateuch perhaps it is better to say, from the religious modernist point of view, that those who, over a long period, came to see the Pentateuch as the Torah were inspired so to do. As Professor Isaiah Leibowitz put it, it is not the Written Torah which gave rise to the Oral Torah but the Oral Torah, the total experience of devout Jews, which gave rise to the Written Torah, i.e. by accepting it as such.[1] Obviously the ancient rabbis would not have put it in this way, yet it is not impermissible to argue that behind the rabbinic formulation is the idea that Judaism was not 'made up' but is a revealed religion and, in this sense, Torah *is* from Heaven.

Liberal supernaturalists do believe in 'Heaven'—in this context, a rabbinic synonym for God—and they believe in the Torah (the Jewish religion taken in totality, not just the Bible) as much as their ancestors did. But in the light of modern knowledge it is, as suggested above, the 'from' in the doctrine that the Torah is from Heaven that has to be understood in terms of divine–human co-operation. In much the same way, as Professor Jakob Petuchowski was fond of saying, the benediction *hamotsi leḥem min ha'arets*—'who bringeth forth bread from the earth'—does not mean that God brings bread ready-made or ready-sliced from the ground, but that He does so through the labours of the farmers, the bakers, and the distributors, and that some types of bread are better baked and more nutritious than others.

What is involved in all this is the comparatively newly discovered sense of history, a better appreciation of what actually happened in the past, not what we are told happened. It is all a matter of plausibility. Think once again of Krochmal on Psalm 137. Prior to serious historical investigation, the 'traditional' view prevailed that King David wrote this psalm as he composed, by the aid of the holy spirit, the whole book of Psalms. For anyone with the slightest historical sense, it is far more plausible to suggest that the book of Psalms contains psalms produced in various periods which were eventually collected under the title 'The Psalms of David', because David, the 'sweet singer in Israel' (2 Sam. 23: 1), was known as the originator of psalm-singing to the glory of God. Why should not a believer say that those who actually composed the book of Psalms, the psalmists, were endowed by God with the holy spirit, unless this endowment is thought of as a divine guarantee of infallibility? A psalmist in a given age must have shared the knowledge and even the moral sense of that age but, because he was inspired, he could still produce exquisite hymns to God and in the process transcend his human limitations.

Likewise, it is now far more plausible to suggest that Moses, the 'law-giver', attracted to his person laws and doctrines given after his day and

[1] For similar ideas expressed by Leibowitz, see Joshua O. Haberman, *The God I Believe In* (New York, 1994), 127–52.

that it is these that are recorded in the Pentateuch as the Torah of Moses. This idea is implicit in Frankel's idea of ancient laws being treated as if they were 'laws given to Moses at Sinai', although, admittedly, Frankel touched only on the rabbinic idea and, no doubt for good reason, felt himself unable to engage in pentateuchal criticism, unlike Zunz. The Torah is not the Bible alone but the whole of Jewish teachings. Even in Orthodoxy, rabbinic institutions belong to *Torat moshe*, 'the Torah of Moses'.

The liberal supernaturalist cannot bring himself to presume how the Almighty should have revealed His Torah. He believes that revelation is a mystery, the full scope of which is beyond the power of the human mind to grasp. What he says rather is that, if we are to preserve our intellectual integrity, a readjustment has to be made in the light of our present knowledge. To say this is not, of course, to claim superiority to the ancients, but simply to recognize that we now have access to facts that were not available to them.

What it all amounts to is this. Faith in God cannot be invoked to deny the facts on the grounds that this is how the ancients saw it, any more than it can be invoked to affirm that—as Maimonides held—the sun, moon, and stars are fixed to concentric spheres revolving around the earth. Even though we can no longer view it that way, we can see—as Maimonides did but in a more wondrous way—God as the Creator of the grander, more immense, more wondrous, and more mysterious universe that modern science has disclosed to us.

A readjustment is necessary, but to make it is not to deny the essential truth of the Torah. On the contrary, our appreciation of the Torah is enhanced when it is seen in dynamic rather than static terms.

Liberal supernaturalists have come to appreciate that the idea of God giving the Torah to Moses—call it 'myth' if you will since the connotation of this term in modern scholarship is truth expressed in non-historical terms—suggests that Judaism developed by using the God-to-Moses paradigm as a way of expressing that Judaism is a developing religion and yet an eternal faith. We can still sing, when the Sefer Torah is joyously raised on high: 'And this is the Torah which Moses set before the Children of Israel according to the commandment of the Lord by the hand of Moses'. It is poetry, to be sure, but poetry so sublime that beside it pedestrian prosaic accounts pale into insignificance.

Orthodoxy, going its own way, largely ignores the historical approach or, on the rare occasions when it does deign to consider it, dismisses it blithely as a heretical denial of *Torah min hashamayim*. Essentially, the Orthodox position is that all that has to be said on this doctrine has already been said by the talmudic rabbis, to question whom is itself heretical. This stance came into conflict with scholarship in the case of Rabbi Moshe Feinstein and Dr I. Lange, which I shall now examine.

The Lange Case

It was mentioned in passing in Chapter 2 that Judah Hehasid of Regensburg (d. 1217) saw no objection to the suggestion that some verses in the Pentateuch were added by authors who lived after Moses. Judah Hehasid's remarks remained in manuscript until they were published by a distinguished medievalist, Dr I. Lange, who was incidentally an Orthodox Jew. Lange, with impeccable scholarship, collated a number of manuscripts in his work.[2] Except for other members of the scholarly world, Lange's book would have been ignored were it not that Rabbi Daniel Levy, a young Orthodox rabbi in Switzerland where Lange resided at the time, detected heresy in the work. No one doubted that the commentaries dated from the Middle Ages, but Levy and others could not believe that they contained the authentic opinions of Judah Hehasid, venerated throughout the Orthodox world as a great saint (*hehasid* means 'the saint'). The work must have been attributed to Judah Hehasid by a medieval heretic anxious to mislead naïve believers. No one accused Lange himself of forgery. The evidence he adduced was too strong for anyone to deny a medieval genesis. Levy brought the matter to the attention of a number of rabbis, including the famed Orthodox halakhist, Rabbi Moshe Feinstein (1895–1986). Rabbi Feinstein faced the challenge in his responsa collection, *Igerot moshe*,[3] and came to the conclusion that the work was indeed a forgery and should be banned. The end of the sorry story is that so much pressure was brought to bear on poor, innocent Lange that he had to issue a bowdlerized edition of the book from which the offending passages were deleted.

What was the cause of offence? In three passages, Judah Hehasid (there is no evidence at all that a medieval forger ever existed; despite

[2] *Perushei hatorah lerabi yehudah hehasid* (Jerusalem, 1975).
[3] *Yoreh de'ah* (Benei Berak, 1981), nos. 114 and 115, pp. 358–9 and 359–61.

rabbis Feinstein and Levy, the work does contain the ideas of the saint) states, quite casually, with not the slightest suggestion that he is presenting daring views, that some few verses of the Pentateuch must have been added by others to the book written by Moses. The following are the verses and the saint's comments on them:

1. 'And he set Ephraim before Manasseh' (Gen. 48: 20). This passage in Genesis speaks of Jacob blessing Joseph's younger son, Ephraim, before blessing the older son, Manasseh. The son of Judah Hehasid, in one opinion which he attributes to his father, says that this does not mean that Jacob set Ephraim before Manasseh since that has already been stated. The meaning of 'and *he* set' is that, in obedience to Jacob's preference, Moses 'set' the tribe of Ephraim before that of Manasseh, i.e. under Ephraim's banner when the tribes journeyed on (Num. 10: 22–3). But in that case Moses should have used the first person: 'and I set', just as he did later on when he said 'Moreover I have given thee one portion above thy brethren' (Gen. 48: 22). It follows that the verse 'and he set' must have been added either by Joshua or *by the Men of the Great Synagogue*!

2. 'Then sang Israel this song' (Num. 21: 17). Judah Hehasid says that the song they sang was that recorded in Psalm 136, known as 'the Great Hallel'. This song was originally in the Pentateuch but David took it, together with other 'orphaned' psalms, i.e. psalms without attribution, and placed them in the book of Psalms. Here is the opposite idea, that a portion of the original Pentateuch written by Moses is now in Psalms because David used it when he compiled the book of Psalms.

3. 'So we passed by from our brethren the children of Esau, that dwell in Seir, from the way of the Arabah, from Elath, and from Ezion-geber' (Deut. 2: 8). This verse seems to mean that the Children of Israel came to Ezion-geber and then left it, as another verse says 'And they journeyed from Abronah, and pitched in Ezion-geber. And they journeyed from Ezion-geber' (Num. 33: 35–6). But, Judah Hehasid's son asks, in the name of his father, since they only went around the land of Edom (Num. 21: 4) and, as our verse says, they passed by the children of Esau, representing Edom, how could they have come to Ezion-geber which belonged to Edom, as stated in the book of Chronicles: 'Then went Solomon to Ezion-geber, and to Eloth, on the sea-shore in the land of

Edom' (2 Chr. 8: 17)? The only conclusion to be reached is that in the days of Moses Ezion-geber did not belong to Edom, whereas in the days of Solomon it did, that is, at some time between Moses and Solomon Ezion-geber became part of the territory of Edom. When did that happen? It was when King Hadar of Edom married 'Mehetabel, the daughter of Matred, the daughter of Mei-zahav' (Gen. 36: 39). Mei-zahav means 'waters of gold'; Ezion-geber was so called because, Judah Hehasid says, like Marseilles, it was a great port from which men sailed in quest of gold. Mehetabel, to whom Ezion-geber had formerly belonged, brought it as a dowry to King Hadar. This did not happen until a king had reigned in Israel (Gen. 36: 31), that is, not before the reign of Saul, the first king of the Children of Israel. Thus the history of Ezion-geber is that in the days of Moses it did not belong to Edom, but that at some time between Moses and King Saul it had passed to Edom through Mehetabel. By the time of Solomon Ezion-geber already belonged to Edom. And here comes the most striking comment of Judah Hehasid. In order to solve the contradiction between our verse, that Ezion-geber did not belong to Edom, and the verse in Chronicles that in the time of Solomon it did, he says that in the time of the Men of the Great Synagogue they added the passage about the kings of Edom to the Pentateuch.

In his first responsum on the subject, addressed to Rabbi Levy, Rabbi Feinstein remarks that since Levy tells him that Lange persists in publishing the book as it is without omissions, he feels obliged to reply at once, even though his state of health does not really allow it. Rabbi Feinstein quotes the passage in Mishnah *Sanhedrin* according to which one who says that even a single verse was not from Heaven despises the word of the Lord, and he quotes Maimonides' famous formulation. While Rabbi Feinstein admits that the talmudic passage only refers to a single verse, in Maimonides' formulation this is extended to include even a single word. This must be correct since what difference is there in this connection between a word and verse? To say, as Judah Hehasid is reported as saying in Lange's book, that Joshua or the Men of the Great Synagogue added the verse 'and he set Ephraim before Manasseh', is to deny that Moses wrote the whole of the Torah, including this verse, at the command of God. Rabbi Feinstein's argument is very weak. The talmudic passage only refers to one who says that a single verse (or word, according to Maimonides) of the Torah did not come from Heaven, but was written by Moses of his own accord. Rabbi Feinstein says that it applies *a fortiori* to one who claims that a verse was not in the Torah in the first place. Judah Hehasid evidently held that there is no *a fortiori*, since the Talmud does not speak at all of one who says that this or that verse had been added later to the Torah God gave to Moses and which then became part of the Torah. At any rate, there were other thinkers in the Middle Ages, as we have noted, who must have taken such a line, different from Maimonides' stark formulation.

The statement in the book that King David took Psalm 136 out of the Torah is sheer nonsense, says Rabbi Feinstein. Moreover, it is worse than the other comments in that there is no reason at all for saying this unless it is simply to be provocative for its own sake. For David to have taken away a portion of the Torah would have meant that he tampered with the words given by God to Moses, and that would have been a worse offence than that of the one who says that a verse was not given by God to Moses.

As for the suggestion that the portion of the kings of Edom was added later, Ibn Ezra refers to a certain Yitshaki, who argued in similar vein, but Ibn Ezra states that Yitshaki's book should be burnt; so we have the *pesak din* ('legal decision') that such a book must be burnt. How, then, dare anyone have had such a book printed in the first place? Rabbi Feinstein must have known that he was going beyond the normal halakhic process when he quoted Ibn Ezra's decision as binding: halakhically, Ibn Ezra is never considered to be a *posek*, only a famous poet and commentator on the Bible.

In the second responsum, addressed to Rabbi Shelomo Zalman Auerbach, Rabbi Feinstein says that he has discussed the matter with Rabbi Levy over the telephone and that he suggested that Levy should try to persuade Lange not to publish the work, but that it should all be done privately lest the present-day heretics, hearing of the existence of such a work in manuscript, should try to have it published and so mislead the innocent. Lange, however, had insisted that the book be published, and many copies had already been sold. Levy had also told Rabbi Feinstein that Rabbi Auerbach and Rabbi Eliashav had made Lange promise to produce a new edition from which the offending passages would be omitted. There would be no objection to such a course provided it was made clear in the introduction to the new edition that the earlier edition contained these three forgeries, which is what Rabbi Feinstein and the other rabbis believed them to be. Against this course, Rabbi Feinstein argued that the detection of these three heresies placed the whole book under suspicion. Who knew what further heresies would be found when the book was closely examined? For instance, it asks why the Torah forbids male homosexual practices, as if a reason was required for the prohibition of acts held abhorrent by all decent people, non-Jews as well as Jews. And the answer, that it is to encourage men to marry women, would only have the effect of further weakening the prohibition, as if the act were no more than a failure to keep the precept to be fruitful and multiply. Since the book had already been published, concluded Rabbi Feinstein, there was nothing they could do about it. But they should protest that the book was a forgery, that Judah Hehasid did not write these things, and that the book deserved to be burnt.

There are now, in fact, two editions of the book: the original edition containing the 'heresies' and the new edition from which they have been omitted. I was fortunate to be given by a friend the uncensored edition, which is now something of a collector's item.

Halakhah and Doctrine

Although, as I have tried to show in my book *Theology in the Responsa*, the great halakhists also dealt with theological matters, discussing these with the same rigour with which they discussed legal matters, it is only in comparatively recent years that theological statements such as that in the talmudic passage and in Maimonides have been treated as if questions of belief belonged to the halakhah. Because Maimonides is the great, though not the sole, expert in halakhah and because the Talmud is the final court of appeal in halakhic matters, this is carried over to the area of theology, in which it has no place. If this analysis is correct, the answer to the questions raised at the beginning of this chapter is clear. For rabbis like Rabbi Feinstein and the majority of present-day Orthodox rabbis who follow the line he takes, the approach of the liberal supernaturalist is not only untraditional but constitutes a heretical denial of *Torah min hashamayim*. Halakhah, now a name not only for what Jews are expected to do but also for what they are expected to believe, regulates thought as well as action. The halakhist has become a theologian, with the difference that he decides in matters of dogma solely on the basis of statements by the great rabbis of the past, which are seen as totally binding with no room for individual dissent. Moreover, there is no room for the exercise of the historical critical approach. It is inconceivable for Orthodox rabbis even to mention in their deliberations scholars like Zunz, Krochmal, Rapoport, and Frankel, whose works do not belong in the category of *sefarim kedoshim* ('holy books') but are seen as secular literature at the best and as heretical at the worst. In his very perceptive and sympathetic sociological investigation, *The World of the Yeshiva*, William B. Helmreich cites as works viewed with suspicion in yeshiva circles Salo Baron's *A Social and Religious History of the Jews* and Heinrich Graetz's *History of the Jews*.[4] Such works were accused of 'lacking in proper Torah *hashkofos* [perspectives]'. The liberal supernaturalist may still claim to be in the tradition. He can no longer lay claim to Orthodoxy. The divide is at present categorical. Whether bridge-building will ever succeed remains to be seen,

If the truth be told, what is really involved in the whole discussion is not the question of biblical criticism, but whether the talmudic rabbis are infallible supermen, or rather whether the talmudic literature—the Babylonian and the Jerusalem Talmuds and the Midrash—contains infallible truth which it is heretical to question. What happened in the history of Judaism, probably in reaction to the Karaites who rejected the Talmud and the whole doctrine of the Oral Torah, is that all the rabbis mentioned in the Talmud were now conceptualized collectively as *ḥazal*, denoting *ḥakhameinu zikhronam liverakhah*, 'our sages of blessed memory', to take issue with whom is to take issue with God Himself, since they are the only true exponents of His word as revealed in the Torah. Thus when Rabbi Moshe Feinstein wishes to prove his case it is not to the Pentateuch itself that he goes but to what the Talmud says (actually, in large measure, to what Maimonides says the Talmud says). In other words the notion has developed that there is a divine guarantee that *ḥazal* can never be wrong in matters of faith. A non-fundamentalist will respect the talmudic sages and, indeed, if he is observant, he will follow their rulings in matters of halakhah, but his intellectual integrity will not allow him to postulate that the great teachers of the past were infallible supermen. Thus, Rabbi Chaim Dov Keller

---

[4] William B. Helmreich, *The World of the Yeshiva: An Intimate Portrait of Orthodox Jewry* (New York, 1982), 169–70.

criticizes Rabbi Emanuel Rackman's contention that there is no dogma to the effect that one has to accept the attribution of the biblical books to the men traditionally regarded as their authors. Keller protests:

Surely, if we cannot accept the word of the *Mesora* [tradition] on so basic a subject as the authorship of Tanach [the Bible], then on what can we? If in this basic non-scientific non-technological area modern archaeology and biblical criticism are capable of superseding the *Mesora* and *Chazal* (who, it would be presumed, were misled somewhere along the line) what then prevents us from assuming they were not misled on the authorship of the Pentateuch, which Rabbi Rackman is not willing to question?[5]

Yes, indeed; if we do not follow the rabbis in their contention that King David wrote the book of Psalms there is no logic in accepting their views on the authorship of the Pentateuch and, as this book argues, we should adopt the historical critical methodology in both instances. If Rabbi Keller is prepared to accept that the rabbis could have been mistaken with regard to scientific and technological matters (I would not use the word 'misled' since the rabbis could not have anticipated the findings of modern science and the advances of modern technology), as is implied by his use of the words 'non-scientific non-technological', it is necessary to repeat that modern biblical and rabbinic scholarship is 'scientific' or is, at least, closer to scientific investigation than to a blind acceptance of past views, which would rule out all historical considerations of how Judaism came to be.

In particular, the now very well known ArtScroll series of biblical commentaries is notorious in rejecting all modern scholarship as applied to the biblical books or, for that matter, to talmudic literature. In his preface to the ArtScroll commentary on the book of Esther, Rabbi Meir Zlotowitz writes:

It must be made clear that this is not a so-called 'scientific' or 'apologetic' commentary on the Megillah. That area has, unfortunately, been too well-covered, resulting in violence to the Jewish faith as well as to correct [*sic*] interpretation. It is in no way the intention of this book to demonstrate the legitimacy [*sic*] or historicity of Esther or Mordechai to non-believers or doubters. *Belief in the authenticity of every book of the Torah* [*sic*] *is basic to Jewish faith, and we proceed from there.* It comes as no surprise to me—nor should it to any Orthodox Jew—that the palace in Shushan, as unearthed by archealogists [*sic*], bears out

[5] Chaim Dov Keller, 'Modern Orthodoxy: An Analysis and a Response', in Reuben P. Bulka (ed.), *Dimensions of Orthodox Judaism* (New York, 1983), 253–71.

the description of the palace in the Megillah in every detail; nor do we deem it necessary to prove, by means of the 'Persian borrow-words', nor by whatever means, that the Book was, indeed, written in that contemporary period.

Rather, the aim was a specifically traditional commentary reflecting the Megillah as understood by Chazal. No non-Jewish sources have even been consulted, much less quoted. *I consider it offensive that the Torah [sic] should need authentication from the secular or so-called 'scientific' sources.*[6]

Zlotowitz's 'so-called "scientific"' is very revealing. He implies that if biblical criticism were scientific he would embrace it, but evidently believes that the interpretations and comments by *ḥazal* demonstrate that all criticism in this area is wrong and hence can only be scientific in a 'so-called' sense. But, if that is the case, why mention the archaeological findings with regard to the palace at Shushan at all? For all its many virtues, attractive presentation, and great popularity, the whole ArtScroll series is so completely fundamentalistic, either entirely ignoring all critical theories or taking a brave swipe at them, that it is hardly necessary to dismiss it as scholarship. But I rubbed my eyes when I first read the Hebrew approbation to the ArtScroll *Book of Jonah* by Mordechai Gifter, a prominent *rosh yeshivah*, who writes (my translation):

The concept of repentance as illuminated by the Torah is as far removed as possible from all the discussions on this subject at all times among all religions. All our present existence is life after Adam's sin and the purpose, according to our holy Torah, of man's service is to return to the marvellous light that existed before Adam had sinned. It follows that even the most perfect saint is engaged in the task of repentance. From this point of view, there is, indeed, 'none righteous upon earth who doeth only good and sinneth not', since there is the taint of the serpent in whatever he does.[7]

This comes very close not only to sheer fundamentalism but to Christian fundamentalism.

When discussing attitudes towards the talmudic sages, it has to be appreciated that not all the medieval teachers believed that *ḥazal* were infallible in all matters. According to Maimonides (*Guide* iii. 14 end) the talmudic rabbis could possess less knowledge of such matters as astronomy than the gentile scholars of his day possessed. The *geonim* noted that the talmudic rabbis only possessed the medical knowledge of their

---

[6] Meir Zlotowitz (ed.), *The ArtScroll Commentary to the Book of Esther* (New York, 1977), p. x.   [7] Ibid.

day, so that no one should rely on remedies for sickness mentioned in the Talmud unless these were approved by contemporary physicians.[8] However, it was not until the sixteenth century that Azariah dei Rossi dared to suggest that talmudic statements about the past need not be accepted literally. In his *Meor einayim*,[9] dei Rossi refers to the talmudic statement (*Gittin* 56b) that the emperor Titus who destroyed the Temple was punished by a gnat which entered his nose and grew in his head into a bird of brass with claws of iron. We know, remarks dei Rossi, that Titus died a normal death. What the Talmud is saying is that a tiny gnat of remorse pecked away at Titus's conscience because he had destroyed the Temple, growing ever stronger until he could no longer live with his guilt. In other words dei Rossi recognized, as did the Wissenschaft des Judentums scholars who followed him, that talmudic and midrashic legends are just that, not sober historical statements but imaginative reworkings of history used in order to convey moral truth. In his comments on King David and Psalm 137, Krochmal was obviously following in dei Rossi's wake.

Thus there is a historical tradition in which the Talmud is not always regarded as an infallible guide in mundane matters. However, it has to be said that no one before the rise of modern scholarship would have considered the tradition, in the form in which it is found in the talmudic literature, to be anything but an infallible guide in matters regarding the authorship and meaning of the biblical books. So, again, since this is so, the view presented in this book is untraditional.

For all that, I did mention in *We Have Reason to Believe* a few typical talmudic passages, which I shall now examine rather more fully, that can be understood without distortion as acknowledging that there is a human element in the Torah, though the rabbis themselves would not, and could not, have put it that way.

The Human Element in Rabbinic Literature

First I shall examine the passage in the Babylonian Talmud, *Eruvin* 13b, on the debates between the rival Houses of Hillel and Shammai who flourished, according to the tradition, in the first century BCE. (It

---

[8] B. M. Lewin, *Otsar hageonim: Gittin* (Jerusalem, 1941), 152 ff.   [9] 2. 16.

matters not for our purpose that the actual historical background to the two Houses is somewhat vague.) The passage reads:

Rav Abba said in the name of Samuel: 'For three years the Houses of Shammai and Hillel engaged in debate [on the following matter]. These said: The halakhah is in accordance with our opinions, and the others said: The halakhah is in accordance with our opinions. A *bat kol* [voice from Heaven] proceeded saying, Both these and these are the words of the living God but the halakhah is in accordance with the opinions of the House of Hillel. But if both these and these are the words of the living God, why did the House of Hillel have the merit that the halakhah should be fixed in accordance with their opinion? [It was] because they [the members of the House of Hillel] were gentle and retiring, referring [always] to their own opinions and to the opinions of the House of Shammai.

First to be noted is that what we have here is a statement by Rav Abba in the name of Samuel (an early third-century Babylonian teacher), reporting on events that were said to have taken place over 200 years before his time. The saying is set in the framework of the final redaction of the Babylonian Talmud—the question regarding why the House of Hillel had the merit that the halakhah should have been fixed in accordance with their opinion probably belongs not to Samuel but to the final editors, though it may just be the view of Samuel himself. In any event, the words 'Rav Abba said in the name of Samuel' belong to the final editors. I mention all this in order to show how difficult it is to date accurately sayings in the Babylonian Talmud and to distinguish between fact and legend. The story of the *bat kol*, for instance, may be a reflection on why ultimately the House of Hillel is followed.

It does not require any acute historical sense to recognize in this passage the idea that the post-biblical debates, of which there are so many throughout the talmudic period and beyond, are themselves part of the Torah. From the historical point of view, what this talmudic passage is implying is that the very contradictions between the Houses of Shammai and Hillel are all part of the halakhic process, part of the Torah, even though, in practice, one can only follow one opinion, the *bat kol* deciding which. Incidentally, the passage also implies that in such debates, while the actual decision must be given in favour of one side in the debate, this is not because that one side is in possession of God's absolute truth—the very existence of the debate means that the absolute truth is unobtainable—but only that, since a decision is called for, it can be decided on grounds of 'merit'. Note, especially, that the 'merit' does not consist in greater proficiency in learning but in superior moral character.

However, it is only right here to refer to the influential remarks on the passage by Ritba, Rabbi Yom Tov Ishbili (d. 1330). In his commentary on the passage Ritba writes:

The French rabbis, of blessed memory, ask: How is it possible for both of them to be the words of the living God, since what one permits the other forbids? They reply that when Moses ascended on high to receive the Torah, he was shown with regard to every topic forty-nine arguments to render it forbidden and another forty-nine arguments to render it permitted. He [Moses] asked the Holy One, blessed be He, about this and He replied that this is given over [for discussion] by the Sages of Israel in each generation and whatever they finally decide is to be followed. This is acceptable as homiletics. But according to the way of truth [Kabbalah] there is a mystery here.[10]

By this latter remark Ritba probably means that stricter views stem from the *sefirot* of the left side on high and more lenient views from those of the right side, but since both right and left, Judgement and Mercy, are combined, the two opposing views are themselves 'the words of the living God'.

The comment of Ritba in the name of the French scholars has often been quoted in present-day Orthodox polemics as a stick with which to beat reformist and other scholars who interpret the talmudic passage to mean not that there is a divine communication to the sages, but that the very human arguments are themselves part of the living Torah, with all the contradictions. Not so, argue the Orthodox. As Ritba says in the name of the French scholars, there are no real contradictions because *both* views were given to Moses on Sinai. Ritba, while praising the view of the French scholars, still considers it to be homiletical, evidently finding it hard to believe that the doctrine of *Torah min hashamayim* includes the contradictions and debates. A non-fundamentalist would feel justified in reading the passage as an acknowledgement that the very debates, human though they are, belong with all their errors and contradictions to the divine Torah, conceived of in terms of divine–human co-operation. Indeed a careful reading of Ritba shows that even the French scholars come close to affirming the same thing.

The Talmud (*Baba metsia* 59b) tells of an oven, the ritual purity of which is debated by Rabbi Eliezer and the sages. I give the passage here

[10] *Ḥidushei haritba* on *Eruvin*, ed. M. Goldstein (Jerusalem, 1980), 107–8.

in paraphrase. Rabbi Eliezer said to the sages: 'If the ruling is as I hold let this carob-tree prove it.' Thereupon the carob-tree was uprooted from its place, but the sages said: 'No proof can be brought from a carob-tree.' Rabbi Eliezer then said: 'If the ruling is as I hold, let the stream of water prove it.' Whereupon the stream flowed backwards, but the sages said 'No proof can be adduced from a stream of water.' Again Rabbi Eliezer argued: 'Let the walls of the House of Learning prove it.' Whereupon the walls of the House of Learning began to totter, but Rabbi Joshua rebuked them, 'If scholars are debating matters of halakhah what has it to do with you?' Consequently, the walls did not fall in out of respect for Rabbi Joshua, but neither did they revert to their former position out of respect for Rabbi Eliezer. To this very day they can be seen in a slanting position. In desperation Rabbi Eliezer said 'If I am right let it be proved from Heaven' and a *bat kol* cried out 'Why do you dispute with Rabbi Eliezer, seeing that in all matters the halakhah is in accordance with his rulings?' But Rabbi Joshua said 'It is not in Heaven' (Deut. 30: 12). The Torah states 'After the majority one must incline' (Exod. 23: 2 in rabbinic interpretation), which means that where the law is in doubt it must be decided by a majority of human sages and no appeal to a *bat kol* is allowed. The passage concludes with the anecdote that when Rabbi Nathan met Elijah the Prophet, who returns periodically to discuss Torah with the rabbis, he asked him, 'What did the Holy One, blessed be He, do in that hour?' Elijah replied 'He laughed with joy, saying "My sons have defeated Me, My sons have defeated Me".'

One would have to be a philistine to dissect and analyse this charming rabbinic fancy as if it were anything like a precise, cold theological statement. There is even a touch of humour in the statement about the walls refusing to fall out of respect for Rabbi Joshua and refusing to go back out of respect for Rabbi Eliezer, and in the addition that if you go there today you will find the walls still standing in a slanting position. It should also be appreciated that the concern of this passage, like that of the previous one quoted, is with halakhah. The implication here is that if you are to have a legal system at all you cannot, whenever the matter is debated, request God to intercede. The development of the system can only be through the exercise of human reasoning, the only kind of reasoning possible for the sages who are, after all, human beings with the imperfections imposed on them by their human nature. Even if God does intervene, as He did in the case of the oven, by declaring that the halakhah is in accordance with Rabbi Eliezer, He is really stepping beyond the boundaries for legal decision He Himself has set in His Torah. This is the meaning of Rabbi Joshua's protest. Rabbi Joshua is saying, in effect, that when God gave the Torah for human beings to decide, it is as if He had said 'From now on do not bring Me into it even if I order you, through a *bat kol*, to appeal directly to Me.' Rabbi Joshua is not denying the authenticity of the *bat kol*. He is not saying that it was an illusion, only that it is irrelevant for purposes of practical halakhah. Elijah's description of God laughing and saying that His sons have conquered Him presumably means that, from the point of view of God's absolute truth, Rabbi Eliezer is right, but that human decision-making is concerned with how humans see the matter, not with how God Himself sees it. It is possible that the whole legend is directed against those who, like some of the Karaites in the Middle Ages, believed that the saints need not be masters of the law but, when in doubt, can have a 'hot line' to Heaven. However we understand the passage, there does emerge from it the idea of divine–human co-operation in the evolution of the Torah in post-biblical times. The talmudic rabbis would not, of course, have applied this to the Torah given to Moses. In post-talmudic times, when, as noted above, the Talmud became a 'canonized' text and the talmudic rabbis (*ḥazal*) were treated as if they belonged to the original Torah, the scope of Torah included the rabbinic interpretations now found in the Talmud.

Though I have referred to it in support of my views in *We Have Reason to Believe*, I now believe that the talmudic passage in *Menaḥot* 29*b* has been overworked. Yet I want to paraphrase it, since it is often used in contemporary discussion of the human element in the Torah. The passage begins with a saying of R. Judah in the name of Rab (an early third-century Babylonian teacher). When Moses ascended on high he found the Holy One, blessed be He, engaged in weaving crowns (the ornaments with which certain letters are decorated) for the letters of the Torah. Moses asked God the meaning of these crowns, and God replied that at the end of many generations there would arise a man, Akiva ben Joseph by name, who would expound upon each point 'heaps and heaps of laws' (here again it is the halakhah that is stressed). 'Lord of the Universe', declared Moses, 'permit me to see that man.' 'Turn around', said God, and Moses suddenly found himself behind eight rows of students in Rabbi Akiva's college. Being unable to follow the discussions,

Moses became ill at ease, but when one of the students asked Rabbi Akiva, 'How do you know that this is so?' and the sage replied, 'It is a law given to Moses at Sinai', Moses was comforted. When Moses returned to God, he said to Him 'Lord of the Universe, Thou hast such a man and yet Thou givest the Torah through me!' God replied, 'Be silent, for thus has it entered My Mind.'

Forty years ago, in *We Have Reason to Believe*, I commented on this gem of a story:

In other words the Torah that Akiba was teaching was so different from the Torah given to Moses—because the social, economic, political and religious conditions were so different in Akiba's day—that, at first, Moses could not recognise his Torah in the Torah taught by Akiba. But he was reassured when he realised that Akiba's Torah was *implicit* in his Torah, was, indeed, an attempt to make his Torah relevant to the spiritual needs of Jews in the age of Akiba.[11]

I now believe that I went rather too far in reading modern ideas into the ancient tale—a constant temptation, which should be resisted when discussing rabbinic views. The story does not in fact speak of the difference between the Torah of Moses and that of Rabbi Akiva, but of the difference between Moses himself and Akiva. It is possible that the intention of those who told the tale was to point to the great humility of Moses, who believed that Akiva was a more powerful *exponent* of the same Torah, hence his protest that the Torah should have been given through Akiva. Yet, having said this, I am not entirely repentant since, when all is said and done, this is an example of a talmudic passage in which the human element in the transmission of the Torah is so strongly appreciated that Akiva could be seen as a greater interpreter of the Torah than Moses himself, although it was Moses' Torah that he was interpreting.

The passage has received many comments from both the right and the left. Some Reform rabbis, not too anxious to read the idea of development into rabbinic texts, have suggested that the whole story was told in jest, very unlikely since anachronisms of this kind are found throughout talmudic literature and, in any event, are evidently treated seriously, although the legendary element should not be overlooked. A year or two ago, some Orthodox rabbis, while admitting that the story implies that Moses was unfamiliar with aspects of his own Torah, adopted

[11] Louis Jacobs, *We Have Reason to Believe*, 4th, rev., edn. (London, 1995), 78.

an ingenious ploy. The story says that all this happened 'when Moses ascended on high', meaning, that it happened as soon as Moses ascended Mount Sinai and before he had been taught the Torah. Had Moses' time-transcending journey taken place *after* he had been taught the Torah he would have had no difficulty in understanding what Akiva was saying. This is clever but wholly fanciful. If that is the meaning, why did God not wait until Moses had become better informed before sending him on his journey through time? Moreover, the expression 'when Moses ascended on high' is used by the rabbis not for the beginning of his experience but for the whole of it. The attempt is pure apologetics, and the contention stands that beneath the surface of this, and, I believe, other talmudic stories, is the tremendous idea, not fully formulated until modern times, that the Torah reaches down through the ages by human co-operation with the divine.

It will not generally do to try to turn the talmudic rabbis into Bible critics before their time. The view of liberal supernaturalism is obviously untraditional precisely because 'liberalism' in this context means a new departure from the tradition in the light of evidence and a methodology unknown until the modern period. All that this chapter seeks to demonstrate is that there are faint glimmerings, at least, in talmudic statements which enable non-fundamentalists to claim that their new theological formulations do not, in essence, do such violence to the rabbinic tradition as to move beyond the parameters of rabbinic Judaism as a whole. The point of quoting talmudic and similar references from the past is to show how much more flexible the rabbis were in matters of dogma than, say, Maimonides, whose stark formulation is often hurled against the legitimacy of the 'liberal' approach. To repeat, what is involved in any new formulation of dogma is a greater awareness of the real history of Judaism. To quote talmudic passages, as do the Orthodox, against this new view is to beg the question. Yet two further talmudic observations are not unhelpful in our quest.

The first is the saying, attributed to the School of Rabbi Ishmael (first to second centuries CE) that 'the Torah speaks in the language of men' (*Sifre* on Num. 15: 31; *Baba metsia* 31*b*). This school is said to have taken issue with those of its contemporaries who derived rules and teachings from a pleonastic word or syllable, for instance, the use of the infinitive absolute form of the verb. According to the School of Rabbi Ishmael no teachings can be derived from such expressions since this is how Hebrew is spoken, the Torah simply recording its teachings in 'the language of men'. The Torah is, according to this view, a divinely authored document, but the language it uses, including stylistic devices, is the language used by the human beings to whom it is directed. Maimonides (*Guide* i. 26) used this principle in order to explain biblical anthropomorphisms, although, in reality, the School of Rabbi Ishmael only applied the principle to the derivation of laws from this kind of expression.

The second passage (*Sanhedrin* 89*a*) states that the same watchword (communication) is revealed to many prophets, yet no two prophets, if they are true prophets, prophesy in identical language. This is a remarkable anticipation of the modern idea that prophetic inspiration is mediated through the personality of the prophet.

We can extend this excursus on the rabbinic tradition by referring to the comment by Rabbi Yom Tov Lipmann Heller (1579–1654) in his famous commentary on the Mishnah, *Tosafot yom tov*. In his introduction to this commentary, Heller remarks that, although Moses handed down a complete exposition of the Torah to Joshua, and Joshua handed it down to the Elders, and so on through the whole chain of tradition, there is no period and no generation in which new ideas were not put forward. But, asks Heller, what of the statement of the Talmud (*Megillah* 19*b*) that the Holy One, blessed be He, showed Moses the minutiae of the scribes and the innovations they introduced, such as the reading of the Megillah, which seems to suggest that there has been no development at all in Judaism, everything having been given to Moses at Sinai? Heller, as early as the seventeenth century, like his contemporary Azariah dei Rossi, could not believe that what amounts to an abolition of human history could have been suggested by the talmudic rabbis. Heller suggests that the Talmud does not say that God *handed down* the later innovations to Moses, only that He *showed* them to Moses, namely, that He allowed Moses to gaze into the future to see the scribes and sages engaging in their innovations *at the time when they did so*. That is to say, God did not actually tell Moses that, in the future, such innovations as the reading of the Megillah would be introduced, but rather allowed him to see into that future when they would be introduced by the sages. The authors of these innovations are the sages themselves. These had no *tradition* from Moses that they should introduce their innovations, but did so because that was what the times required for the Torah to be realized in its fullness. Whether or not Heller's subtle distinction between Moses being shown and Moses being given is a legitimate reading of the talmudic passage is beside the point. Whether or not this was intended by the rabbis, we find, at least, a great talmudist holding such an idea, one, surely, with relevance to our investigation.

FOUR

IS IT SCIENTIFIC?

So FAR I HAVE ARGUED that faith cannot be invoked to deny facts established by scientific demonstration and that, since the historical critical method is scientific, the attitude which persists in rejecting the method on grounds of faith amounts to a rejection of scientific investigation. This means that to affirm belief in the Pentateuch as the inerrant word of God given in its totality to Moses, together with the Oral Torah, involves a rejection of the facts uncovered by the scientific approach, the scientific, historical critical method having established to the complete satisfaction of unbiased students that the Pentateuch is a composite work compiled by various hands at different periods, and that the idea of the inerrancy of the Pentateuch and hence of the creation narrative in Genesis runs counter to the scientific accounts of the age of the earth and the history of mankind. If we use fundamentalism, reluctantly, but as the most convenient term, for the attitude which affirms both the traditional belief in divine authorship of the Pentateuch and its consequent inerrancy, we have to conclude that fundamentalism is unscientific and unhistorical.

Fundamentalism and Science

A fundamentalist aware of the conflict between the two views—some fundamentalists go their own sweet way without caring about it and good luck to them—can, of course, reject the scientific view as unfounded. He may argue that if, indeed, faith really ran counter to science, honesty would oblige us to prefer science, but, in fact, what is supposed to be the scientific picture of the universe and the Bible is not scientific at all. This was the attitude of many devout Christians in the nineteenth century in the science versus religion controversies. Another fundamentalist argument may be that every scientific hypothesis is only guesswork, to accept the results of which as established facts is sheer folly in that the facts are those stated by God Himself in Scripture. The late Lubavitcher Rebbe, for example, used to argue that to establish the vast age of the earth on the basis of the fossil records is to ignore the 'fact' that God may have placed the fossils there for reasons of His own. That what appear to be the remains of the dinosaurs have been discovered should not lead us to conclude that dinosaurs actually existed on earth millions of years ago since, as part of His creative processes, God may have created the fossils during the six days of creation. Why He should have done this we do not know, but then who are we to probe the divine purpose? To be fair, the Lubavitcher was too good a theologian to suggest that God placed the fossils there as a test of faith, that is, to see whether men would be suffi- ciently steadfast in their faith in Genesis to resist the blandishments of science. Presumably he did not argue in this way because that would mean that God intentionally planted false clues. But, then, to reject all the results of scientific investigation also ultimately involves the notion that God has given us the reason to discover the facts but expects us to believe that our reasoning is faulty, despite the extremely high plausibility of its conclusions, and, surely, this also involves a belief that God has planted false clues. Nor was the Lubavitcher able to conclude that Genesis can be squared with science on the grounds that the six days of creation represent vast periods of time for, if that were the case, what are we to make of the command to keep the Sabbath because God rested on that 'day', which means an actual 'day', the seventh day of the week on which we keep the Sabbath? It is also surprising that this notion, popular among fundamentalist scientists, that the 'days' of Genesis represent vast periods of time, fails utterly to explain what are the 'nights' of Genesis.

Another ingenious fundamentalist ploy is to follow the idea of Philip Gosse in his once famous book *Omphalos* (Greek for 'navel').[1] Gosse, a distinguished nineteenth-century scientist and a member of the Plymouth Brethren, at first found the scientific picture to be at variance with the Genesis narrative. As a believer in the literal truth of the Bible he could not reject Genesis, but as a scientist himself nor could he deny the results of proper scientific enquiry. Pondering over the matter, he resolved the contradiction by asking the question: Did Adam have a

[1] See the excellent survey in Berel Dov Lerner, '*Omphalos* Revisited', *Jewish Bible Quarterly*, 23 (1995), 162–7.

navel? Presumably he did, even though he was not born of a woman but was created from the dust of the earth. Since all men ever since Adam have navels, Adam, too, must have had a navel in order to be a proper human being. By the same token, the trees at the beginning of creation must have had the rings which determine the age of trees simply in order to be trees, even though these original trees were created spontaneously, not after the period of growth by which we now determine the age of trees. Gosse applies this idea to the world as a whole. He argues that the world as a whole that was created in six days by the divine fiat had the *appearance* of having emerged over a very long period of evolution. Thus the geologists in their study of the different strata of the earth's surface were right in detecting such phenomena as volcanic eruptions and ice ages, as were the astronomers in their exploration of the age of the solar system, and the evolutionists in describing the ascent of man from amœba and so forth, but all this evolution did not take place in real time but in what Gosse calls prochronic time, that is in the hypothetical time-scale in which the world would have emerged had God decided to create the world in the evolutionary stages it now exhibits. Some Orthodox Jewish scientists have recently followed a similar line, comparing the long evolution of the world to a film made to run from beginning to end in a minute or two. The trouble with this type of argument is that it fails to account for the Genesis narrative of Adam and Eve, who are created in real time and have no connection with prochronic time. Why should there be the appearance of primitive man in diverse places on earth in order to give the appearance of growth since Adam was a new creation? Why did Adam have to have the appearance of having emerged from primitive man as he had to have a navel in order to resemble his descendants as human beings? And this is to say nothing about the evidence that human civilizations existed *on earth* long before the approximately six thousand years ago when, according to Genesis, Adam and Eve were created.

The truth is that the great battles over science and Genesis among Christians in the nineteenth century seem to have left Orthodox rabbis unmoved, either because they were not interested in the question as being of any relevance to Jewish religious life or because they felt, as Rabbi A. I. Kook (1865–1935) said, that the Genesis narrative belongs to the 'secrets of the Torah' and hence should not be taken literally. In his work *Orot hakodesh* Rabbi Kook writes:

The theory of evolution now busy conquering the world is more in accord with life's mystery as understood by the Kabbalah than with any other philosophical theory. The notion that there is an evolutionary path upwards provides the world with a basis for optimism, for how can one despair when one sees that everything is evolving to ever greater heights?

Rabbi Kook courageously accepts the theory of evolution, believing that this idea of constant progress towards greater heights, hitherto confined to the élite, should now be taught to the masses, despite the apparent contradiction between the theory of evolution and Genesis. Rabbi Kook continues:

It is not the difficulty of reconciling certain statements in the Bible or in other traditional sources with the theory of evolution that encourages the masses to remain indifferent. It is easy enough to see how the two can be reconciled. Everyone knows that these topics, which belong to life's mystery, are always dominated by metaphor, riddle, and hint. Even the ear of the masses is attuned to hearing the brief formula that this or that verse or statement belongs to the secrets of the Torah which are on a higher plane than the simple meaning would suggest. The masses are quite content to accept such a solution and their opinion is in accord with that of the thinkers who assess the high poetical content that is ever-present when ancient mysteries are expounded.[2]

A remarkable statement by an Orthodox rabbi, for which Rabbi Kook was severely taken to task by his Orthodox contemporaries. Yet he, too, fails to deal with the question of Adam and Eve. If these figures also belong to the mysteries of the Torah, why are they treated in the whole of the Jewish tradition as real historical figures from whom all human beings are descended?

In their attempt to reconcile Genesis with science, some Orthodox writers nowadays are fond of quoting early rabbinic statements, such as an opinion in the Midrash (*Genesis rabbah* 3: 7) that the Holy One, blessed be He, created worlds and then destroyed them because they did not satisfy Him until He created this one—upon which the great sixteenth-century kabbalist, Isaac Luria, based his system. Or they refer to the statement (*Ḥagigah* 13b–14a) that before God created this world He had intended to create 974 generations but did not create them. But by no stretch of the imagination can these statements be squared with the age of this world and of primitive man, quite apart from the anachronism involved in the idea that the ancient rabbis anticipated modern

[2] (Jerusalem, 1938), vol. ii, part 5, 19–22.

scientific theories. The rabbinic statements belong to the trend in ancient rabbinic thought to see God as planning His creation, put forward in the well-known statement in *Pirkei avot* (5: 1): 'The world was created by ten sayings. But surely it could have been created by one saying? It is in order to punish the wicked who destroy a world created by ten sayings and to reward the righteous who sustain a world created by ten sayings.' In Luria's schemes the 'worlds' created and then destroyed by God before He created this world represent processes in the divine unfolding and have nothing to do with the evolution of this world.

The famous talmudist and commentator on the Mishnah, Israel Lipschütz (1782–1860), the first Orthodox rabbi to deal with the evidence for the existence of primitive man, drew on the early kabbalistic notion of a series of six-thousand-year cycles one after the other, in each of which the world is created anew, the Torah speaking only of the creation of the world in the present cycle.[3] Thus, according to Lipschütz, the skeletons of primitive man are those of men who lived in a previous cycle. This whole doctrine of cycles was rejected by the later kabbalists, but, in any event, the meaning of the doctrine is that this world was created afresh during the six days of creation so that there are no remains of earlier creatures belonging in a different cycle. All that such suggestions amount to is that there are ancient theories about the world before the 'beginning' of Genesis, and that is known since it is widely acknowledged that ancient cosmological theories and myths were used by the rabbis, unconscious of their origins, in their speculations. It is hard to see how such speculations can be of any help with regard to reconciling Genesis with science.

A valiant modern attempt at reconciling science with Genesis is that of Joseph Herman Hertz (1872–1946), the British chief rabbi, in his note entitled 'The Jewish Attitude towards Evolution'.[4] Hertz states that there is nothing inherently un-Jewish in the evolutionary conception of the origin and growth of forms of existence from the simple to the complex, and from the lowest to the highest. Hertz is even more specific:

Nor is the Biblical account of the creation of man irreconcilable with the view that certain forms of organized being have been endowed with the capacity of developing, in God's good time and under the action of a suitable environment,

---

[3] *Derush or haḥayim* (printed at the end of his commentary on the Mishnah, *Tiferet yisrael* on *Nezikin*).

[4] In his *The Pentateuch and Haftorahs* (London, 1950), 194–5.

the attributes distinctive of man. 'God formed man of the dust of the ground' (Gen. 2: 7). Whence that dust was taken is not, and cannot be, of fundamental importance. Science holds that man was formed from the lower animals; are they not too 'dust of the ground'?

Hertz goes on to say that the Bible's purpose is not to explain the biological origins of the human race but its spiritual kinship with God. And Hertz quotes the statesman Arthur James Balfour, who observes that the Bible 'neither provides, nor, in the nature of things, could provide, faultless anticipations of sciences still unborn. If by a miracle it had provided them, without a miracle they could not have been understood.' But if Hertz is prepared to accept that the Bible is not a scientific textbook and that man did evolve from lower forms, under the guidance of God, where do Adam and Eve come into the picture? If Adam represents the human race as a whole as it had evolved from the 'lowest forms', it cannot have been in the form of a single man and then a single woman from whom all mankind evolved. Perhaps Hertz would say that the story of Adam and Eve is a myth, but once one is prepared to go as far as this, why not accept the idea, stressed repeatedly in this book, that there is a human element in the Torah, that the Genesis narrative was composed by human beings, albeit inspired human beings, as a great hymn to the Creator, a hymn expressed in the language of its day and in accordance with the pre-scientific thought patterns of its day? The high religious significance of the narrative is not affected if we see it in this way.

On biblical criticism, too, there are differing attitudes among what we have called fundamentalists. One of these is to deny that the historical critical approach deserves to be called scientific, a term which, they maintain, is only applicable to the physical sciences which are based on empirical investigation. In the physical sciences, hypotheses can be tested and shown to be wrong where they are contrary to the facts, whereas historical questions belong to a past that, by its very nature, is no longer available to us for direct investigation. All historians can do is present educated guesses, so to prefer guesswork to tradition is to be thoroughly unscientific. The fallacy here is the denial that the documents of the past *can* be investigated to yield results with a very high degree of plausibility. Biblical criticism, for example, is based on an attempted objective consideration of what the Bible actually says and how what it says emerged. It is true that we cannot prove that the Pentateuch is a composite work but that it is, as the critics hold, seems very plausible on the internal evidence. What this objection really amounts to is that since what the tradition seems to say about the composition of the Pentateuch is guaranteed by God Himself to be completely accurate, and since it is a divinely authored document, all investigation into its origins is automatically ruled out of court. Such a stance is question-begging— the tradition is 'true' because that is what the tradition says—and is thoroughly unscientific in that it does not allow any investigation into whether or not the tradition is true.

It would be logical, though puzzling, to maintain that scholarly investigation has no place in the study of the Pentateuch, but if this is the stance adopted one cannot go on to argue that, for instance, the Documentary Hypothesis has been attacked by scholars on the Jewish side like M. H. Segal, Yehezkel Kaufmann, and Umberto Cassuto, favourites among 'scientific' fundamentalists. For if scholarship has no voice because we have a divine guarantee that the Pentateuch is a unity, it cannot be invoked to defend the traditional view, scholarship having no say either way in the matter. You cannot rule out scholarly method as irrelevant to faith and in the same breath rely on those who themselves use that method to show that the scholarship of Wellhausen and the like is faulty. Whether Wellhausen is correct is a matter of scholarship, to be decided on scholarly grounds.

In point of fact, as noted earlier in this book, the Documentary Hypothesis is still the dominant one for biblical scholars, albeit with various degrees of refinement. Nor is the fact that much emphasis is placed in contemporary biblical scholarship on the literary analysis of the pentateuchal text as we now have it of relevance to the issue. No literary critic of note rejects the idea that the Pentateuch is heterogeneous. What the literary critic is doing is to examine the document as it emerged as a unity from the hands of the final editors.

Moreover, had those who invoke the three scholars I have mentioned read their works they would have seen that their supposed attacks on the Documentary Hypothesis are based on scholarly grounds, not on grounds of faith, and that their views are as much at variance with the fundamentalist view as they are with the Documentary Hypothesis. Segal argues for the Mosaic authorship of the bulk of the Pentateuch, but he admits that many passages must have been added after Moses.

Segal's stance seems to be that Moses *could have been* the author of a good deal of the Pentateuch but not of all of it. Many passages must have been added later. But in that case Segal's view is a documentary hypothesis of its own, only the documents are not those detected by Wellhausen and his forerunners. The way Segal approaches the question, as anyone who studies his work must come to realize, is even more destructive of the doctrine that the real Author of the Pentateuch is God. To defend the tradition it is not enough to demonstrate that a good deal of the Pentateuch could have been written by Moses with many later additions. The traditional view is that every word was conveyed by God to Moses. Segal, operating on purely scholarly grounds, completely ignores the theological question, as he was, indeed, obliged to do as a scholar, but, if that is the case, he is of no help whatsoever to the fundamentalists, the majority of whom are, in any event, honest enough never to dream of calling in desperation on Segal in their defence.

Cassuto relies a good deal on the Ugaritic texts, on which he was a great expert. But to say that the Pentateuch was influenced by its Canaanite background and that Exodus was written by a poet in the time of David hardly supports fundamentalism. To give one example among the many that could be adduced, in connection with the great ages of the antediluvians in Genesis, Cassuto notes that none of them, not even Methuselah, lived for a thousand years—a 'day' in the life of God: 'For a thousand years in Thy sight are but as yesterday when it is past' (Ps. 90: 4). This is because the Torah is reacting to the notion found in the ancient Babylonian myths that in the remote past there lived supermen who became gods. No, says the Torah, even the supermen of old never lived for a 'day of God', and they were human beings, not gods. If this means anything it is that there were no actual antediluvians who lived to a great old age, but that the whole narrative is a device to promote monotheistic belief. A fundamentalist would say that these men really did exist and really lived for the years they are recorded in the Torah as having lived.

As for Kaufmann, he is the least likely scholar to be called on for the rejection of the Documentary Hypothesis. Kaufmann, in fact, accepts the division of the Pentateuch into the documents JE, D, and P. The three law codes in the Pentateuch, says Kaufmann, contradict as well as complement one another, and the only way these contradictions can be resolved is by converting rabbinic Midrash to the plain meaning of the text. Kaufmann's scholarly novelty consists chiefly in postulating that P is earlier than D, not later as did Wellhausen. Nor is the Uppsala school, often invoked in this connection, any help to the fundamentalist. This school is uneasy about speaking of actual documents, preferring to think of streams (tradents) of oral tradition from different sources. This is a kind of affirmation that what the rabbis call the Oral Torah preceded the Written Torah. There is only one conclusion to be drawn from all this: that there is a human element in the Pentateuch and the idea of verbal inspiration has had its day.

It is more than a little odd to find some scholars prepared to employ the historical critical method on the other books of the Bible as well as on rabbinic literature but who stop short when it comes to the Pentateuch. Even at the Jewish Theological Seminary, whose approach is that of Frankel and the Breslau school, critical theories were avoided, at first, with regard to the Pentateuch, but followed in connection with the rest of the Bible.[5] But if the method is sound it is illogical not to apply it to the Pentateuch. If it is not sound, how can it be used in connection with the rest of Jewish sacred literature? If you come to the conclusion, through the application of the historical critical method, that the prophet Isaiah could not have written the second part of the book attributed to him nor David the whole of the psalms attributed to him, how can you still hold that Moses must have written 'his' book, since the application of the same method shows that he did not? The method used is the same in both instances.

In recent years, conclusions reached by the use of computers are increasingly hailed to demonstrate that to understand the doctrine of *Torah min hashamayim* in the fundamentalist way, far from being unscientific, is in accord with the most up-to-date method of scientific enquiry. Through computers, word and letter associations in the Bible can be detected which were inaccessible to unaided investigators simply because no unaided student could detect these complexities. At first, studies were made of the book of Genesis to show that the style of the book is uniform, there being no stylistic differences between the supposed documents JE, P, and D of the critics. The trouble with this is, first, that the study was limited to the book of Genesis. It would have been more impressive if, say, the book of Deuteronomy had been compared stylistically with Leviticus. Secondly, the study did discover stylistic differences in the book of Genesis itself, but these were said to be due to the differ-

---

[5] See Jack Wertheimer (ed.), *Tradition Renewed: A History of the Jewish Theological Seminary of America* (New York, 1997), index s.v. 'Higher Criticism'.

ences between human speech, divine speech, and narrative, ignoring the fact that all three of these differ in the supposed sources. Moreover, it is bizarre to analyse the stylistic differences of a document said, according to the fundamentalist view, to have a divine Author, as if the Almighty has a special style of writing. This alleged proof of unity has now been abandoned. In its stead it is now claimed that the computers have un- covered hidden codes in the Pentateuch which so accurately foretell events of the future that they must have been placed there by the One who alone can foretell the future.

It all began over fifty years ago when a Rabbi Michael Weissmandel, long before the computer revolution, discovered through his own studies of the text that if one counts forty-nine letters from the first *tav* in the Torah (the last letter of the first word, *bereshit*) the fiftieth letter is a *vav*. If another forty-nine letters are counted, the fiftieth letter is a *resh*, and counting forty-nine after that yields *hé* as the fiftieth letter. These four letters form the word Torah (*tav, vav, resh, hé*). The same result is obtained when we count from the first *tav* in Exodus. In the book of Numbers we find the word Torah in reverse order: *hé, resh, vav, tav*, but to achieve the result we have to start not with the first *hé* of the book but the third. In Deuteronomy we again find the word Torah spelled back- wards but here the jumps must be of forty-nine letters and we have to start with the twentieth, not the first, *hé*. The book of Leviticus yields a different word at spaces of eight from the first *yod*—the word YHVH, the Tetragrammaton. Thus the first two books of the Pentateuch con- tain the word Torah in equidistant spacing of the letters, and the last two books the same but in reverse order. In the middle book, Leviticus, the Tetragrammaton appears—thus the code contains the idea that God is the author of the Torah. It is easy to see how flexible is the approach. The letters are not all spaced at the same distance and the word Torah is twice spelled differently. One can produce such results from almost any book with a degree of selective adaptation. It has been noted that the forty-sixth word from the end of Psalm 46 in the Authorized Version of the Bible is 'shakes' and the forty-sixth word from the beginning is 'spear'; it presumably could thus be argued that Shakespeare had a hand in the AV translation and put his name there.

In 1989 an Israeli physicist, Doron Witzum, published in collaboration with a professor of mathematics, Eliyahu Rips, the book *Hameimad hanosaf* ('The Additional Dimension'). In the book Witzum claimed that, by means of the computer, it was possible to demonstrate that the method of equidistant letter sequence (ELS) revealed in close proximity in the text of the Torah words that could not possibly be coincidental and must have been placed there by intention. For instance, they discovered the names of famous rabbis such as Maimonides in close proximity in the Torah to words which give the date of birth or death of these rabbis. In 1994 Witzum and Rips published their findings in the prestigious *Statistical Science* journal, the editors of which admitted, without actually endorsing the study, that it did present a 'statistical puzzle'. If, by proper statistical research, the dates of rabbis in the Middle Ages are found to be recorded in the Torah in code, this proves that the author of the Torah is God since no human could have inserted such codes into his work. The Aish Hatorah Yeshiva, in its efforts to win over Jews to Orthodoxy, has regular courses on the Codes in order to prove the doctrine *Torah min hashamayim*.

In 1997 a journalist, Michael Drosnin, relying on the work of Witzum and Rips, went further in using the method of ELS in order to show that, for example, the Torah foretold the assassination of John F. Kennedy in the close proximity of the words 'Kennedy', 'to die', and 'Dallas'. Drosnin's book, *The Bible Code*, in which he tried his hand at forecasting the future, is currently a runaway best-seller which Warner Brothers are to make into a film! There is no accounting for credulity in an age clamouring for certainty and wishing to find it in the Bible, suddenly restored as a divinely inspired work. Witzum and Rips claim to have used the best statistical methods, but critics of their work have shown that it is possible to gain similar results from any lengthy work provided the investigation lends itself, if not to cheating, at least to flexible adaptation of the words.[6] In fact the Masoretic text, the present text of the Bible, was not established until the early Middle Ages, and even the tradition acknowledges that in matters of full and defective words we do not necessarily have the original text. This has led some defenders of the Codes to postulate that even if the present text was not the text received from the hand of Moses it was divinely inspired, so the Codes detected in it are authentic. A curious notion to say the least, that the original God-given text was supplanted by a later text which corrected the earlier text's errors, all done by the holy spirit.

[6] See the detailed treatment by David Horovitz, 'Busting the Bible Code Breakers', *The Jerusalem Report*, 4 Sept. 1997, pp. 14–18.

What are we to make of all this? Leaving aside the statistical question, it is hard to see how the fundamentalist case is enhanced by a reduction of the Torah to a kind of ancient *Old Moore's Almanac*, to say nothing of the theological problem in the very idea of God providing detailed accounts in the Bible of events that were to happen well over three thousand years later. And there are conclusions that are so preposterous that it is unnecessary to show the faultiness of the premises on which they are based. According to Witzum and Rips the Codes spell out 'Hitler' in connection with the Holocaust. Even more weird and wonderful is the 'discovery' of the word formed from the letters *alef, yod, dalet, samekh*, forming the word or, rather acronym, AIDS, in close proximity to the words for 'monkeys' and 'Africa', thus foretelling that the AIDS virus would stem from monkeys in Africa! It would all be a colossal joke deserving to be dismissed out of hand were it not that so many fundamentalists find that it helps them to prove the divinity of the Torah, with the implication that the Torah is not divine because of its teachings but because it can be shown to be divine by a conjuring trick.

Isaac Breuer (1883–1946), grandson of Samson Raphael Hirsch and foremost exponent of his grandfather's philosophy of Judaism, adopted a very much more sophisticated approach to the question we are considering in this chapter: how Orthodoxy can be squared with the findings of science, including the scientific study of the Bible and rabbinic literature.[7] For our purpose, we can examine a selection from Breuer's *Neue Kasari*, in which he uses Kantian categories in order to establish the epistemological basis of the doctrine *Torah min hashamayim*. The book is in the form of a dialogue. An imaginary discussion takes place between a Mr Weiler and Alfred Roden, the son of a completely assimilated Jewish banker in Germany, who has won his way through to the strict Orthodoxy of German separatism and who encourages Weiler, sincere in his Judaism but plagued by religious doubts, to follow the same path. In particular, Weiler has serious misgivings about the doctrine that the Torah is divine, a belief that has been undermined for him by his acquaintance with biblical criticism, among other things.

Breuer's basic thrust is to apply Kant's famous distinction between the *phenomena* and the *noumena* not only to our knowledge of God and the physical world but to the Torah. According to Kant, all we can know of

[7] For Breuer's views in English, the selection in Jacob S. Levinger, *Concepts of Judaism* (Jerusalem, 1974) cannot be bettered.

the world is things as they appear to us. The world we perceive is one we construct by our thought patterns. This is not the 'real' world. Since we are incapable of getting out of our own skins, as it were, we can never know things as they are in themselves. By the same token, Breuer makes his hero argue, we can never know the Torah-in-itself, only the Torah as revealed to us in the *word*. All we can understand—all, indeed, that we need to understand—is this *word*, through which we perceive how the Torah-in-itself wishes us to regulate our lives. It follows, continues our friend Alfred as he wills poor, benighted Mr Weiler into fundamental-ism, though, naturally, he does not label it thus, that all biblical criticism is as absurd as an attempt to criticize nature for its enigmas and contra-dictions. The Bible critics arrive at their conclusions because they treat the Torah like any other book. But, in the process, they deny the Torah-in-itself and are, therefore, as misguided as those few natural scientists who refuse to accept the 'givenness' of the natural world instead of doing their proper job, which is to investigate thoroughly how this 'givenness' makes its impact on our sense perception. If the Torah were only a purely human production the reasoning of the Bible critics might well be convincing, but that is precisely the point. The Torah is not a human production at all, but is in the form of words, by means of which God communicates with us. As Alfred puts it:

For the Jewish nation, the Torah is the sum of the letters that were written down at God's command and by God's dictation. The words that are com-posed of these letters produce a meaning which our reason can appreciate. For God has availed Himself of man's language for His revelation of the word. But the Torah has not become the language of men on the strength of this circum-stance. The Torah as the language of men is only the visible form of the Torah as the language of God, in just the same manner that the world as conception we have perceived is only the visible form of the world-in-itself.

At this stage it becomes clear that Alfred, and through him, Breuer, is trying to have his cake and eat it. Biblical criticism is rendered taboo and the Torah made immune from all its findings by invoking the concept of Torah-in-itself. But, by definition, no human being can understand the Torah-in-itself, so how do we study the Torah and how can we know what its demands are? How, indeed, can Torah-in-itself make any de-mands? The answer is that the Torah-in-itself operates, as it were, through the Torah as written word and we are capable of understanding this word. But then we are back where we started, since, if the written word can be understood by humans, on what grounds can we reject categorically the human understanding of the Bible critics which, on the human level at least, Breuer seems to admit is plausible?

Breuer is too astute a thinker to ignore this difficulty, and seeks to solve it by making Alfred call to his aid the oral teaching, the Oral Torah, which is the self-authenticating interpretation of the written word by 'Kenesset Israel' (the community of Israel):

Alfred: I mean the oral teaching, the 'Torah of the spoken word', which forms the link between Torah-in-itself, the 'Torah of the written word', and comprehended Torah.

Weiler: Well, tradition then. The 'Torah of the spoken word' can only be preserved by tradition, being passed on orally from one generation to the next. The Torah of the written word resides with the 'primal foundation' of things; it is creation, just like the world-in-itself.

Alfred: The 'Torah of the spoken word' resides with the eternal Jewish nation which, as the transcendental custodian of the word which was addressed to it by God through Moses and has been guarded by it, is called 'Kenesset Israel'. In its unity, formed by God's spoken word, it represents God's 'kingship'.

But this begs the question with a vengeance. For this is precisely what we are discussing—the correct understanding of how the Torah, including the Torah of the spoken word, actually came to be. The massive researches of modern rabbinical as well as biblical scholarship surely demonstrate, as we have noted especially, that there is a *history* of the whole concept of Torah so that, nowadays, to think of the community of Israel as merely passive recipients of a divine body of truth, unchanged and unimpaired throughout the ages, is not to accept the idea of a 'metahistory' but to be completely unhistorical, to fly in the teeth of history.

This takes us to the heart of the matter. Breuer seems to have a mistaken notion of what biblical criticism is about. It is unfortunate that the terms 'higher' and 'lower' criticism, taken from the study of the Greek classics, were used for the discipline of biblical studies. The aim of every self-respecting critic (that some of them were biased and less than objective is to be deplored, but does not affect the argument) is not to sit in judgement on the Bible but to investigate how the Bible came to be. 'Criticism' in this context means no more than investigation by methods tried and tested in other disciplines, which yield extremely plausible results. To be sure, Breuer is right that the natural scientist is behaving childishly if he 'criticizes' the universe for not being a better place. He must accept the universe as it is, in all its 'givenness'. In pre-Copernican astronomy, it was held to be 'given' that the earth is at the centre of the universe. It was not a denial of the 'given' but a better understanding of it that demanded a new picture based on the results of empirical investigation and human reasoning, themselves part of the 'given'. One need not deny either the transcendental aspect of the Torah or the special role of the Jewish people and the Jewish tradition in its interpretation in order to follow modern scholarly method, even if the results seem to suggest that, at times, there has been misunderstanding. After all, the real aim of scholarship in this area is to discover what the texts originally meant, how they were put together, and how ideas developed. To deny all this in the name of an alleged monolithic structure of an alleged unassailable truth is, as noted more than once in this book, to believe in the God who plants false clues to mislead those who use the reasoning powers He has given them.

Science and Belief

More than once in his book Breuer refers to Bible critics and the disloyal Jews who adopt the critical approach. But, again as we have noted earlier, modern critical investigation into the sources of Judaism is not a rival religious philosophy. It is a tool, a newly fashioned instrument, a method of discovering what happened in the past, yielding results that are to be questioned and further refined but which possess a very high degree of probability with regard to the basic findings. In this sense, criticism is reasonable, but it certainly does not imply that reason alone is the sole key to religious truth. The Jew prepared to adopt the critical approach need not deny the transcendental aspects of the Torah. His findings will no doubt be untraditional in that not every construction put on Jewish history by past teachers of Judaism necessarily holds water today. But far from this being an act of disloyalty to Judaism, it can be an act of supreme faith in Judaism's ability to accept the truth from whichever source it comes; faith in God, who is not bound by the way we imagine that He must work to fulfil His purposes; and faith in human reasoning, which is, no doubt, a very poor thing but the only means we have for distinguishing between superstition and well-founded belief, between obscurantism and valid submission to a mystery beyond all our puny efforts at understanding, in a word, between error and truth, which is 'the seal of the Holy One, blessed be He'.

Do I hear an indignant protest? You are prepared to be bravely 'liberal' and 'scientific' in connection with the findings of the historical school, dismissing your opponents as unscientific and unhistorical fundamentalists, and yet, when it comes to the 'supernaturalist' part of the equation you suddenly become a blind believer for whom criticism has no place? Why accept religious belief at all, since it is certainly not susceptible to scientific proof? You accuse others of trying to have their cake and eat it: are you yourself not trying to do this impossible thing? If it is unscientific to adopt a fundamentalist stance with regard to the content of revelation, how do you know and why do you constantly claim that revelation actually took place? You have argued that all you are trying to do is to explore the meaning of 'from' in the doctrine 'the Torah is from Heaven', but why stop at the 'from'? Why not, in all honesty, admit that by casting doubts on the traditional understanding of 'from' you are thereby doubting whether there is a 'Torah' and a 'Heaven'?

My reply is to make a distinction between facts, open to scientific, empirical investigation, and basic beliefs, beyond these. I called my book *We Have Reason to Believe* to denote that, while belief must be reasonable, in the sense that it must not be in flat contradiction to the known facts, to believe is not the same as to prove. There has been much discussion on how religious people arrive at their beliefs. In my book *Faith* I have tried to examine this question from the Jewish point of view. But, to put it simply, however belief is attained, it is held to be reasonable to hold it. No religious believer ever says that his belief is unreasonable, in the sense that he knows his belief to be untrue but insists on it nonetheless. Your believer is usually faced with a bundle of religious beliefs, not all of which seem necessarily cogent and, whether he is conscious of it or not, he is selective, choosing those beliefs the truth of which seems highly plausible and rejecting those that seem either implausible or simply impossible. Of course, there is an element of subjectivity in such an assessment, but then this element is present in all our decisions. If, for instance, I am faced with the 'traditional' belief that there are demons at work in the universe and the other traditional belief that God is in control of the universe, I choose to believe in the latter because it coheres with the rest of my puny understanding of how things are, and to reject the former because it raises more questions than it solves. I believe in the existence of

God because this seems to me and to so very many of my peers and my ancestors to be how the universe makes sense. But I cannot accept fundamentalism because such beliefs are an affront to reason. It is not that I do not believe that, say, the world is only six thousand years old. It is rather that I know that the world is much older.

Although this chapter has the aim of defending liberalism in religion against the claim that such a stance is unscientific, I do not wish to conclude without any further consideration of the relationship between science and the basic belief in God. Essentially, science has nothing to say one way or another on the truth of this basic belief, any more than science has anything to say about moral questions. The social scientist may, indeed, tell us about the mechanics of why some people behave badly and others well, but unless we are complete determinists, if we are moral persons, we strive, not always successfully, to lead good lives. In a word, we ought not to equate science, which is a tool for the investigation of particular facts, with reason, which is the only tool we have for making sense of the world we inhabit and our role within it.

There have been, and still are, religious philosophers whose faith is based almost entirely on reason. The medieval thinkers who advanced proofs for the existence of God 'believed' that these proofs decided the matter once and for all. Richard Swinburne tries to work out, using the tools of science, a modern argument that belief in God is more plausible than any other hypothesis to describe how the universe works and came into being.[8] Modern scientific theories about the Big Bang are sometimes said to be strictly relevant to religious faith, but only in the sense that the Big Bang theory seems to imply that the universe had a beginning (what was before the Big Bang?) and is thus in accord with the idea that the universe has a Creator.[9] If the Big Bang theory indicates that the universe must have had a beginning 'out of nothing' (out of Nothing, as the kabbalists would have styled it if they had used English, i.e. out of the Ineffableness of God) it supports the medieval cosmological argument that an infinite regress is impossible. All this has more to do with philosophy than with science, involving philosophical or theological reflection on the facts *as a whole* uncovered by scientific investigation.

---

[8] *The Existence of God* (Oxford, 1979); cf. Alan G. Padgett (ed.), *Reason and the Christian Religion: Essays in Honour of Richard Swinburne* (Oxford, 1994).

[9] For a recent discussion of this question, see William Lane Craig and Quentin Smith, *Theism, Atheism and Big Bang Cosmology* (Oxford, 1995).

This is why I still stand by the view I tried to express in *We Have Reason to Believe*, that belief in God is entirely reasonable but that belief in the inerrancy of Scripture or the rabbinic tradition is not, which is certainly not to deny that the Bible is our Torah and the ancient rabbis our teachers. There are difficulties in the liberal supernatural view, but once the tremendous idea that God really *exists* is believed to be true, that God co-operates with humans for the fulfilment of His purposes, then all the rest follows. Critical theories about how the Bible came to be and how the rabbis came to hold the opinions they did can then be seen, problems and all, as belonging to the process by which God reveals Himself to us. The 'from' sheds light on the meaning for us of 'Torah' and 'Heaven'. Liberalism redeems supernaturalism from primitiveness. Supernaturalism redeems liberalism from banality and crude historicism.

Obviously, not everything that is claimed to be supernatural is really so. Whether or not, for instance, there is such a thing as extra-sensory perception, ESP, has been considered extensively in fairly recent years and attempts have been made to investigate this scientifically; whether the conclusions are valid is another matter. But if it is established that ESP is real it does not necessarily prove the supernatural, since ESP would then have been established as part of the natural order, i.e. part of the way the universe functions. However, it would defeat a completely materialistic philosophy by establishing that mind is not part of matter but can function independently of matter. By the same token science cannot prove that miracles cannot happen, since miracles themselves can be an in-built feature of nature. Attempts at a scientific proof that ghosts are real have usually failed, but even if they had succeeded it would only show that there is the possibility of communication with the dead and would not have much relevance to the doctrine of the afterlife if this is understood as a realm beyond space and time. There is no escape from the contention that science deals with the facts of the universe while religion seeks to reach that which transcends the universe. Or, as C. S. Lewis put it, the scientist does not believe, he knows.

Of course, once biblical criticism has done its work, the theological question is not whether miracles *can* happen but whether they did in fact happen. As Hume said long ago, it is a question of evidence. The liberal supernaturalist who, on 'scientific' grounds, holds that we do not have the direct guarantee of God that the biblical miracles actually occurred but only that this is how the human record sees it, is left with the view that human beings in the past believed that God did perform miracles for His people or His saints. We should, therefore, treat with a strong degree of scepticism the claim that, say, hasidic *rebbes* can perform miraculous cures, but we ought not to deny on *a priori* grounds that some persons, by their holy living, can influence the course of nature. It is undoubtedly true that, before the rise of modern science, the ancients had little awareness of nature proceeding by cause and effect and tended to interpret unusual events as the result of direct divine intervention. That moderns no longer do this is no reason for denying that God can and does intervene to set aside His own 'laws'.

I am aware that the above is too bald a statement to satisfy the enquiring mind. One would have to call attention to the rich literature, Jewish and non-Jewish, on the relation of the natural order to the supernatural. All I wish to do in this chapter is to show that a liberal is not guilty of self-contradiction if he affirms at the same time that he is a supernaturalist. So, while science and religion are essentially two quite different areas of human thought and experience, the marvellous universe science has revealed to us—the immensity of space; the complex structure of the atom; the intricate patterns of the leaf; above all, the workings of the human mind—increases our sense of wonder, and if it does not lead to an irrefutable argument for design, shows at least how extremely plausible is the traditional Jewish belief that the glory of God fills the universe He has created.

Even the traditional proofs for God's existence—the ontological, the cosmological, the teleological, the argument from man's moral sense and from religious experience—have not been entirely demolished, and moderns have no right to look upon the medieval thinkers who advanced them as benighted. If they are put forward as 'proofs' it is hard to see why more than one should be required. Moreover, if each one is faulty, how can they all be sound? But if they are treated as arguments rather than proofs, if the inductive method is used rather than the deductive, each argument lends support to the others, as I wrote in my book *Faith*:

An archaeologist, for example, may be able to date his finds accurately by discovering absolute proof of the date. He may, for example, discover a coin that bears a recognisable emblem to which a fixed date can be ascribed. This would constitute proof of the date. But if no such proof were available the archaeologist would then proceed to advance a number of arguments for his dating. He would then perhaps point to the strata in which his discoveries were made, to the type of pottery excavated, to literary sources which seem to tally with his dating. If he found that the arguments from various premises converged to suggest a particular date it would become extremely plausible to suggest that this was in fact the date of his material.[10]

Swinburne, the renowned exponent of theism in the philosophical vein, is particularly good on this.[11] Antony Flew remarks:

A failed proof cannot serve as a pointer to anything, save perhaps to the weaknesses of those who have accepted it. Nor, for the same reason can it be put to work along with other throwouts as part of an accumulation of evidences. If one leaky bucket will not hold water that is no reason to think that ten can.[12]

But, observes Swinburne, if you put three weak arguments together you may often get a strong one, perhaps even a deductively valid one. If you put ten leaking buckets together in such a way that the holes in each are squashed against the solid parts of the others you may, indeed, get a bucket that holds water.

As I noted at the beginning of this chapter, Orthodox Jews are generally silent on the whole question of biblical criticism. There are, however, three essays dealing with the topic from the scientific point of view in *Challenge: Torah Views on Science and its Problems*, edited by Aryeh Carmell and Cyril Domb.[13] This publication is sponsored by the Association of Orthodox Jewish Scientists, an intriguing title, which surely implies that it is possible to be an Orthodox Jew and a scientist at the same time, and that the apparent 'challenge' science presents to Orthodoxy can be met successfully. The three essays in this volume on biblical criticism are relevant to the theme of this chapter, that of the scientific, that is, the historical critical, approach to the classical sources of Judaism. It might be helpful to look at these three essays, by Cyril M. Abelson, Max Kapustin, and Emanuel Feldman. Abelson attended my lectures at the New West End, but later on sided with the opposition at the time of the 'Jacobs Affair'. Although his essay, 'Bias and the Bible',[14] appears in a volume devoted to scientific considerations, Abelson, in fact, is content to issue a diatribe against the 'critics', accusing them of antisemitic bias. The editors preface Abelson's essay with the words 'Cyril Abelson documents some interesting correlations between high-level critical scholarship and virulent anti-Semitism, particularly in the Nazi era', as if an

---

[10] *Faith*, 46.   [11] *The Existence of God*, 13–24.
[12] Antony Flew, *God and Philosophy* (London, 1966), 167.
[13] Jerusalem, 1978.   [14] Pp. 412–20.

argument *ad hominem* has any relevance to the question of how to meet the scientific challenge to fundamentalist Orthodoxy. The other two essays are much more judicious, and deserve to be studied.

In his essay, 'Biblical Criticism: A Traditional View',[15] Kapustin rightly remarks that biblical criticism in itself merely represents a scientific methodology which in principle contradicts the approach to the Bible that has been cultivated in traditional Judaism from time immemorial to our own day: 'For the Bible critic, the Torah is not word for word and letter for letter direct divine relation.' Kapustin continues: 'On the basis of this fundamental assumption they then proceed to the conclusion that the text as we have it is a composite work covering many centuries and derived from many different individuals and "schools of thought".' Kapustin asks, 'What should be the approach by traditional Jews to this whole area?' He significantly replies: 'The answer is to be found in the clear and binding position of the tradition, combined with an *objective scientific* evaluation of Biblical Criticism' (emphasis mine). Thus biblical criticism, when examined 'with an objective scientific evaluation', is bad science and should hold no terrors for traditional Jews. Instead of examining the whole critical theory, Kapustin simply quotes David Hoffmann's scholarly attack on both literary and textual criticism as if this were sufficient to demolish the whole critical edifice *on scientific grounds*. Kapustin, in contrast to Abelson, sounds a note of caution. It is one-sided to evaluate all aspects of non-Jewish 'Old Testament' scholarship on the grounds that it is a means for the depreciation of the Jewish religion. Such an evaluation, he observes, is neither historically nor factually correct. Kapustin, therefore, hails modern biblical studies, but believes that they now tend to support the traditional view. I have already noted the attempt to use Yehezkel Kaufmann to buttress the traditional view on grounds of pure scholarship, whereas, in reality, Kaufmann adopts a critical theory of his own. Kapustin, aware of this, remarks 'Yechezkel Kaufman [*sic*] (who accepts the basic critical premises regarding the composite nature of the Pentateuch) has made a most impressive effort to show that the Torah precedes the literature of the Prophets', thus accepting Kaufmann's *scholarly* views on the Torah preceding the prophets but rejecting Kaufmann's *scholarly* view that there are three sources in the Pentateuch. Are we engaging in objective scholarship or

---

[15] Carmell and Domb (eds.),*Challenge*, 422–31.

are we using it to buttress positions already held by tradition or on the basis of faith?

Kapustin's effort amounts ultimately to the contention that biblical scholarship should not be totally rejected, since elements in it tend to support the traditional view. 'The case for the unity of the Pentateuch today', he writes, 'does not have to rely on the authority of tradition alone. It is supported by sound scientific argument. The evidence for the possibility of "Mosaic" authorship is mounting.' If the evidence is really mounting for the Mosaic authorship of the Pentateuch, where is this mounting evidence mentioned in any modern scholarly publication?

The best essay of the three and the most 'scientific' is that of Feldman, entitled 'Changing Patterns in Biblical Criticism'.[16] The editors preface Feldman's contribution by observing: 'This article traces in detail the course of biblical criticism from the earliest times to the present day, showing with examples how recent archaeological discoveries have revolutionized critical attitudes in many respects. He envisages an eventual rapprochement between "traditional" and "critical" modes of study.'

Feldman first notes that traditional Jews still view biblical criticism with strong suspicion and as of utter irrelevance to one who is immersed in the study of God's word. Yet, though it may be helpful to one's faith to deny that it exists at all, biblical scholarship should be given at least a *de facto* recognition. Feldman argues, as many have done before him, that the whole critical theory was a reflection of the times in which Hegelian notions of thesis, antithesis, and synthesis prevailed, so that the evolutionary nature of pentateuchal religion could easily be detected. The trouble with this is that the evidence that the Pentateuch is a composite work from different periods does not depend at all on the Wellhausen thesis of evolutionary progress from lower to higher. Very few, if any, contemporary biblical scholars adopt evolutionary theories to explain the Pentateuch, but all, as mentioned earlier, accept that the evidence of compositeness is overwhelming. In fact in Feldman we find the idea, of which Orthodox teachers are increasingly fond, that all you have to do to dismiss all criticism, lower as well as higher, is to show that the Documentary Hypothesis, the fruit of nineteenth-century German scholarship, has now been abandoned.

[16] Ibid. 432–44.

Feldman points to the evidence provided by archaeological discoveries which show that conditions described in the patriarchal narratives actually obtained in that period. Thus, for instance, the discovery of the fifteenth-century BCE archive during the 1925–31 excavations at the site of Nuzi in northern Mesopotamia sheds light on biblical narratives. For instance, in relation to the episode of Rachel's taking of her father's *terafim* in Genesis 31: 19 and 30, the Nuzi tablets enable us to see the historical background to the narrative, since we learn that property could pass to a son-in-law in certain circumstances, but in order to give it the proper sanction the father had to give the household gods—*terafim*—to his daughter's husband. Or when, in the Pentateuch, a patriarch's wife is referred to as his sister (Gen. 12: 10–20; 20: 2–6; 26: 1–11) this can be understood against the background of the Nuzi tablets' evidence that marriage was considered most sacred when the wife had the legal status of sister. Hence, by referring to their wives as sisters, Abraham and Isaac were actually protecting their wives.

It is hard to see how the uncovering of the background helps the fundamentalist view. All it shows, which must be obvious to any student of the Bible, is that the 'background' to the narratives is real. Far from helping the fundamentalist it ought to puzzle him since, according to his view, it was all 'dictated' word for word and letter by letter by God Himself. Did God use the Nuzi background for the purpose? Or is it not far more plausible to hold that the very fact that the patriarchal narratives are told against the background of ancient civilizations shows that the stories were told by humans who knew of this background? And what of the duplicates? Why are there two narratives, each with its own vocabulary, of the patriarchs calling their wives their sisters? And if the aim of calling a wife a sister was to increase her status, why did Abraham not do this long before he came to Egypt and saw that his wife was so beautiful that the Egyptians might desire her?

Feldman is to be admired for issuing a caveat. Archaeology, he says, is not the handmaiden of the Bible, and it is not invariably a support to Torah.

For the believing Jew, scholarly and scientific support for Torah is pleasant, but it is not indispensable to his faith. Similarly, apparent contradictions to Torah do not disturb him. He remembers only too well that just forty years ago Torah had been 'scientifically' disproved, only to find the disprover itself become the disproved.

Thus, in the final analysis, Feldman falls back on faith, failing to see, as I have suggested more than once, that if the facts are so, faith can only be invoked to deny them if we can believe that God has planted false clues.

Far more objective is the essay by Steven Shaw, 'Orthodox Reactions to the Challenge of Biblical Criticism' in the journal *Tradition*.[17] Shaw, a graduate student in Near Eastern Studies at the University of Pennsylvania when he wrote the essay, is far more familiar with what biblical criticism is and what it purports to be doing than the other Orthodox writers mentioned. Shaw first quotes Louis Rabinowitz's three 'basic and inviolate principles' in the matter: that the Torah is from Heaven; that the Masoretic text is the only *textus receptus* of the Torah; and that the only valid method of interpreting the Torah for Jewish purposes is the one based on the Oral Torah. If these principles are accepted, says Shaw, it would mean that Modern Orthodox efforts in the field of biblical scholarship may be severely curtailed.

Shaw notes that the term *Torah misinai*, used frequently nowadays, is actually only a loose appellation for the more exact phrase *Torah min hashamayim*, since, from the internal evidence, it is obvious that many of the events related in the Pentateuch are said to have taken place during the forty years the Israelites journeyed through the Sinai wilderness. On the reliability of the Masoretic text, Shaw observes that modern biblical scholarship is inclined to attribute greater reliability to the Masoretic text than to other versions, but then quotes me as saying that:

It is quite impossible to dismiss every emendation of the Massoretic text contained in Kittel's *Biblia Hebraica*, based on the ancient versions. And there is no serious Bible scholar in the world who would consider such an outright dismissal as anything but a complete betrayal of the scholarly ideal. That the Massoretic text is always correct and that all ancient variants are due to error is a belief so preposterous that it would hardly have been necessary to refute it were it not for the fact that it is implied in the standard formulation of the eighth article of the faith.[18]

As for the doctrine of the Oral Torah, Shaw believes that, while in matters of halakhah the interpretation of the text of the Torah is, indeed, inviolate, in other matters the student is free to interpret the Torah even if the interpretation does not accord with the Oral Torah. But since

[17] 10 (Spring 1969), 61–85.
[18] Louis Jacobs, *Principles of the Jewish Faith* (London, 1964), 259.

Orthodox Jews live by the halakhah it is hard to see how the halakhic interpretation accords with the original text, since historians of the halakhah have shown that the halakhah itself has developed in response to the social, economic, and even political background of its practitioners. Since this is so, it is hard to see how a defence of the Mosaic authorship of the Torah is relevant to the issue. Indeed, if it is established that the Torah was given word for word by God to Moses, how could the rabbis interpret that word so differently from its plain meaning? To reply that the rabbis possessed the authentic interpretation involves the idea of an undisturbed and unqualified tradition from generation to generation; not only is there no evidence at all for this position, but all the available evidence points in the opposite direction.

Shaw refers to the view that the findings of archaeology support the tradition. But they certainly lend no support to fundamentalism. Nor, as I argued at the beginning of this chapter, is it fair to invoke Umberto Cassuto, as Shaw does, in favour of the unity of the Pentateuch, since Cassuto does not believe in either the unity of the Pentateuch or its Mosaic authorship.

Shaw, honestly facing the problem, quotes Joseph Heinemann,[19] with whom he evidently agrees. According to Shaw, Heinemann, after granting that Orthodoxy is often placed in a difficult position by biblical criticism, declared that perhaps the only thing left for the Orthodox Jew is to admit sincerely that he is unable to be 'a man of science' in this area. With the great respect due to the memory of a great scholar, I must confess that I am unable to make sense of these remarks of Heinemann. Being a 'man of science in this area' only means that one pursues scientific method with regard to uncovering how Judaism developed. Either such a method yields good results, which are open to empirical examination and criticism, or it is completely useless wherever it is undertaken. Once one admits that the method can be convincingly applied in other areas, one cannot simply opt out of applying it in this.

In this whole discussion, I fail to see why observant Jews cannot take the necessary step of adopting, as many others have done and as I have tried to do in this book, the view that the practical observances of Judaism have as their sanction that this is how the Torah has been de-

---

[19] I knew Joseph Heinemann well. He was a strictly Orthodox Jew but realized that biblical criticism and modern rabbinic scholarship—Heinemann was himself a distinguished practitioner of the latter—do seem to pose severe problems for Orthodoxy.

veloped by human beings in response to the divine will, albeit conveyed through the historical experiences of the Jewish people; that there is a human element in the Torah, which can no longer be seen as an infallible text but still belongs to the way in which God has communicated His will to mankind. If such an approach is not that of Orthodoxy so be it. There is no such doctrine as 'Orthodoxy *min hashamayim*'.

FIVE

THE *MITSVOT*: GOD-GIVEN OR MAN-MADE?

AN OBJECTION levelled again and again to views such as mine is: if what you say is true, that the *mitsvot* are not direct commands given by God but the result of human reflection and adaptation over the ages, why should Jews obey them? Why should contemporary Jews be fettered by the tradition? It is rational to keep *divine* laws, for who is man to question the will of God? But why should human beings follow laws ordained by other human beings? Why should our lives be governed by the teachings of the masters of old, no matter how eminent, wise, and saintly they were? To reply to this challenge, it is necessary to consider the meaning that can be given to the distinction between God-made and man-made laws.

The ethical precepts of Judaism present less of a problem than the purely ritual precepts in that the former are, in the main, those which human beings can understand and to which they respond of their own volition; those which they would carry out even there were no divine commands. I discussed the relationship between religion and ethics from a Jewish point of view some years ago.[1] I repeat here only the salient points relevant to the theme of this chapter.

The Ethical Basis

A question much discussed by religious thinkers is whether the good in the ethical sense is good because God wills it to be so, or rather whether God wills it to be so because it is good. In other words, is there an

[1] 'The Relationship Between Religion and Ethics', in Gene Outka and John P. Reeder (eds.), *Religion and Morality: A Collection of Essays* (Garden City, NY, 1973), 155–72.

autonomous ethic with only an indirect association with religion? To take the fifth commandment as an illustration, is it proper to honour parents because God has so commanded, or does God command it because it is right and proper? If the former is true, then conceivably if God had commanded us to despise our parents that would be right. But if the latter, then God, being God, could not possibly command us to despise our parents. Or, with regard to the eighth commandment, is it wrong to steal only because God has declared that it is wrong, or is it wrong to steal because it is intrinsically wrong and that is why God commands us not to steal? Although the biblical prophets were not systematic philosophers and would not have formulated the question in the form mentioned, yet from the prophetic books in the Bible it would seem that, for the prophets, justice and mercy are to be practised because human beings understand of their own accord that this is how they ought to behave, and the burden of the prophetic call in the name of God is for humans to be true to that which they already know is right. This is not, of course, to say that human beings always respond to what they know to be good. The prophetic demand is directed to people who know what is right but do not follow it in their lives. As Abraham Lincoln once said, 'It is not that which I do not understand in the Bible that bothers me. It is that which I understand only too well.'

In many of the pentateuchal laws the reason for their observance is stated, a reason which appeals to man's innate ethical sensibility:

And a stranger thou shalt not oppress; for ye know the heart of a stranger, seeing ye were strangers in the land of Egypt. (Exod. 23: 9)

If thou at all take thy neighbour's garment to pledge, thou shalt restore it unto him by that the sun goes down; for that is his only covering, it is the garment for his skin: wherein shall he sleep? And it shall come to pass, when he crieth unto Me that I will hear; for I am gracious. (Exod. 22: 25–6)

Thou shalt not have in thy bag diverse weights, a great and a small. Thou shalt not have in thy house diverse measures, a great and a small. A perfect and just weight shalt thou have; a perfect and just measure shalt thou have; that thy days may be long upon the land which the Lord thy God giveth thee. For all that do such things, even all that do unrighteously, are an abomination unto the Lord thy God. (Deut. 25: 13–16)

Thou shalt not abhor an Edomite, for he is thy brother; thou shalt not abhor an Egyptian, because thou wast a stranger in his land. (Deut. 23: 7)

A plain reading of the famous passage in the book of Micah (6: 7–8) similarly suggests that man knows how he should behave and that that is what God wants him to do:

Will the Lord be pleased with thousands of rams, with tens of thousands of rivers of oil? Shall I give my first-born for my transgressions, the fruit of my body for the sin of my soul? It hath been told thee, O man, what is good, and what the Lord doth require of thee; only to do justly and to love mercy, and to walk humbly with thy God.

So, too, does Isaiah appeal to his people:

Wash you, make you clean, put away the evil of your doings from before Mine eyes, cease to do evil, learn to do well; seek justice, relieve the oppressed, judge the fatherless, plead for the widow. (Isa. 1: 16–17)

The prophet Amos castigates Damascus, Gaza, Tyre, Edom, Ammon, and Moab for atrocities they have perpetrated, even though these peoples had received no divine law, the implication being that man is capable of discerning right from wrong by the natural light that is within him (Amos 1–2). Indeed, nowhere in the prophetic books are the 'nations' condemned for worshipping their gods—only for the ethical abominations such as child sacrifice associated with worship.

That to behave ethically does not require the authentication of a divine command is implied, too, in the rabbinic idea (Jerusalem Talmud, *Rosh hashanah* 1: 3) that God obeys His own laws. Quoting the Greek saying (the quotation is in Greek in Hebrew characters) that the law is not written for the king, the passage continues that a human king decrees laws for his subjects but he himself is not obliged to keep them, whereas God orders man to rise before the aged, and He did this Himself, as it were, out of respect for Abraham. The Babylonian Talmud (*Yoma* 67b) gives as examples of commandments 'which if they had not been written in Scripture should by right have been written' the laws concerning idolatry, immorality, bloodshed, robbery, and blasphemy. There is also the oft-quoted saying of the third-century Palestinian teacher, Rabbi Johanan (*Eruvin* 100b): 'If the Torah had not been given we could have learnt modesty from the cat, honesty from the ant, charity from the dove, and good manners from the cock who first coaxes and then mates.'

Particularly relevant is the discussion in Sa'adya Gaon's *Sefer ha'emunot vehade'ot* ('Book of Beliefs and Opinions'), compiled in 933.[2]

---

[2] Part 3, chs. 1–3; trans. into English by S. Rosenblatt as *Beliefs and Opinions* (New Haven, Conn., 1948), 146–7.

Sa'adya classifies the *mitsvot* of the Torah into the *rational* and the *revealed*, in which classification he was followed by subsequent Jewish thinkers. The rational precepts, which include the ethical, would be recognized as binding even without revelation. Revealed precepts (such as the dietary laws) are not irrational (there is a reason for them and they are not arbitrary), but here God's will is paramount. Obviously man would not know that he has to obey these precepts if it had not been revealed to him. He would not wear tefillin or refrain from eating pork if he were not *commanded* so to do, for how would he otherwise know that this is what God would have him do? But, Sa'adya asks, what need is there for revelation in connection with the rational precepts? If man can know them without revelation, if, as we say nowadays, they are autonomous and are kept because it is right to do so, not because they are enjoined in Scripture, why are they, in fact, revealed through prophecy? Sa'adya's basic answer is that revelation is required to avoid all uncertainty and for the precise details of how the rational precepts are to be carried out to be given. Thus, for example, it is true that man would know by his own reason that it is wrong to steal, yet revelation is still required in order to inform man how property is to be acquired. Sa'adya seems to be saying that even without religion's precise teachings man's moral sense would still function, but it would be confused when it came to application. In Sa'adya's own words:

A further example is that, although reason considers stealing objectionable, there is nothing in it to inform us how a person comes to acquire property so that it becomes his possession. It does not state, for instance, whether this comes about as a result of labour, or is effected by means of barter, or by way of inheritance, or is derived from that which is free to all, like what is hunted on land or sea. Nor is one informed by it as to whether a sale becomes valid upon the payment of the price, or by taking hold of the article, or by means of a statement alone. Besides these, there are many other uncertainties pertaining to this subject which would take too long and would be too difficult to enumerate. The prophets, therefore, came along with a clear-cut decision for each instance. Another example is the question of the expiation of crime. Reason considers it proper, to be sure, that whoever commits a crime should expiate it, but does not define what form this expiation ought to take: whether a reprimand alone is sufficient, or a malediction should go with it, or a flogging should be added. In the event that the punishment takes the form of flogging, again, the question is how much, and the same applies to the malediction and the reprimand. Or it is possible that no satisfaction will be obtained except by the death of the criminal.

And again it might be asked whether the punishment should be the same for whoever commits a certain crime or whether it should vary from person to person. Then the prophets came and fixed for each crime its own penalty, and grouped some of them with others under certain conditions, and imposed monetary fines for some. For these considerations, then, that we have enumerated and other such reasons, it is necessary for us to have recourse to the mission of God's messengers. For if we were to defer in these matters to our own opinions, our views would differ and we would not agree on anything. Besides that, we are, of course, in need of their guidance on account of the precepts prescribed by revelation, as we have explained.

Sa'adya does of course believe in a direct divine revelation not only for the revealed precepts but also for the details of the rational precepts, and is no help for a non-fundamentalist approach. Yet Sa'adya's idea, followed by all who accept his distinction between the two types of precept, that there are precepts that do not in essence require a divine revelation because to observe them is innate to human nature, enables even those who prefer, for good reason, to think of revelation through the people rather than directly to them, to say that for the observance of the ethical precepts no direct revelation is necessary. As for Sa'adya's details of the precepts, these are indeed provided by the halakhah. What is required is to extend Sa'adya's 'the prophets' to the rabbis who teach the laws, to the Oral Torah. It may even be that Sa'adya himself included the rabbinic tradition in his use of the term 'prophets', since he was the great opponent of the Karaites, who rejected the whole talmudic tradition, and some of the instances to which he refers are, in fact, rabbinic, not biblical.

A further idea in connection with the relationship between religion and ethics is that, granted the autonomy of ethics, religion is required to give an added dimension to human life. The religious man sees his ethical concern as part of his total relationship with his God. This should not be taken to mean that there is a conflict between love of God and love of man, as George Orwell did, for instance, when he pronounced that you cannot love both God and man. On the contrary, the love of man is part of what is meant by the love of God. But, by introducing the love of God into the picture, a different quality is imparted to man's ethical strivings. Man has no need for the God hypothesis in order to appreciate the claims of the ethical side of human life. If a man has to invoke his religion in order to be good in the ethical sense, he is remote from the good as religion sees it. But the religious man believes that God *is* and that God's nature is such that every act of justice, love, and compassion makes for the fulfilment of His purpose, every act of cruelty and oppression for its frustration. Man is to live, it can be put, both horizontally and vertically, open to earthly needs and responding to them as any other ethical man would do, but with his religious beliefs to add to the scene the glories of heaven. Such a way of looking at the matter does not depend on any fundamentalist understanding of *Torah min hashamayim*.

The Jewish mystics appear to see it in this way. Take, for instance, the great compendium of the Jewish religion *Shenei luḥot haberit* ('The Two Tablets of the Covenant'),[3] known as the Shelah, by the German kabbalist, Isaiah Horowitz (?1565–1630). At the beginning of the book (44*b*–45*b*), Horowitz discusses the obligation to love all God's creatures and its connection with the other great commandment to love God. Horowitz discusses the well-known story in the Talmud (*Shabbat* 31*a*) of the prospective convert to Judaism who requested Hillel to teach him the whole of the Torah while he stood on one leg. Hillel replied 'That which is hateful unto thee do not do unto thy neighbour. This is the whole of the Torah. All the rest is commentary, go and learn.' The medieval commentators were puzzled by this tale. What of the religious obligations of the Torah? Rashi suggests that Hillel was referring only to the ethical precepts, or that by 'thy neighbour' Hillel meant God. Horowitz draws on this to suggest that, in fact, both loves—of God and of one's neighbour—are really one, since God is One and all derives from Him. The love of one's neighbour is part of the love of God who created the neighbour. By loving one's neighbour one fulfils God's purpose. Horowitz adds a more mystical note. Since man is created in God's image, there is a divine spark in every human soul, so that the love of one's neighbour is quite literally the love of God.

Horowitz's summary of his view is interesting in itself, but also because it calls attention to character dispositions, which there is certainly no direct command in Scripture to cultivate:

In truth, if you will examine the matter carefully, you will find that the majority of the precepts depend for their fulfilment on the command to love one's neighbour. First there are all the precepts regarding alms-giving, leaving the forgotten sheaf and the corners of the field to the poor, tithing, honesty in business, the prohibition of usury, and many others of a like nature. Then there are

---

[3] [Amsterdam, 1648]; 2 vols. (Jerusalem, 1963).

all the virtuous traits of character: compassion, kindliness, patience, love, judging others charitably, running to help them when they are in danger, not slandering them or bearing tales, not scorning or hating them or feeling envious of them, not flying into a rage, not being over-ambitious, these and thousands of other virtues depend on loving one's neighbour and only then can one become perfect by keeping both the positive and negative precepts. And even with regard to those precepts which have no connection with one's neighbour—the prohibition, for example, of forbidden food and of eating leaven on Passover—a man will keep them *a fortiori*. For if he loves his neighbour as himself, how much more will he love God Who loves him with an unqualified and true love, Who is Lord of the universe and to Whom all belongs, blessed be He. So you see that the command to love thy neighbour as thyself is the leg [referring to the would-be convert's demand that he be taught the whole Torah while standing on one leg] upon which the whole world stands. So you can see that 'thou shalt love thy neighbour as thyself' brings about 'thou shalt love the Lord thy God'.

The Ritual Precepts

So far we have considered what Sa'adya calls the rational precepts. These do not necessarily need the spur of a direct divine communication for their authentication. But what of the precepts of which, Sa'adya says, we only know through revelation? Let us first examine the dietary laws as an example. The fundamentalist argument runs somewhat as follows. To observe the dietary laws, the laws of *kashrut*, involves a good deal of self-denial. It is hard to be scrupulous in matters of diet, to refrain from eating certain foods, to have separate dishes for meat and milk, never to eat even kosher food in a non-kosher restaurant, but we willingly make the sacrifice because, we believe, this is what God will have us do. As the well-known rabbinic saying has it, 'A man should not say "It is impossible for me to eat swine flesh" but should rather say "It is truly possible, but what can I do since my Father in Heaven has so decreed?"' (*Sifra* on Lev. 20: 26). But why submit to *kashrut* if the whole discipline may have originated in primitive taboos and was, in any event, not commanded by God but created by human beings, however spiritually gifted? The simple answer is that, indeed, there is little point in observing *kashrut* and the other ritual requirements of Judaism unless the motive for the observance is to obey a divine imperative. Where views such as mine deviate from fundamentalism is not on whether the precepts are commanded by God—many non-fundamentalists also believe that they are—but on how the command was conveyed. Historically considered, what the rabbinic saying is aiming at is that there is little religious value in otherwise apparently valueless observances unless these are undertaken out of a religious motivation.

Strictly relevant to this theme is the acute analysis of Maimonides in his *Shemonah perakim* ('Eight Chapters'—Introduction to *Pirkei avot*, ch. 6). Maimonides discusses Greek and Hebraic ethical ideals when these are in conflict. (Such a discussion could only have been held once Greek ways of thinking had begun, in the Middle Ages, to be considered in relation to Judaism. It was not, of course, and could not have been, possible in rabbinic times.) Who is the better man, asks Maimonides: the one who has no desire to do wrong or the one who wishes to do wrong but refrains by exercising constant self-control? The Greek thinkers appear to be saying that the better man is the one who has no desire to do wrong, no murder in his heart, no urge to take that which does not belong to him, no hateful or harmful thoughts. The talmudic rabbis, on the other hand, as in the quotation from the *Sifra*, seem to be saying the exact opposite. The rabbis seem to be saying that, ideally, a man should have the desire to do wrong, to eat forbidden food, for example, but should not do the wrong because his Father in Heaven has so decreed. Maimonides resolves the conflict by a neat (some might say, a too neat) distinction between religious and ethical laws. The rabbis are thinking of purely religious laws and here the element of obedience to God's will be paramount. The man who has no desire to eat forbidden food because, for example, he dislikes the taste or what he imagines to be the taste, does not abstain out of religious conviction and, since the act in itself is ethically neutral, his abstention has no religious value. His motive for abstaining is not for religious reasons. But the Greeks are thinking of ethical demands, and the rabbis would here agree that to refrain from murder by exercising self-control is to fall short of the purpose of the ethical laws, which, from the ideal point of view, seek to promote the good character which will ensure that its possessor has no wish in his heart to harm others.

From Man-Made Institutions to Divine Commands

In point of fact, most of the details of *kashrut* are not found in the Pentateuch at all. There is no reference to the laws of *sheḥitah*, which, say the rabbis, were given to Moses at Sinai. The prohibition on the cooking and eating of meat and milk together is derived by rabbinic hermeneutics from the verse which forbids seething a kid in its mother's milk, and the prohibition on cooking chicken in butter is said to be rabbinic. That one does not eat meat and milk at the same meal is also said to be rabbinic, a precaution against cooking them together. Again, according to the rabbis, the biblical prohibition on eating or drinking blood does not apply to blood that has been boiled or cooked, so that the whole procedure of salting meat before cooking is rabbinic. There is no escaping the view that a fundamentalist attitude involves the acceptance not of the literal words of the Pentateuch, but that the rabbinic interpretation is the authentic meaning of the pentateuchal laws, so that what non-fundamentalists are saying is that, seen historically, these rabbinic laws did not simply drop down from Heaven but are, like the pentateuchal laws themselves, the result of human co-operation with the divine in the creation of the Torah. Our approach is, indeed, new, and a departure from tradition, but does not involve any rejection of the *mitsvot* as the word of God.

In a lecture in Manchester a year or two ago I said, and it has been held against me by fundamentalists ever since, that I wear tefillin because my grandfather wore tefillin. This was taken to imply that the only reason I wear tefillin is because the tradition so demands, a position of ancestor worship I have never entertained for one moment. What I said was that the average Jew who wears tefillin does so as part of the pattern of his religious life, but that the sociological aspects of a ritual do not preclude the recognition of the ultimate religious sanction for its observance. True, I wear tefillin in the first instance because my grandfather wore them and my grandfather because his grandfather wore them. But, while the wearing of tefillin has now become sacred habit, it is a sacred habit by means of which Jews come nearer to God. Jews, before donning the tefillin, do, after all, recite the benediction 'Who has sanctified us with His commandments and has commanded us to wear tefillin'. They are saying in so many words that they wear tefillin because it is a religious obligation, an important part of traditional Jewish observance, even though they do not normally feel obliged even to consider how this particular practice came to be. The theological aspect is only relevant so far as the actual observance is concerned, not for any doctrine as to how the ritual came about. I do not deny that the attitude of the

Breslau school, upon which my view is based, departs from the medieval philosophy of the *mitsvot* as direct commands of God. But it is a departure forced on us by the new knowledge of the history of Judaism. Fundamentalism may provide the certainty that many require in order to be observant, but history has shown that fundamentalism is untenable. A new philosophy of the *mitsvot* is required, but it is one still within the tradition itself (as discussed in Chapter 3 above) which can now be seen to be a developing tradition.

The best illustration of what is meant by revelation through the experiences of the people of Israel is provided by the institution of the synagogue. Even the fundamentalist, who holds that for religious institutions to be binding a direct divine command is necessary, has to admit that there is no such divine communication for Jews to frequent the synagogue. The whole institution of the synagogue has developed largely as a response to the destruction of the Temple, when communal prayer took the place of the sacrifices. Communal prayer itself is a later development. All the prayers in the Bible are individual prayers. The liturgy of the synagogue can be traced from its early beginnings. Many of the hymns were composed by medieval poets. The ever-popular *Lekhah dodi* hymn for welcoming the sabbath was composed by Solomon Alkabets as late as the sixteenth century.

With regard to the music of the synagogue, each community of Jews has its own melodies. Sephardi melodies are in the Arabic or Oriental modes, Ashkenazi ones in the German mode. In Western synagogues musical compositions go back to sixteenth-century Italy but, of course, there were musical accompaniments to the Temple service, and there has been a host of composers of synagogue music in the nineteenth and twentieth centuries. Even the mode of cantillation of the Torah differs from one community to another: the Sephardi differs from the Ashkenazi, and, in the Ashkenazi mode itself, there are differences between the German and the Lithuanian styles.

Architectural styles differ very widely from synagogue to synagogue. Rabbi Ezekiel Landau of Prague (d. 1793) was asked whether it is permitted to build an octagonal-shaped synagogue. He wrote in reply:

With regard to the question whether it is permitted to build a synagogue with eight walls and eight corners or whether a synagogue must have only four walls and four corners and must be greater in length than in breadth. I am surprised at the questioner. What reason can he have had for supposing that it is forbidden? You were quite right to tell him that there is no reference to this in the *Shulḥan arukh*. I go further and say that we do not find in any of the early Codes or in the Babylonian Talmud or in the Jerusalem Talmud that a synagogue is required to have any particular shape.[4]

There are many reasons why Jews go to the synagogue. Some go for social reasons or because they like the traditional melodies or the rabbi and the cantor (these institutions themselves having developed over time). But the majority go to synagogue, in addition to other reasons, in order to worship their Creator. They do believe that it is the will of God that they should do so but, ultimately, that will is discovered through the very practice of worship in the synagogue. Jews go to the synagogue because that is what Jews do and since that is what Jews do, how Jews worship God, it can be said that this is what God would have them do and is hence a divine command, albeit one not conveyed directly to passive recipients. To put it somewhat crudely, the synagogue is man-made, the institution itself, its forms, its liturgy, its melodies, its architecture, and everything else about it. But the men who made it were God-seekers who were followed by popular consensus, itself under the guidance of God. It is but a step—a very big step to be sure—to the application of this to the whole idea of revelation, a mystery even for the fundamentalist, as it is bound to be since no human mind can grasp the workings of the divine will.

Let us examine further the thought-provoking passage in the Talmud (*Shabbat* 23a) on the benediction to be recited when kindling the Hanukah lights. The passage reads: 'What is the benediction? Who sanctified us with His commandments and commanded us to kindle the light of Hanukah. And where did He command us? R. Avia said "Thou shalt not turn aside" [Deut. 17: 11]. R. Nehemiah said: "Ask thy father and he will shew thee; thine elders and they will tell thee" [Deut. 32: 7].' On this passage there is a huge debate between Maimonides and Nahmanides, concerning how it relates to laws introduced by the rabbis.[5] According to Maimonides, the passage means that the Torah itself orders us to obey rabbinic law. He ridicules, however, the notion that the passage means that one day this and that will occur in the days

---

[4] *Noda biyehudah*, second series (Jerusalem, 1969), no. 18.
[5] See Maimonides, *Sefer hamitsvot, Shoresh rishon* (Warsaw, 1883) and Nahmanides' comment ad loc.

of the Maccabees, and that they will ordain that the Hanukah light has to be kindled, and that their ordinance must be obeyed. The passage should rather be understood to mean that there is a divine command that the ordinances of the sages of Israel should be obeyed whenever and for whatever reason they ordain them. Thus, in Maimonides' view, and this is repeatedly stressed by Orthodox thinkers today, all rabbinic law is ultimately biblical law. It follows that, in Maimonides' view, the only reason why a Jew is obliged to obey a religious law is because there is a command in the Torah for him so to do, and there is such a command to obey rabbinic law in the two verses quoted.

Nahmanides (Ramban), in his comments on this section of Maimonides' work, demurs. The two verses in Deuteronomy do not really deal at all with the question of laws ordained by the later rabbis. The first verse quoted, according to Nahmanides, deals with obedience by one of its members to the decision of the great court, the Sanhedrin. This does mean that there is biblical warrant for some teachings of the rabbis, but only when they are in the position of a Sanhedrin, that is, in their basic interpretation of the laws of the Torah, and in no way does this refer to institutions that are of post-biblical origin. The second verse is not in a legal context but is a simple plea to take note of the people's past. For Nahmanides, the two verses are what is known as an *asmakhta*, the term for an idea pegged onto a verse which is not its real meaning. For Nahmanides rabbinic law is precisely that, rabbinic and not biblical. Nahmanides does not tell us why, in that case, rabbinic law should be obeyed. Presumably he would have said that rabbinic law has to be obeyed, even in the absence of a direct divine command, because the Jewish religion requires later legislation by the sages in order for it to be preserved. Something of the sort is implied in the comment of the great twentieth-century *rosh yeshivah*, Rabbi Simeon Shkop (1860–1940):

The Rambam holds that according to the Torah we are obliged to keep all that we have been commanded through *ḥazal*, and with regard to this it is said 'Thou shalt not turn aside'. But the Ramban, disagreeing with him, holds that this negative prohibition is only stated in the Torah with regard to that which *ḥazal* interpreted as the plain meaning of the Torah or that which they derived by means of the thirteen hermeneutical principles by which the Torah is expounded. But with regard to that which *ḥazal* innovated in order to provide a fence and a protection [i.e. rabbinic ordinances with the aim of protecting the Torah] there is nothing whatsoever in the Torah that we are obliged to obey their words. How I am astonished by such a statement! Can it be right that we are obliged to listen to the words of *ḥazal* without an admonition to do so in the Torah? Who is Lord over us except our Father in Heaven? If He did not decree that we must listen to the voice of *ḥazal* who obliged us to do so? These things break the roofs [a talmudic expression to denote a very startling statement] and there is neither a carpenter nor a carpenter's apprentice ['carpenter' is a rabbinic synonym for a scholar] who can solve the problem. But I find a solution to this. According to the Ramban's theory we are obliged to obey *ḥazal* because our reason tells us so. Since they believed it to be good to ordain this and enact that then that is what is true and good for us. Just as our reason concurs that we should listen to the word of the Lord, so does it decree that we should keep all that *ḥazal* and our holy teachers decree.[6]

Be that as it may, historically considered we have in all this an anticipation of the idea that, whatever its origins, a ritual should be observed if its observance enhances the spiritual life of the Jew, though I am far from suggesting that either Nahmanides or Rabbi Simeon Shkop would even have thought of expressing such an idea. Yet, here too, when Jews kindle the Hanukah lights, they do so as part of their quest for the divine Will and that is how the command is conveyed. There is also more than a hint here that the doctrine of the Oral Torah applies not only to actual laws given at Sinai but to the institutions of the rabbis, although, of course, the rabbis did believe in actual laws given to Moses at Sinai and they obviously would not have held that the Written Torah is itself a creation, so to speak, of the Oral Torah.

It has to be admitted, however, that the modern way of looking at the whole question of observance involves a strong degree of selectivity. On the fundamentalist view, to observe each *mitsvah*, together with every one of its details, is a divine imperative. The medieval thinkers did discuss the reasons for the *mitsvot*, but that the *mitsvot* must be kept in their entirety they did not and could not question. Before the Emancipation, Judaism presented itself as a package complete in itself. The medieval Jew followed the pattern of Jewish life which he was obliged to accept as totally binding in all its details, unless he wished to opt out of Judaism, which comparatively few ever thought of doing. The Emancipation and the Enlightenment brought in their wake an unravelling of the package, later aided and abetted by the introduction of the historical critical study of Judaism. The tendency among modernist Jews, even

6 *Sha'arei yosher* (Warsaw, 1928), section 1, ch. 7, 18–19.

among those who kept the *mitsvot*, was to ask not so much why God ordained that we should keep the *mitsvot*, but rather why we should keep this or that *mitsvah* and, for the first time, the idea of relative value was introduced into the equation. To refer, again, to the question of *kashrut*, the modernist Jew who keeps the dietary laws will seek to discover what religious value there is in adherence to these laws. He will see such value in the preservation of the Jewish people or, in a more religious vein, in the promotion of holiness in daily living. This is, after all, the reason implied in the biblical injunction regarding these laws. But once the question of value is introduced an element of selectivity is bound to be present.

It is all very well to argue, as I do in this book, that the *mitsvot* provide the Jew with a vocabulary of worship, but some of our values are those of Western society, and when the *mitsvot* are assessed against these values they do, not very often but certainly at times, come into conflict with the informed Jewish conscience. One thinks in this connection of attitudes towards women, or non-Jews, or the law of the *mamzer*, in which there is severe discrimination against innocent children.[7] Many non-fundamentalist but observant Jews have tried to face this acute problem. I have tried to deal with the vexed question, admittedly without too much success, in my book *A Tree of Life*. Here one can only say that it is possible, given the will, for the non-fundamentalist Jew to find the way to a solution by an adaptation of the halakhah, the legal system of Judaism, which, as historical investigation has shown, has been flexible and creative. After all, Jews no longer practise polygamy (even those Sephardi communities who did so until recently), no longer have slaves, and no longer avail themselves of the *ḥerem*, nor do they treat heretics as if they are utterly beyond the pale, nor do Orthodox doctors refuse to treat non-Jewish patients on the sabbath.

It might be useful at this stage in the argument to examine Jewish life as it is actually lived. There are theoretical problems in connection with Jewish institutions, observances, feasts, and fasts, once the history of these has been discovered through scholarly research but, as I have argued in this book, the history of how Jewish institutions came to be is irrelevant to Jewish religious life today. For practical purposes we need a vocabulary of worship. Let us see how this works.

---

[7] A *mamzer* is the child of a seriously forbidden union, and is only allowed to marry another *mamzer* or a proselyte.

Take the festival of Hanukah. We have noted the use of 'Who has commanded us' in connection with the benediction over the Hanukah lights, which can, without too much distortion, be understood as being commanded through the experiences of the Jewish people. Now, so far as this festival is concerned, the events it celebrates really happened. The Maccabees really did wage the wars and really did rededicate the Temple. But did the miracle of the oil really take place or is it a legend? The arguments for the latter view are well known: the sole reference is in a comparatively late talmudic passage; there is no reference to it in the liturgy of the day; from the book of Maccabees it appears that the eight days of Hanukah are based on the eight days of the festival of Sukkot, which would have been celebrated had the Temple been in Jewish hands. And yet, legend or no legend, the celebration of Hanukah came to centre on the miracle of the oil. Homiletical discourses throughout the ages have interpreted the miracle of the oil as a symbol of the power of the spirit. On the sabbath of Hanukah the *haftarah* is from the book of Zechariah, containing the verse 'Then he answered and spoke unto me, saying: "This is the word of the Lord unto Zerubbabel, saying: Not by might, nor by power, but by My spirit, saith the Lord of hosts"' (Zech. 4: 6). Moreover, there is much evidence that the kindling of the lights on Hanukah precedes by centuries the story of the miracle of the oil, and the connection of this with the pagan kindling of lights at the time of the winter solstice has often been noted. So what! Yes, Hanukah has had a history. Hanukah is man-made. Hanukah, and the stress on the miracle of the oil, is a creation of the Jewish people. But this creativity has inspired Jews to keep alive the flame of Judaism, and that is the best reason there can be for Jews to continue to celebrate this festival.

The festival of Purim presents problems of its own from the historical point of view. Did the events related in the book of Esther actually take place? Did King Ahasuerus really rule over the whole world, as some rabbinic *midrashim* seem to suggest, and did he wish to destroy all Jews at the request of Haman? Why is there no mention in any external sources of King Ahasuerus having a Jewish consort? Is the book of Esther a 'nationalistic' rather than a 'religious' book, as is suggested by the absence of the name of God? This kind of question has been aired in scores of books. And yet Jews, even if they allow themselves to doubt its historicity, still keep Purim. Why? Surely it is because the festival represents the persistence of Jews in surviving as Jews under the guidance of God. Haman has become a symbol of the vicious antisemite who cannot bear to live in a world in which there are Jews. As for the alleged vindictiveness of the story, for which reason some Reform Jews no longer celebrate Purim, it is a moral duty to rejoice at the defeat of tyranny. True, if the story in all its details really happened, there are questionable moral elements in it, but precisely here history helps us. In all probability it did not really happen, but antisemitism really happened and tyranny and oppression really happened and still happen, and it is the hope that these will one day be overthrown that is being celebrated on Purim. Yes, Purim is man-made and being man-made has questionable elements, but Jews have managed to override these elements in joyous celebration. The danger in the celebration of Purim is real. It could have led to an attitude of unbridled nationalism or exclusive particularism, to hatred of non-Jews or suspicion of their motives. That it did not do so is due partly to the 'fun' element in the festival: the Purimspiel, dressing up, imbibing strong drink, the parodies of classical Jewish literature, the Purim Rov and Purim 'Torah', all of which allow aggressive instincts to be expressed without getting out of control. The horrible massacre in Hebron by Baruch Goldstein was, alas, provoked by the Purim story, but was an abominable act of murder decried and utterly repudiated in the name of Judaism by the whole of Jewry, except for the hateful fanatics who erected a stone in memory of the murderer.

It is when we come to the three biblical feasts—Passover, Shavuot, and Sukkot—that the historical question looms large. It is now axiomatic among biblical scholars that these were originally agricultural festivals in ancient Israel, transformed by being connected to historical events. With regard to Shavuot the transformation did not take place until fairly late rabbinic times, when it became the 'season of the giving of our Torah'. Also, the archaeological evidence points to the sojourn in Egypt of only some tribes, not all the Children of Israel. The question is, then, how much of the biblical story of the Exodus is in conformity with what actually happened in the past? Were there really around two million Israelites in the Exodus, and how could the seventy souls that came into Egypt have become such a large number of persons at the time of the Exodus? Again this kind of question is not relevant to practical Judaism. Historically minded Jews may express their puzzlement at these and similar aspects of the *seder* on Passover, but they do so as part of the *mitsvah* to retell the story, not as biblical critics or historians or archaeologists. Of course, if Israel was never in Egypt and no Exodus ever took place, it would be more than a little bizarre to celebrate a deliverance from an evil that never existed. To this our reply must be that, poetry or not, the story of the Exodus embraces the living tradition of a living people that the Exodus did happen, although the story received many embellishments through the ages. As Martin Buber put it, in the story of the Exodus we have 'sacred history', *Heilsgeschichte*. It is saga rather than chronicle, poetic reflection on the facts of history rather than a sober account of them. And the message of freedom from bondage is a universal theme and is so considered by Jews who celebrate Passover, even while, as Jews, thinking primarily of their own freedom and giving thanks for it.

If Judaism is seen as having evolved through human co-operation with the divine, great caution should be exercised in drawing too neat a distinction between divine and man-made *mitsvot*. But if the question is raised whether Passover is man-made, the answer is that most of the features of the festival are acknowledged as human creations in the tradition itself. The prohibition on leaven and the obligation to eat matzah are both in the Bible, but it is in the rabbinic literature that we find the definition of leaven and when to eat matzah. That rice cannot become *hamets* is debated in the Talmud, the ruling being given that a dough made of rice does not constitute *hamets*. In the Middle Ages Jews in Germany, for various reasons, took it upon themselves not to eat rice or legumes on Passover, so that to this day pious Ashkenazi Jews do not eat rice or legumes on Passover, though for Sephardi Jews there is no prohibition. From the Bible it might appear that matzah has to be eaten during the whole of Passover, but as the rabbis understand it, the *mitsvah* to eat matzah is only binding on the first night of the festival. That one has to drink four cups of wine at the *seder* is a rabbinic rule, and the whole order of the *seder* night is based largely on Jewish custom in the sense that this is how Jews do it. And, here again, since it is man-made the divine element only enters because Jews worship God on Passover in this, rather than any other, manner. A fundamentalist would object to the use of the word 'rituals' to describe the *mitsvot*. They are for him direct divine commands, and to call them 'rituals' is to cheapen them. But the non-fundamentalist, uneasy with the notion of a direct divine command because his knowledge of history does not allow him to see it that way, gladly employs the term 'rituals' to denote that they are the creation of human beings reaching out to God. And yet they are still *mitsvot*, divine commands in the sense that, if one can speak of what it is that God wishes Jews to do, this is what He wishes Jews to do.

In connection with Sukkot, all the details of how a sukkah is to be constructed—its minimum and maximum size, its shape, its covering, and the regulations regarding eating and sleeping there—are all as recorded in the Talmud and are not found in the Bible. That four species of plant have to be taken on Sukkot is mentioned in the Bible—though the idea that they have to be taken in the hand and waved to and fro is rabbinic. That the phrase 'fruit of a beautiful tree' means the *etrog* is stated only in the rabbinic literature, as are all the details regarding the size and shape of the four species. The festival of Simhat Torah is a new creation, dating from the geonic period (sixth–eleventh centuries), with its rituals developing in different ways among the Jewish communities of the world. That Sukkot has two days of festival at its beginning and end in the Diaspora is acknowledged to be rabbinic. In fact, the observant fundamentalist is misguided, from his own point of view, in stressing the idea that God gave every word and every letter to Moses. If this is the case, the question must present itself to him: how does it come about that, today, in our celebration of the festivals and in so many other matters, we practise our religion in a manner so different from the actual command of God? And it is not only the Orthodox who are fundamentalists. Some Reform Jews in the last century used to argue, as did the Karaites, that to keep two days of the festivals is sheer blasphemy in that it purports to improve on God's word. There is no recourse here and elsewhere but to accept that the festivals and all their details are manmade, in the sense that they are the result of human creativity, but, since they are directed to God, they are divinely commanded.

The man-made element in the festivals is seen most of all in Shavuot. As remarked above, the festival in the Bible is entirely agricultural and is an adjunct (*atseret*) to Passover, with no special rituals of its own except for the special sacrifices in Temple times. Even in the Mishnah Shavuot is still known as 'Atseret'. But eventually Shavuot became the anniversary of the giving of the Torah, since, according to the book of Exodus, the theophany at Sinai took place on this date, in the third month of the year. Historically speaking, the whole idea of *the* Torah, comprising the whole of the Pentateuch as well as the Oral Torah, is not found at all in the

Pentateuch itself, as I have noted previously. But once the Torah had come into its own, so to speak, in rabbinic times, Shavuot became the day *par excellence* on which is celebrated Israel's choicest gift—a gift, the non-fundamentalist would say, received not by passive recipients but through creative co-operation with the divine. From this point of view, Shavuot is truly the 'season of the giving of our Torah', but the expression is not, for the non-fundamentalist, a statement about a particular date in history. It is rather a statement or declaration of what the Torah means for Jews in terms of the eternal verities. According to any reading of the situation, the later elaborations of Shavuot—the decorating of the synagogue with plants, the eating of dairy foods, the all-night vigil introduced by the kabbalists—are the result of Jewish creativity and are certainly man-made, yet no one thinks of rejecting them on these grounds.

Or take the festivals of Rosh Hashanah and Yom Kippur. There is no clear statement in the Pentateuch that the *shofar* has to be sounded on Rosh Hashanah. Since there is no pentateuchal basis for this, the Karaites did not blow the *shofar* on this festival. And, certainly, the details about the type of *shofar* that has to be blown, its size and the kind of notes to be sounded, as well as the accompanying benedictions and scriptural verses to be recited, are known to us from the rabbis, who provide us with the 'vocabulary of worship' to be used, and which Jews everywhere use, on this great day. For Jews, the sounding of the *shofar* means a call to repentance and to mending one's ways, as Maimonides said, although he refers to it only as a 'hint'.

Yom Kippur, in the Pentateuch, is chiefly a day of service in the Temple and this is what it remained in Temple times. After the destruction of the Temple, the Temple service was referred to in the Avodah service of the Musaf prayer, but the emphasis became one of sincere repentance required of the individual Jew, the culmination of the Ten Days of Penitence, themselves the creation of the rabbis. To afflict oneself is enjoined in the Pentateuch, but it is the rabbis who explained this injunction to mean that we have to fast and who added the other 'afflictions'—to abstain from bathing, anointing with oil, wearing leather shoes, and marital relations. Jews who still observe these practices do so not necessarily because they are mentioned in the Bible, which, in fact, they are not, but because it has seemed very reasonable that this is the way a day of prayer and spirituality should be observed. The magnificent hymns of the day—well, some of them—are recited because, whoever were their composers, they still speak to our souls. Devout Jews know that these hymns and the melodies which accompany them are man-made, but refuse to see that as any reason for discarding them. On the contrary, if I may put it like this, a recognition of the human element makes it all the more religiously significant by calling constant attention to the fact that, in our religious life, we are reciting words composed by human beings like ourselves, even if we consider them to have been spiritually superior. In point of fact, a number of the *piyutim* are 'man-made' in another sense, in that they found entry into the prayerbook by a whim of the printers. It might also be noted that a feature of Yom Kippur mentioned in the *Shulḥan arukh*, which used to be widely practised among the Ashkenazim, is hardly practised anywhere today, so far as I am aware, even among the *ḥaredim*, with few exceptions. This is the practice of receiving a symbolic flogging on the eve of Yom Kippur. Why it has dropped out of practice can only be conjectured—maybe because it tended to invite ridicule—but drop out it did. This is a trivial matter in itself but is nonetheless relevant to our enquiry. To see the Jewish people as following practices that are man-made, by calling attention to the human element in the development of the Jewish religion, is also to see Jewish creativity in the omission of rituals which have had their day. Naturally, this latter principle has always been adopted with great caution, otherwise the Jewish people would have been in danger of allowing the whole house of Judaism to collapse by subjecting it entirely to its builders rather than its actual users. Behind it all lies the consensus of the Jewish people on what should be preserved of the tradition and what can safely be rejected. To call attention to the role of the Jewish community in the creation of Jewish institutions is not to adopt an attitude of ancestor worship or one which believes that the Jewish people can never be wrong. But how can we know when and where the Jewish people have created wisely or foolishly except by faith in the sound religious sense of the Jewish community as a whole, which, indeed, may at times have got it wrong but which has usually got it right? There is not much point in asking, for instance, whether the Karaites were right or wrong in their interpretation of the verse in the Pentateuch about not kindling lights on the sabbath, which, for them, means that Jews are obliged to sit in darkness all through the sacred day. Since our argument is that human consensus determines our ways of worship, then, indeed, the Karaites were right, in that their interpretation provided them with their vocabulary of worship, while the Rabbanites, whom we follow, were right in that their interpretation provided them with such a vocabulary. To ask 'but which of them does God Himself want?' is a little childish since Karaites and Rabbanites, Orthodox Jews and Reform Jews, all ask the same question, to which, short of a direct revelation, there is no answer. Yet, when all is said and done, history has decided, or, better, God has decided through history, that the Rabbanites have won out and that this, therefore, is the admittedly man-made Torah that God wishes us to keep if we wish to be faithful to Judaism as a religion.

We should, at this stage, look at the institution of the greatest significance to Jewish religious life, the sabbath. Whatever the origins of this tremendous day, without which, as the rabbis saw, there could be no Judaism worthy of the name, it appears in the Pentateuch, especially, as everyone knows, as the fourth commandment. Yet there are only one or two references in the Pentateuch to what constitutes *melakhah* ('work') on the sabbath. The Mishnah lists thirty-nine main classes of work:

There are forty save one main classes of work: sowing, ploughing, binding sheaves, threshing, winnowing, cleansing crops, grinding, sifting, kneading, baking, shearing wool, washing or beating or dyeing it, spinning, weaving, making two loops, weaving two threads, separating two threads, tying [a knot], untying [a knot], sewing two stitches, tearing in order to sew two stitches, hunting a gazelle, slaughtering or flaying or salting it or curing its skin, scraping it or cutting it up, writing two letters, erasing in order to write two letters, building, pulling down, putting out a fire, lighting a fire, striking with a hammer, and taking [something] from one domain to another. (Shabbat 7: 2)

It can be seen at a glance that these thirty-nine main categories of work are those which were involved in daily life in mishnaic times. They all have to do with the provision of food, clothing, and housing. Out of these there emerged, in the history of rabbinic Judaism, numerous applications of these main categories. The much later idea that it is creative work that is forbidden in order to hail God as Creator is fine, but, it must be said, there is no evidence for it in rabbinic literature.

In addition to the rabbinic development and interpretation of what constitutes work forbidden on the sabbath, there are prohibitions clearly of rabbinic origin such as *muktsah*, the handling of tools or money which may lead to the carrying out of forbidden work. To recite kiddush

on the sabbath is derived from the injunction to 'remember the Sabbath', but the derivation is of rabbinic origin, as is the injunction to eat
three, instead of the usual two, meals on the sabbath. Also of rabbinic
origin is the lighting of sabbath candles—*ner shabat*. In rabbinic times
this meant that the home should be well lit on the sabbath but, in the
Middle Ages, probably to counter the Karaite view that the home
should be in darkness, special sabbath candles were introduced, over
which the benediction is recited: 'Who has sanctified us with His commandments and has commanded us to kindle the sabbath lights'. This
benediction is of importance to our investigation. Over a ritual unknown in both the Bible and the rabbinic literature, a benediction is recited in which God is thanked for *commanding* us. Can there be a better
illustration that man-made laws are considered to be divine commands?
The non-fundamentalist Jew who keeps the sabbath does not feel himself obliged to believe that all the thirty-nine types of work are to be refrained from on the sabbath because this was the direct divine command
in the Torah. His sense of history will not allow him to accept this,
which is why he is not a fundamentalist. But that in no way prevents him
from seeing the sabbath, in all its details, in the language of tradition, as
being a divine imperative.

At this stage in the argument, another cogent question can be put.
Are you saying, then, that there is no difference between the fundamentalist and the non-fundamentalist? Is not your house of Judaism really
only the same old house, except that you have entered it from the back
door, while the fundamentalist, more honestly, has approached it from
the front? What is the significance of your constant harping on direct
versus indirect divine communication? Does it not all amount to the
same thing? To vary slightly the metaphor of the door, are you not,
without being aware of it, an Omar Khayyam?

> Myself when young did eagerly frequent
> Doctor and Saint, and heard great argument
> About it and about; but evermore
> Came out by the same Door wherein I went.

The differences between the two approaches may not, indeed, be too
obvious at first glance, but unless I believed them to be real and important I would not have bothered to write *We Have Reason to Believe* and
this book, and would have to conclude that Zechariah Frankel and the

Breslau school were engaged in a colossal theological, though not historical, waste of time. In the realm of theory, even if there were no consequences for practice, it is surely important to know the history of Judaism. According to the fundamentalist understanding, Judaism has had no history except one of simple transmission from generation to generation of basically unchanging formulations. It is important to free the doctrine of *Torah min hashamayim* from the fetters of mechanistic fundamentalism. If it may be put in this way, it seems far more plausible and more true to the facts to say that God works through human beings in the disclosure of His word than that the Torah is an heirloom to be placed reverently on the shelf with only an occasional dusting. To see Judaism in historical terms also enables us to study the Torah in a new but refreshing way. It is no accident that fundamentalist Jews usually view historical studies with a strong degree of suspicion. They are right to do so from their point of view of static transmission. The idea of an unfinished Torah to be completed by humans does not affect in essence the doctrine that the Torah is divine. What is required is a new philosophy of halakhah, in which this creation of the Jewish people has not lost its dynamics. Yet, as I have said, there are problems in the new approach, especially in that it allows for selectivity.

If we examine the institution of the sabbath in this light, there is no logical objection to the acceptance by a non-fundamentalist of all the details of sabbath observance, since for him as well as for the fundamentalist the sabbath is mandatory. He will not smoke on the sabbath because he can appreciate that the discovery of how to make fire was one of the greatest steps towards civilization, and he will refrain from smoking on the sabbath as an acknowledgement of God as Creator. But he will find it hard to accept the notion, found in the sources, that to light a cigarette on the sabbath involves the death penalty, and that if he were to do this in the days of a restored Sanhedrin he would be sentenced to be stoned to death. He would be free from the crushing burden of direct divine communication that there is, in theory at least, the death penalty for this religious offence, flogging for another, and he would be glad that history has decided that such divine threats can no longer be operative.

Since, according to his view, the non-fundamentalist is free to choose which sabbath and other observances awaken a response in him, he may, in his personal life, though without any wish to offend others, choose, say, to switch on the electric light on the sabbath though he might not use electricity to cook or bake or shave. This is because the latter activities have long been part of sabbath observance, whereas a case has been made that switching on an electric light, since there is no combustion, does not fall under the heading of making fire. But that would be his personal choice and he would do it in order to enhance his enjoyment of the sabbath. For the same reason he might decide that, whatever the halakhists say, to carry a handkerchief in the pocket on the sabbath does not involve the carrying from domain to domain referred to in the Mishnah, since people did not have pockets in their garments in mishnaic times. He will agree, if challenged, that he is not operating within the boundaries of the halakhah, but might feel free to depart from the halakhah in his personal life. Admittedly there is a grey area in all this and there are undoubtedly severe tensions in the life of a non-fundamentalist who still believes it is right to be observant. I shall discuss this issue further in Chapters 6 and 11 of this book.

To give a different illustration of the non-fundamentalist attitude, we can take the Shema. The fundamentalist, in the unlikely event of being asked why he recites the Shema, would reply somewhat as follows: 'In Deuteronomy (6: 4–7) Moses says: "Hear O Israel: The Lord our God, the Lord is One. And thou shalt love the Lord thy God with all thy heart, and with all thy soul, and with all thy might. And these words, which I command thee this day, shall be upon thy heart; and thou shalt teach them diligently unto thy children, and shalt talk of them when thou sittest in thy house, and when thou walkest by the way, and when thou liest down, and when thou risest up." Deuteronomy is the fifth book of the Torah delivered by God to Moses and I therefore recite the Shema because God has told me to do so. I am aware that there is an opinion in the Talmud (*Berakhot* 21a) according to which "these words" mean words of the Torah and hence the duty to recite the Shema twice daily is rabbinic but, then, I consider rabbinic law as laid down in the Talmud to have ultimate biblical and hence divine sanction. I know that I have to recite the Shema in the evening and the morning because the rabbis tell us that this is the meaning of "when thou liest down, and when thou risest up", which, say the rabbis, means at the time of lying down and at the time of rising up, that is, in the evening and the morning. Thus whenever I recite the Shema I am using God's actual words communicated (I know that God has no vocal organs and does not literally "speak") to Moses.'

The non-fundamentalist will put it all rather differently; he will say something like this: 'Deuteronomy was originally a separate book, probably the book discovered in the days of King Josiah and compiled shortly before then but, in any event, long after the days of Moses. It does contain the words of God for that time but is not itself the *word* of God. This it cannot be since it only became part of the Pentateuch when it was combined with the other pentateuchal books by an editor or series of editors, which means, since there are contradictions between Deuteronomy and other sections of the Pentateuch, that the Shema is not the words of Moses himself but what the Deuteronomist said that Moses said. I do not see the rabbis as infallible authorities but as great teachers, yet I must respect their ruling that one must recite the Shema daily, not so much because the rabbis say so but because all the evidence goes to show that the Shema was recited as part of the Temple service and has been recited by Jews throughout the ages. As a historically minded Jew, I am interested in how the Shema developed, but as a religious Jew the development is irrelevant to me. I recite the Shema because the words constitute a glorious affirmation of Jewish belief and, when reciting it, I share in the experiences of my fellow-Jews, belonging to a community of faith reaching back to Deuteronomy and beyond. Since it is good to do this and since it provides me with a Jewish "vocabulary of worship", the only one that makes sense to me as a Jew, I believe that to recite the Shema is a divine command, albeit one communicated through the experiences of my people. By the same token I recite the words following the first verse of the Shema, which everyone admits were added in rabbinic times: "Blessed be the name of His glorious Kingdom for ever and ever".'

In effect, then, not only do both the fundamentalist and the non-fundamentalist Jew recite the Shema; they both do it in obedience to a divine command. The truth is that neither usually bothers to spell it all out. The religious Jew, fundamentalist or non-fundamentalist, is not necessarily concerned with theological or historical niceties. For all our discussion in this chapter on man-made versus divine precepts, it is the sociological factor that is decisive. A Jew acts out his Judaism within the context of the particular fraternity to which he belongs. A hasid will probably shout aloud the words of the Shema, and this will not only be tolerated but admired by his fellow-worshippers. A different, contemplative type of hasid may be lost in silent contemplation during a good part of his recitation of the Shema. A Lithuanian-type Jew will probably recite the Shema with clear enunciation of each word, as the rabbis advise. The custom of covering the eyes when reciting the Shema is observed by many Jews, but some Western Jews seem to believe this to be an ostentatious form of piety. What matters is that Jews recite the Shema in worship of the One God. By so doing they transform a man-made institution into a divine command.

SIX

ORTHODOXY

ORTHODOX JEWS at the end of the twentieth century are divided into a number of groupings, each following its own specific pattern of religious conduct. The Sephardi Jews are generally content to have their religious life modelled on the traditional behavioural norms of their ancestors without too much reflection on its theological underpinning, while Ashkenazi Jews have been compelled to become more theologically inclined, the result of the greater impact made on European Jewry by the Emancipation and the Enlightenment. It is no accident that no real Reform movement has emerged among the Sephardim. The Ashkenazim are divided into the *haredim*, or ultra-Orthodox, as they are now often called, and the Modern Orthodox. The term *haredim* is taken from the verse 'And trembleth [*vehared*] at My word' (Isa. 66: 2) and the verse in the same chapter 'Hear the word of the Lord, ye that tremble [*haharedim*] at His word' (Isa. 66: 5). The *haredim* usually claim that they are not a new group of especially pious folk but are simply continuing what has always constituted authentic Jewish piety.[1] Orthodox Jews have two things in common: they all affirm allegiance to the doctrine of Torah from Heaven, conceived of in what we have called the fundamentalist understanding of the doctrine, and they all seek to lead their lives according to the halakhah as recorded in the standard codes of Jewish law.

Unity and Diversity in Orthodoxy

It has to be appreciated, however, that all these groups, when claiming to follow the Jewish tradition, are in reality devotees of a particular

[1] Amnon Levi's *Haharedim* (Jerusalem, 1988) is a lively and vivid journalistic account of the various manifestations of *haredi* life in Israel. Similar works in English are David Landau, *Piety and Power: The World of Jewish Fundamentalism* (London, 1993) and Samuel Heilman's sociological study, *Defenders of the Faith: Inside Ultra-Orthodox Jewry* (New York, 1992).

tradition, that of their immediate ancestors and teachers. Nowadays, when the Ashkenazi/Lithuanian mode of learning has spread throughout the Orthodox world, there is an increasing trend for Sephardi youngsters to become, as it were, honorary Ashkenazim, even to the extent of speaking Yiddish and adopting Ashkenazi mores. But in former times it was virtually unheard of for a Sephardi to become an Ashkenazi or vice versa. Such an exchange of allegiance would have been seen as an act of sheer disloyalty to the community to which one belonged. The differences between Sephardim and Ashkenazim are not, in fact, doctrinal in any way, so that one could decide to switch to a different doctrinal position because it seemed more cogent than one's own. Doctrinal truth was never the issue, any more than filial piety depends on whether or not parents are in philosophical harmony with their offspring. I would maintain that even while, among the Ashkenazim, instances are found of *haredim* becoming Modern Orthodox or the other way round, the basic allegiance of each group is based not so much on truth content but on family tradition or the particular institution in which a person has been educated. Let us examine the different patterns of life of the various Orthodox groupings.

Haredim

The most prominent *haredi* group is that of the Lithuanians, that is, Jews who themselves or whose forebears hail from Lithuania, or those who have studied in Lithuanian-type yeshivas. There has been a great proliferation of yeshivas of this type in the USA, Israel, and Europe. Many more young men study in Lithuanian-type yeshivas than in the whole of pre-war Lithuania itself. Whereas the comparatively few yeshiva men in Lithuania were on the defensive against the Haskalah, the yeshiva world today is proudly on the offensive, believing that the Torah studied in the yeshiva is supremely important not only in preserving the ideal of study for its own sake, but also as a protection from harm, spiritual and material, for the Jewish people a whole. Utter devotion to study of the Torah, it is held, releases a tremendous outpouring of divine grace which, in the language of Kabbalah, 'sweetens the world' and gives the power to the Jewish people to exert a cosmic influence. Nowadays, the Lithuanian pattern has spread to many other yeshivas formerly unaware of the whole Lithuanian methodology.

The Lithuanian *derekh* ('way') consists of the new methodology invented by Rabbi Hayim Soloveitchik of Brisk (Brest–Litovsk) (1853–1918), also known as Reb Hayim Brisker, and followed by his disciples and their disciples. In addition to intense Talmud study by this analytical method, the yeshivas introduced *musar* into their curricula, despite opposition at first. The *musar* movement was founded in nineteenth-century Lithuania by Rabbi Israel Salanter. The word *musar* is found in the verse 'Hear, my son, the instruction [*musar*] of thy father' (Prov. 1: 8). The term came to denote the moralistic literature developed in the Middle Ages, but in Salanter's novel approach this literature was not so much studied as employed in an attempt to change the character by the recital in mournful tones of two or three passages repeated over and over again. In the larger yeshivas of this type, lectures (*shiurim*) in Talmud are delivered by the yeshiva head (*rosh yeshivah*), but the main studying is done in the large study hall by pairs of students exploring the texts together. A study partner is known as a *havruta* ('partner'). The study of Talmud in this way is based on the rabbinic idea that it is extremely undesirable to try to study the Torah on one's own, since it is only through the honing of mind against mind that the complexities of the subject can be fully grasped. In addition to the yeshiva heads, each yeshiva has a *mashgiah* ('overseer'), a moral tutor whose job is to deliver *musar* discourses and generally direct the students in the right way. The study of Talmud is engaged in for most of the day and a good part of the night, but a half-hour or so is set aside for *musar* in the sense of individual reflection on the student's own shortcomings (not in partnership as in the study of Talmud). The yeshiva students are bachelors who devote their youthful years entirely to the study of the Torah. But many students continue their studies after marriage in the institution attached to the yeshiva known as the *kolel* (a term meaning 'all-embracing', i.e. embracing a number of married students). While at the yeshiva the youths are discouraged from thinking of a career, even a career in the rabbinate. However, in the *kolel* some of the married men do prepare themselves for the practical rabbinate. It must, however, be appreciated that preparation for the rabbinate in this context means the acquisition of the knowledge required to render decisions in Jewish law. The main function of the rabbi in the *haredi* world is precisely that, to decide in matters of, chiefly, religious law. The modern rabbi who delivers sermons, does pastoral work, offers counselling, engages in dialogue with non-Jews, and so forth is not only unknown but severely frowned upon in *haredi*

circles. Indeed, the brighter students in the yeshiva are often discouraged
from entertaining the prospect of becoming rabbis, even of the traditional order, in the belief that a rabbi nowadays is bound to accept various dubious compromises in order to pacify the less strict members
of his community. Even in Lithuania there was a marked tendency for
rabbis to be lenient if they could within the parameters of the halakhah.

The emergence of the yeshiva world is an amazing phenomenon.[2]
Yeshivas existed, of course, in earlier times, but they usually consisted of
a comparatively small number of students who came to study with a rabbi
renowned for his learning, the yeshiva being supported by the townsfolk
as part of their contract with the rabbi. Rabbi Hayim of Volozhin (1749–
1821), disciple of the famed Gaon of Vilna, founded what Alon calls
'Lithuanian and Russian Jewry's great beacon of light', the yeshiva of
Volozhin, which existed for nearly a hundred years (1793–1892). Students
flocked to this yeshiva from all parts of Russia, Poland, and Lithuania,
and even from the USA, and it became a new kind of institution, in which
emphasis was placed on the academic study of the Talmud. Volozhin,
and the yeshivas which followed a similar pattern, Slobodka, Mir, Telz,
Novogrudok, Radin, and Ponevezh, were not colleges for the training
of rabbis. The aim was the study of the Torah 'for its own sake', that is,
the study of the Talmud, because it is the clear duty of the most brilliant
minds to study the word of God without, at first, any thought of a career,
not even a rabbinic career. Naturally, many of the students did eventually
become rabbis, but they studied the sections of the Codes a rabbi is required to know by themselves and received *semikhah* ('ordination') not
from the yeshiva but from a well-known rabbi outside the institution. At
Volozhin the aim of the students was to acquire complete familiarity
with the whole of the Talmud. But, as stated above, under the influence
of the 'Brisker way', the analytical approach was adopted and, instead of
covering the whole of the Talmud, only a number of talmudic tractates
were studied in depth through the application of this analytical methodology. To this was added the study of *musar*, as described above, and
this pattern still prevails more or less in all Lithuanian-type yeshivas.

[2] The best study of the Lithuanian yeshivas in the Old World is that of Gedalyahu
Alon, 'The Lithuanian Yeshivot', trans. Sid Z. Leiman, in Judah Goldin (ed.), *The
Jewish Expression* (New Haven, Conn., 1976), 452–68. For yeshiva life today there is the
excellent sociological study by William B. Helmreich, *The World of the Yeshiva: An
Intimate Portrait of Orthodox Jewry* (New York, 1982).

A few examples of the Lithuanian 'way' can be given here, though for full understanding it would be necessary either to attend a Lithuanian yeshiva as a student or to study the published works of Rabbi Hayim Soloveitchik, Rabbi Simeon Shkop, Rabbi Avigdor Amiel, Rabbi Joseph Leib Bloch, and many others. Essentially the method consists of scrutinizing halakhic definitions and concepts in the Talmud to see where they can be applied and where not (the method is applied chiefly to the halakhah).

Often the analysis is almost certainly implied in the text itself; at other times, the reading into the text is questionable. For example, according to the Talmud, a distinction is made, in cases where compensation has to be paid, between payment as pure compensation (*mamon*, 'money') and payment purely as a fine (*kenas*, 'penalty'). For instance, if A steals something from B and two witnesses testify to his guilt, A is obliged to pay double the worth of the item which he has stolen. If, say, he has stolen one hundred *zuz* and is found out, A is compelled by the court to pay B two hundred *zuz*, but only one hundred is pure compensation, since that is all he has stolen; the payment of the second hundred is in the nature of a fine. Now a further rule is that if A admits that he has stolen, he obviously must pay B one hundred *zuz* to compensate him for the loss he has suffered, but he is exempt from the payment of the second hundred. A man must pay *mamon* if he admits his guilt, but he is not required to pay *kenas*. This is formulated as 'If one admits that he has committed a crime for which payment is in the nature of a fine, he is exempt'—*modeh bikenas patur*. Now there is a debate in the Talmud (*Baba kamma* 74*b*) on a case where A has freely admitted his guilt but later witnesses have also testified to it. One opinion has it that in this case he is exempt from payment since he has admitted his guilt, but the other opinion holds that he is liable if witnesses testify to his guilt after his own admission. The analytical school, with justification from the text even though this is not explicit there, understands the debate to be on whether, when it is said that one who admits to his guilt in cases of *kenas* is exempt, it means that he is truly exempt—that the law frees him because he has admitted his guilt—or whether it simply means that he cannot be made to pay *kenas* on his own admission but is not exonerated, so that, if witnesses testify to his guilt later, he is still liable.

Another example comes from the debate in the Talmud (*Kiddushin* 43*a*) on whether an agent can serve as a witness in a case in which he acts as an agent. For example, a man appoints an agent to deliver a *get* (a bill of divorce), the divorce taking effect as soon as the *get* has been delivered into the wife's hands. Now the delivery of the *get* is invalid unless it is in the presence of two witnesses. Can the agent serve as one of the witnesses? One rabbi argues, why not? Indeed, there can be no better testimony than that of the agent involved. But the other rabbi argues that, since there is the principle 'a man's agent is as the man himself', it follows that just as the husband himself cannot serve as a witness in his own case so, too, his agent cannot so serve. The analytical school explains it in this way. When the law states that the act of an agent is as if the act were carried out by the man who appointed him, this can mean either that the act, to be valid, need not be carried out by the man himself but can be carried out by the agent, or it can mean that the act has to be carried out by the man himself but that the act of the agent is considered to be the act of the man himself. In other words, in the act of agency, is it the act of the agent that is transferred to the principal or is it the person of the principal that is transferred to the agent? If the former, there is no reason why the agent cannot serve as a witness, but if the latter the agent cannot serve as a witness any more than the principal himself.

It is important to appreciate the background to the Lithuanian methodology. The yeshiva heads in Lithuania were engaged in a constant struggle against the Haskalah, the Enlightenment movement. Many of the most brilliant youths were attracted to general non-Jewish culture, and some students left the yeshiva in order to avail themselves of whatever opportunities were to hand—few indeed generally—for the study of science, mathematics, and especially European literature. In reaction the yeshivas tended to look inwards, but apparently realized that the way to win the yeshiva students over to traditional learning was to study the Talmud by this new methodology. In a comprehensive study Norman Solomon goes so far as to suggest that the method was itself, in part at least, the result of the teachers assimilating ideas from modern jurisprudence which they had learned from students at the yeshiva familiar with this discipline.[3] In fact a number of the more traditional rabbis were opposed to the analytical methodology on precisely these grounds, that it was a foreign importation into Judaism. There is some truth

---

[3] *The Analytical Movement: Hayyim Soloveitchik and his Circle* (Atlanta, Ga., 1993).

in this contention. One of the reasons why the *musar* movement was allowed to make inroads into the yeshivas appears to be that *musar* was a kind of 'kosher' Haskalah. In any event, in the Lithuanian-type yeshivas to this day the tendency to avoid all secular learning is very strong. In later years, the blame for the Holocaust was increasingly placed at the door of Western civilization, so powerfully attractive even to Orthodox Jews in Germany. If this was the fruit of Western culture, the yeshivas declared, Jews are far better advised to have nothing to do with it and should devote their minds to Talmud and their hearts to *musar*.

In Germany before Hitler it was quite usual for Orthodox Jews, under the influence of Samson Raphael Hirsch's slogan 'Torah together with *derekh erets*' (in this context 'Torah together with Western culture'), to study at German universities. The Lithuanian yeshivas identified such study with the Haskalah, their bitter foe. A young Orthodox Jew, Simeon Schwab (later Rabbi Simeon Schwab) asked a number of famous eastern European rabbis whether it was permitted, and under which conditions, to study secular culture.[4] Space does not permit lengthy quotes from their interesting and later very influential replies, but sections of the reply by Rabbi Abraham Isaac Bloch, *rosh yeshivah* of Telz, can be mentioned.

Rabbi Bloch, like the others, permitted the study of 'secular wisdom' where it was for the purpose of earning a living, i.e. the study of the sciences in order to obtain an academic post. But he refused to permit any extensive study of Western philosophy because it contained many heretical ideas. The conclusion of this letter is particularly germane. He wrote:

With regard to the study of literature and the reading thereof, and this applies to all popular studies which have no practical use, it is obvious that it is not worthwhile to spend time on these when self-development can be attained from our Holy Torah, especially since in the literature of the nations there are lustful and forbidden notions. In any event, it is not worthwhile to search for gold in a place in which there is filth and mud when it is possible to gather pearls from a pure source, the source of living waters, the Written Torah and the Oral Torah, concerning which it is said [in *Pirkei avot* 5: 25], 'Turn it [the Torah] over and over again for everything is in it'.

---

[4] Their replies are given at length in Yehudah Levi, *Sha'arei talmud torah*, 2nd edn. (Jerusalem, 1982), 295–312.

All that we have written above is only for the purpose of clarifying the topic in a general way. However, in connection with the needs of the hour which devolve now on the great ones of the generation and the leaders of the communities, especially in Germany, now that the Lord has shown us all this, Providence teaches us that those who attached such great significance to the wisdom of the nations were in error, since through this scholars [*lomedim*] have suffered a decrease and the later generation has become remote from the Torah. Now it is essential to revolutionize all customary educational methods there, to root out the outlook that prevails even among the *ḥaredim* [i.e. the German Orthodox] to think of the wisdom of the nations in relation to our Holy Torah. We have to return, therefore, to the eternal ways of our ancestors, to establish schools in which sacred studies are the main course, to teach our sons Scripture, Mishnah, and Talmud. Also [it is necessary] to establish Talmud houses, in which the Talmud and its commentators will be studied by the way of understanding [i.e. by the analytical method] so that they sense the pleasantness of the Torah in her true way, also to acquaint them with the Torah opinion [*da'at torah*] and the light of the Torah. Then we shall be confident that the most talented of them will have a desire to grow in Torah learning and go to study in the great yeshivas. As for those who are unsuited to do this, they will acquire in these Houses of Talmud sufficient Torah and understanding to qualify as *bar urian* ['son of the Torah'], and will then proceed to engage in a profession armed with Torah and *derekh erets*. It is also possible for them to be taught there topics they will require to lead their practical lives, but the main topics should be only Torah and the fear of Heaven. And if a few are found who sense that they are capable of developing in the sciences of the nations, they will find a way to do this apart from us. For our duty is to teach our sons the Torah of the Lord which renders those who possess it happy in this world and the next.[5]

Thus the yeshiva world, which still follows this kind of advice, has set itself off from the Modern Orthodox as truly inhabiting a different 'world'.

Before leaving the yeshiva world, we must also take a look at *musar*, the movement founded by Rabbi Israel Salanter and still followed in this world. So much has been written on the *musar* movement that it is only necessary to touch on some of its ideas in order to see why it cannot be an adequate way for modernists, despite its many insights and lofty ethical stance.

Rabbi Israel Salanter's aim was to promote greater inwardness, religious piety, and ethical commitment among traditionally minded Jews. In the yeshiva world, the movement became élitist, its aim being

[5] Ibid. 296–301.

to add *yirat shamayim* ('fear of Heaven'), here denoting religiosity as well as the striving for greater self-improvement and devotion to learning. The yeshiva man was to become a God-fearing scholar. This aim is achieved by intensive reflection on a number of moralistic and religious texts from the past and by severe introspection.[6]

Two disciples of Israel Salanter were particularly influential, each developing his own particular *musar* 'way'. These were Rabbi Nathan Tsevi Finkel (1849–1927) in Slobodka and Rabbi Yosef Horowitz (1850–1920) in Novogrudok. The Slobodka way, now dominant in present-day Lithuanian-type yeshivas, stresses the basic nobility of the human character; Novogrudok stresses the proneness of human beings to evil. (My teacher, the *rosh yeshivah* of Manchester, was trained in the Novogrudok way.) The difference between the two schools has been stated as 'Slobodka says: man is so great, how dare he sin; Novogrudok says: man is so lowly, how dare he sin'. A frequently voiced complaint against the whole *musar* approach is that constant introspection is unhealthy and self-defeating. Katz refers to an essay by one of the *maskilim* in which he describes a student of a *musar* yeshiva before whom a plate of luscious fruits was placed. His first impulse was to take the most appetizing of these, but he stayed his hand because he thought to eat it was to pander to his fleshly desires. But then he thought to himself 'If I refrain from taking this fruit I shall be guilty of pride in my exercise of self-control.' This *musar* idea of 'working on the self', as it is called, certainly tends to produce a sombre and even an obsessive character. It has been noted more than once that those Lithuanian rabbis, like Rabbi Hayim Soloveitchik and Rabbi Yitshak Elhanan Spektor, who were not devotees of *musar*, were, in fact, more kindly and caring than the adherents of *musar* who stressed these virtues. There is much truth in this, which is an additional reason why *musar* fails to be attractive to modernists.

[6] The now classic work on the *musar* movement is Dov Katz, *Tenuat hamusar* ('The Musar Movement'), 5 vols. (Tel Aviv, 1958), in which the author surveys the ideas of all the main *musar* exponents. Katz's *Pulemos hamusar* ('The Musar Controversy'), 4 vols. (Jerusalem, 1958) deals with the attacks on the movement mounted by the traditional rabbis and the *maskilim*, the former objecting to the idea that the Torah, considered by them to be sufficient in itself as balm to the 'evil inclination', needs any supplementary doctrine, and the latter objecting to the *musar* teachers decrying secular learning. Aaron Soresky's *Marbitsei torah umusar* ('Disseminators of Torah and Musar') (Brooklyn, NY, 1977) surveys 'the yeshivas of the Lithuanian type from the period of Volozhin down to our own day', but, unlike Katz's works, is entirely laudatory.

To be fair, the personality of Rabbi Nathan Tsevi Finkel, the 'Old Man of Slobodka', is an excellent demonstration of *musar* at its best. A Yiddish journalist, M. Gerz, formerly a student at the Slobodka yeshiva, gave a vivid description of Finkel's teaching.

Man was created in the image of God. The sages say that when man was created the angels took him to be a god and wanted to sing his praises. The source of man is God. God was Lord of the world before even the world was created, yet God created the world. For what purpose did God do this? He did it out of great love, to bestow upon man a wide and beautiful world. Is love a human trait? As God is filled with mercy, so man is filled with good. If man does a good deed, he does so for himself, for that is his nature. He cannot do otherwise. He is weighed down with goodness and before he can spend it, he does good for his own sake because he is filled with love and wants to find an outlet for it, for his own pleasure. Then why need someone else know about it?[7]

Finkel practised what he preached. Some students once followed him and found him setting out with a band of gypsies. The astonished students asked him the meaning of it, to which he replied, 'Gypsies are the most forlorn people in the world. They do not know of rest or home. They torture themselves and their families in their wretched travels. So they ought to be heartened by a cheerful mien, a friendly smile in their roaming and wandering.' Because he believed that wanderers were the most forlorn people, he would often steal out to the nearby railway station, where he would help people by carrying a bag, by giving advice or comforting them with a kind word, cheering them with a chat and sometimes giving them a loan. He could, however, be fierce in defence of the Torah and *musar*. When, in 1905, the students at Slobodka, egged on by Jewish revolutionaries outside the yeshiva, rebelled, demanding greater freedom and secular studies, the Old Man put down the mutiny with a firm hand. He excommunicated some of the students. No one would rent them rooms or sell them food and they were forced to leave the town. But while, in Slobodka and the other yeshivas, *musar* was on the defensive, there is no longer any struggle in the modern yeshiva world. The battle against the Haskalah has been won, but at the price of exclusiveness.

The struggle between the values of *musar* and the admirers of modern culture is conveyed in Chaim Grade's short story 'My Quarrel

[7] M. Gerz, 'The Old Man of Slobodka', in Lucy Dawidowicz (ed.), *The Golden Tradition: Jewish Life and Thought in Eastern Europe* (London, 1967), 179–85.

with Hersh Rassayner'.[8] The tale concerns a bitter debate which took place after the Holocaust between the writer and Hersh Rassayner, a former student at the Novogrudok yeshiva and a musarist in that vein. Rassayner argues that the German nation was renowned for its great thinkers and writers, and yet the most fiendish event in all Jewish history, the Holocaust, was not prevented by their vaunted culture. Yes, the great thinkers and writers produced profound and noble ideas, but it was all talk. It is impossible to reproduce the whole of this poignant story. It should be read as one of the best examples of a debate between the *musar* outlook and modernism. Many readers will find themselves, as I do, a little on both sides in the debate, disagreeing with secularism because it is secular and with *musar* for seeing no value in the secular world.

Another important *haredi* group is that which hails originally from Hungary. This group, with representatives all over the Jewish world, comprises followers of the Hungarian champion of Orthodoxy, Rabbi Moses Sofer (the Hatam Sofer, 1762–1839), whose slogan, obviously directed against Reformist tendencies, was 'anything new is forbidden by the Torah', i.e. Judaism permits no departure from any of its ancient practices and teachings. Unlike the Lithuanians, who place the stress on theoretical studies, the Hungarians are more interested in practical Jewish law. The distinction must not be overemphasized. The Lithuanians, as observant Jews, have a keen knowledge of practical law, and the Hungarians, influenced by the Lithuanians, have adopted the theoretical approach in their yeshivas. For all that, it remains true that the only influential Lithuanian *posek* (one who renders practical decisions) in recent years was Rabbi Moshe Feinstein, whereas the Hungarians (and the Polish scholars allied to them) have produced scores of responsa collections offering practical guidance.

Then there are the various hasidic groups—Lubavitch, Satmar, Ger, Belz, Vishnitz, Bobov, and other smaller hasidic groups, each owing allegiance to its own *tsadik* or *rebbe* and each with its own religious lifestyle. Hasidism will be examined further in Chapter 9.

The relationships between the various groupings in *haredi* life are very complex. By now the hasidim, formerly regarded by the Lithuanians as heretics, have made common cause with them against the secularists in

---

[8] Trans. Milton Himmelfarb, in Irving Howe and Eliezer Greenberg (eds.), *A Treasury of Yiddish Stories* (London, 1956), 579–609.

Israel and against non-Orthodox Jews in the Diaspora. It is extremely unusual for a hasid to give up his hasidic way to become a 'Lithuanian', but many hasidic youths do spend some time studying in Lithuanian yeshivas. Hasidim still retain a little of the older hasidic attitude in which the Lithuanians are seen as cold fish, lacking the spiritual warmth and conviviality that hasidism provides. The Lithuanian tends to retort that the hasidic emphasis on keeping one's mind on God, even while studying, effectively prevents the hasidim from acquiring a real mastery of the texts, hence the old taunt that hasidim are unlearned. An interesting development has taken place in the Agudat Yisrael movement. From its inception the Agudah had hasidic members. Originally anti-Zionist, the Agudah has accommodated itself, if not to Zionism, at least to the State of Israel. Agudat Yisrael representatives now sit in the Knesset and, together with other religious parties, exert considerable influence on the Israeli government. The institution known as the Council of Torah Sages is, officially at least, the rabbinic guiding voice in political matters, there having developed the notion, based, in fact, on hasidism, that the Torah sage has a kind of built-in sensitivity to the requirements of the Torah, enabling him to produce the *da'at torah* ('Torah opinion') on every topic, even on those where the traditional sources have nothing to say. On this body hasidic *rebbes* appear, together with the Lithuanian and Hungarian rabbis, as 'Sages of Israel'.

Though there is no such thing as an association of *haredim*, and despite the differences and sometimes fierce rivalries among the *haredi* groups, the *haredim* constitute an identifiable, though unorganized, entity. *Haredim* would say, if asked what constitutes a *haredi*, that a *haredi* Jew is one who follows Jewish law unquestioningly in the belief that the halakhah is the word of God, though, naturally, he will acknowledge that there are differing opinions, often contradicting one another. When this happens, the *haredi* will follow the opinions of his own rabbi, as do all Orthodox Jews. The *haredi* will, however, be extremely scrupulous in his observances, far more so than the ordinary Orthodox Jew, especially with regard to *tseniyut* ('modesty') in matters of comportment and dress, especially of women. All *haredi* married women are obliged to cover completely the natural hair of the head, whether with a *sheitel* (wig) or with a headdress covering all the natural hair. Hungarian married women often follow Rabbi Moses Sofer's extreme ruling that the scalp should be shaved completely before putting on the hair-covering. Women's dresses have to cover the whole of the body. Short sleeves and trouser suits are taboo. In the Me'ah She'arim district in Jerusalem, a stronghold of the *haredim*, posters are displayed urging 'daughters of Israel' to dress modestly when entering the neighbourhood. At wedding banquets and the like, the sexes are completely separated, the bride and groom alone sitting together with the women on the bride's side, the men on the groom's, with a curtain or other form of partition stretched between the two sets of guests. In an issue of the *haredi* newspaper the London *Jewish Tribune*[9] there appeared a notice signed by prominent *haredi* rabbis in Israel and supported by English *haredi* rabbis, to the effect that it is forbidden for women to wear transparent stockings or tights, the thickness of which to satisfy the requirements of the law should ideally be 70 denier but at least 40 denier. The reference is, of course, to stockings which appear below the knee. The rest of the body is in any event covered. A glimpse of stocking is, indeed, held to be shocking by the *haredim*, and not only in 'olden days'. All this has not prevented some *haredi* women wearing elaborate wigs in the latest fashion. This reportedly prompted the former Sephardi chief rabbi of Israel to preach that a married woman who wears a *sheitel* will go to hell.

It is impossible not to admire *haredi* piety and its utter devotion to the study of the Torah. *Haredi* Jews have an unparalleled commitment to Judaism. Often at great sacrifice to themselves, they recite the prayers three times a day in a congregation; unless they are ill, they fast on all the fast-days of the year (even those such as the Monday, Thursday, and Monday after the festivals); they always wait six hours after a meat meal before eating dairy products; most are very chaste even in the bedroom, where artificial methods of contraception are generally eschewed and the missionary position advocated for marital relations; most will not have a television in their house and will never go to the cinema or the theatre; they keep the sabbath as the Codes demand: they will never use the telephone on the sabbath and will remove the light from a refrigerator so that they will not turn it on by opening the door on the sabbath. They are especially scrupulous in their observance of *tseniyut* ('modesty' or 'chastity'). Their womenfolk dress in garments that cover the whole body, including the arms and the neck up to the chin, and their menfolk

---

[9] Thursday, 7 Nov. 1996.

usually avoid gazing at women; certainly, they will never shake hands with women. Moreover, anyone familiar with *ḥaredi* life will not make the mistake of assuming that, while *ḥaredim* are so particular in their religious observances, they are less scrupulous in their ethics. This is a canard by which the *ḥaredim* as a whole are denigrated for the faults of the few. Furthermore, the *ḥaredim* are ready to help and care for all Jews, whether observant or not, and this care is not infrequently extended, as the Talmud enjoins, to non-Jews as well.

As for *ḥaredi* devotion to the study of the Torah, one has only to enter the study hall of a great yeshiva like Ponevezh in Benei Berak in Israel to witness the 'glory of the Torah'; hundreds of youths singing to themselves the words of the texts on which they ponder or engaging in fierce debate over the content of the *rosh yeshivah*'s recent lecture. And this application to study is by no means confined to the yeshiva or to rabbis. The Daf Yomi ('daily page') was introduced by Rabbi Meir Shapira of Lublin (1887–1934) at the 1923 Congress of Agudat Yisrael. Those who follow Rabbi Shapira's plan take it upon themselves to study a new folio page of the Babylonian Talmud each day, completing the whole gigantic work in seven years. Over seventy years later a mass celebration was held in Madison Square Garden in New York, in which it was estimated that no fewer than 25,000 men participated, most of whom had completed the Talmud during the tenth cycle. Every *ḥaredi* synagogue has a *beit midrash* ('study hall') in which there are lectures and discussions on the Talmud and other sacred texts. If the *ḥaredi* world is anything to go by, the Torah is alive and well even, or especially, after the Holocaust.

When contemplating all this, the non-*ḥaredi* Jew is tempted to say 'This is the real thing. If I am to be a faithful Jew this is where I have to be; there is no other course for me but to embrace a *ḥaredi* lifestyle.' Having myself studied in a yeshiva for several years and having observed the beauty and fidelity of *ḥaredi* life at first hand, I admit that I still have occasional twinges of regret at having been compelled to move away from it. Why do I, and many others, observant though we may well be, feel obliged, if not to reject entirely or attack the *ḥaredi* world, at least to distance ourselves from it? The general answer is that while the *ḥaredim* may conquer our hearts they leave us with our heads outside. It would be absurd to suggest that *ḥaredi* study of the Torah does not involve acute thinking of the most rigorous kind. The *ḥaredi* ideal is not only to attain to knowledge of the texts but to investigate them thoroughly by means of reasoned argument. Yet there is no evidence that the critical mind is at all involved in the process. The sacred texts are studied by the *haredim*, but the historical critical methodology of which we have spoken repeatedly is totally ignored and, indeed, treated as heretical. The fundamentalist stance is adopted axiomatically. *Haredim* do study the Talmud and its commentators intensely and, with regard to the post-*Shulhan arukh* authorities, the *aharonim*, criticism of their views is tolerated and, at times, even advocated. But *haredim* never allow themselves to question how the Talmud came to be or whether its teachings should be followed, to say nothing of their attitude to the Bible in its rabbinic interpretation. The whole exercise of Torah study, for the *haredim*, is engaged in as if the Torah is a given, a complete package, the study itself being part of the package. Some of the *haredi* attitudes noted above may strike non-*haredim* as bizarre but, granted the *haredi* postulate that it is all based ultimately on the direct word of God, *haredi* ways must be followed, whatever modernists may think of them. This applies, though to a lesser extent, to Modern Orthodoxy, whose theological attitude we must now examine.

The Modern Orthodox

Like the *haredi* world, Modern Orthodoxy or neo-Orthodoxy refers more to a particular cast of mind than to an organized movement. The basic difference, in theory at least, between the *haredim* and the Modern Orthodox consists of an acceptance by the latter of the values and to some extent the mores of Western society. The real founder of Modern Orthodoxy (though the actual term was first coined in the twentieth century in the USA) is Samson Raphael Hirsch, the famed nineteenth-century German rabbi whose slogan was 'Torah and *derekh erets*'. The actual expression 'Torah and *derekh erets*' is found in the Mishnah (*Pirkei avot* 2: 2), where *derekh erets* (literally 'the way of the earth') denotes either good manners and etiquette or, more probably, having a worldly occupation in addition to the study of the Torah. Hirsch, however, extended the term to mean the way of Western society, i.e. that the devout Jew is by no means called upon to reject Western life, his particular *derekh erets*. On the contrary, just as, for example, the medieval Jewish thinkers managed to accommodate Judaism with Greek thought in its Arabic garb, so, too, a Jew today can be fully observant while participating in the new way of life that has become his own now that the Jews have emerged from the ghetto. Although this attitude often results in a hybrid that is neither really Orthodox nor modern, Modern Orthodoxy does strive to adopt Western values without detriment to the tradition; Hirsch says, in effect, for the enrichment of the tradition. Thus Modern Orthodoxy holds that Western literature, music, and the arts are not merely aids to the good life but, for the modern Jew, contribute greatly to the cultivation of the good life.

One of the best statements of the Modern Orthodox position is an article by the English rabbi Michael Harris, 'An Inventory of Modern Orthodox Beliefs'.[10] I have chosen this article for comment both because it is a honest account of Modern Orthodox beliefs and because it appeared in *Le'ela*, a journal published by Jews' College, where, as described above, my own struggle began.

Harris first observes that, because of the confusion inherent in the term Modern Orthodoxy, Walter Wurzberger prefers the term 'post-Modern Orthodoxy', while the best-known representative of the position, Norman Lamm, prefers 'Centrist Orthodoxy'. Harris himself quotes with approval the view that exaggerated concern about labels is itself symptomatic of Modern Orthodoxy's inner malaise. Harris proceeds to describe Modern Orthodoxy as he understands it. He is probably correct in affirming that many who call themselves Modern Orthodox share in his broad views. Here I chiefly want to address Harris's statement on Modern Orthodoxy and secular studies. Harris writes:

A key characteristic of Modern Orthodoxy is its positive attitude. The positive orientation extends beyond those areas of secular study which may ease the path to a vocation and embraces disciplines such as philosophy and literature which are capable of reinforcing the message of Torah and can undoubtedly furnish the student with tools to enhance his or her Torah study.

Harris refers in a footnote to the book by Norman Lamm, *Torah Umadda: The Encounter of Religious Learning and Worldly Knowledge in the Jewish Tradition*,[11] but Lamm goes further than Harris in advocating 'secular' learning as good in itself, not only because it is useful for the study of the Torah, as stated above.

[10] *Le'ela*, 43 (Apr. 1997), 20–2. See also the response by Arye Forta, 'Progressive Orthodoxy: A Direction for the Future', *Le'ela*, 44 (Oct., 1997), 33–8 and Michael Harris, Arye Forta, and Aryeh Newman, 'Modern Orthodoxy: The Debate Continues', *Le'ela*, 45 (Apr. 1998), 33–7.   [11] Northvale, NJ, 1990.

It is precisely in this matter of 'secular' learning that the stance of Modern Orthodoxy is inadequate. In all the writings of the Modern Orthodox I have yet to find any suggestion that biblical criticism can be reconciled with Jewish observance. The Modern Orthodox seem to be saying that you can be a devout Jew even if you do read Shakespeare or Kant or Wittgenstein, and if you enjoy classical or modern music, or if you have an appreciation of Picasso or other modern artists. Fair enough. But what of history, especially biblical and rabbinic history, the result of studying which is to call into question some of the postulates of the tradition itself? Harris and the others would probably say that, not to put too fine a point on it, Orthodoxy demands a fundamentalist approach to the sources of Judaism. You are allowed to read and even enjoy English literature but on no account are you to read Wellhausen, except, possibly, in order to refute him completely. Here the *ḥaredim* are more logical in opposing all study other than that of the Torah. The Modern Orthodox are selective in how much of 'secular' studies is compatible with the entity they call 'the Torah', without any awareness that the real challenge is posed by the historical critical methodology, an important aspect of secular studies. It is beyond my understanding how highly intelligent Orthodox Jews who embrace general learning wholeheartedly can, at the same time, blithely ignore or meet in a totally inadequate manner the challenge presented by this branch of secular learning.

With regard to the State of Israel, varying attitudes have emerged both among the *ḥaredim* and among the Modern Orthodox. The *ḥaredim*, formerly opposed to Zionism as a secular movement irreligiously usurping the role of the Messiah, came to accept, with a few exceptions, that participation in the political life of the state is mandatory to some extent; the religious parties represent them in the Israeli government. The Modern Orthodox, however, always Zionistic in principle, are now divided between those who simply follow the old line and those who have become more aggressive on the vexed question of surrendering land for peace. The basic theological divide on this issue between the *ḥaredim* and the Modern Orthodox is on whether there are messianic aspects to the state itself. The *ḥaredim* tend to acknowledge the state *de facto*, but still postpone the idea of the final redemption to the advent of the Messiah. The Modern Orthodox tend to see the emergence of the state as the 'beginning of the redemption'—*atḥalta dege'ulah*—that is, the State of Israel is the beginning of the messianic process. In the prayer for the State of Israel introduced by the Israeli chief rabbinate, the emergence of the state is referred to as *reshit tsemiḥut ge'ulatenu* ('the beginning of the sprouting of our redemption'), thus adopting an equivocal attitude. We acknowledge, say the Modern Orthodox, that there is already a numinous quality to the state while awaiting the advent of the Messiah for the complete redemption. The dangers in this notion of a partially realized eschatology are evident. If God is at work directly in the process of redemption, say some of the Modern Orthodox, to surrender land for peace is to frustrate God's plan for His people and for the whole world. All this is based ultimately on the fundamentalist view that we can rely even in political matters not on what the Israeli government decides is the required option but on what various sacred texts, biblical or rabbinic, are imagined to declare about God's will for the state. One can hardly think that it is really a question of bandying texts. Rather, there seems to be at work in this and other areas the unconscious motivation that, as a religious Jew, my understanding of the demands of my religion is that of my particular group. Each group in Orthodoxy—the same applies, of course, to the non-Orthodox as well—has set for itself parameters beyond which it is unthinkable to move. A *ḥaredi* Jew knows that he can only be tolerant of diversity within the confines of *ḥaredi* life. He cannot allow himself to become a Modern Orthodox Jew, not because he has really surveyed the arguments, but because to do that would be virtually to step out of himself, to lose his true identity. By the same token a Modern Orthodox Jew realizes, subconsciously at least, that he can never go over to the *ḥaredi* world without sacrificing his entire religious outlook. Attitudes have hardened to the extent that argument in these matters has become largely irrelevant. The *ḥaredi* way of life is the *ḥaredi* way of life and Modern Orthodoxy is Modern Orthodoxy, period, as Americans say.

Reference must here be made to the *ba'al teshuvah* movement. The term *ba'al teshuvah* (literally, 'one who belongs to repentance') means a penitent, a sinner who has resolved to sin no more, in the talmudic and moralistic literature. But the term has come to refer to one who turns back (*teshuvah* means both 'repentance' and 'turning back', i.e. away from sinfulness to a life of virtue) from a non-observant Jewish life to the practice of the *mitsvot*. Many, especially young, individuals in the USA, disillusioned with what they rightly considered to be the emptiness of mere formal attachment to the Judaism of their parents, resolved to find their way back to a full Jewish life. Institutions with the slogan of outreach seek to cater for these enthusiasts by introducing them gradually to the niceties of Jewish observance. There are, at present, special yeshivas at which young men and (often) women are taught as much of Judaism as they are capable of adopting. The pace is usually gradual with a degree of tolerance and compromise in order not to put them off by an attempted precipitation. The term *ba'al teshuvah*, hitherto referring to the repentant sinner, now becomes a kind of status symbol. The abbreviation BT is now set against that of FFB ('*frum* from birth'), with not only an acceptance of the former but with an amusing recognition of its superiority. The FFB has always been there, whereas the BT has had to struggle in order to find the true way.

It has to be repeated that the Judaism to which the BT is encouraged to return is fundamentalist Orthodoxy. There may be an initial tolerance of non-Orthodox questioning, but it is hoped in BT institutions that eventually all doubts will be stilled and the complete Orthodox package will be seen as the sole option. The students in BT institutions are expected to become familiar with the 613 *mitsvot* and then to put these into practice so far as is possible (some of them, such as the laws of the sacrificial system, are obviously inapplicable today). All 613 are said to be the direct commands of God. Apologetics, in which it is demonstrated that the doctrine of Torah from Heaven is true in its literal sense, is put forward in order to convince the student that it is all unmediated divine truth. Naturally there are tensions in the life of the BT. He may, for example, come into conflict with his parents and decide not to eat anything at all in the parental home because of his newfound adherence to the dietary laws. With the zeal of the convert, he may be stricter in his observance of the *mitsvot* than the FFB. Some *ḥaredi* families are none too happy for their children to marry a BT, believing that the novelty may eventually wear off, leaving their son or daughter with a spouse who has become less observant or even hostile to Judaism. Some *ḥaredi* families have another reason for objecting to their children marrying *ba'alei teshuvah*. This is because the parents of the latter did not observe the laws of family purity (i.e. their mothers did not go to the *mikveh*) and hence their offspring were conceived in impurity. However, Rabbi Unterman, former chief rabbi of Israel, has gone on record as reassuring *ḥaredim* in this matter. Just as a Sefer Torah, said the rabbi, is kosher even when written on inferior parchment since it is redeemed by the sacred letters, so, too, the very fact that the child has become a *ba'al teshuvah* provides the element of sanctity that redeems it from its tainted origin. Yet in many cases the BT does fit fairly easily into the new pattern, with a resulting increase of Jews loyal to Judaism.

A non-fundamentalist, without a patronizing attitude, may entertain a fond appreciation of the BT movement. After all, he himself may be committed to Jewish observance. But, in the belief that truth is important, he will have the same reservations with regard to the movement that he has towards fundamentalist Orthodoxy in general. He will refuse to accept the whole package as the word of God for him and will wish to allow his reason to be selective. He will ask 'What does God want me to do in my situation?' rather than 'What does the tradition say that God says I must do?' This is the main reason why non-Orthodox groups frown on the whole BT movement and have not developed much of an outreach programme. Also at work here is a lack of complete certainty that all the truth has been given, a lack that makes for tolerance.

Orthodox Publishing Activity

During the second half of the twentieth century there has been a publication boom in books in Hebrew and English in all Orthodox circles. A phenomenon especially to be noted is the massive production in the *ḥaredi* world of Festschriften and memorial volumes, hitherto known only as tributes offered by universities and similar institutions to scholars in the modern critical historical vein. A pioneering volume in this connection was the jubilee volume in honour of the famous *rosh yeshivah* Rabbi Simeon Shkop, *Sefer hayovel*, published in Vilna in 1936. In it Rabbi Hayim Ozer Grodzinski offers an 'apology' for the novel feature, implying that Rabbi Shkop only agreed to the quite atypical exposure because it would produce profits for his yeshiva. Rabbi Grodzinski writes:

Behold, many of the best disciples of the great *gaon*, our master Rabbi Simeon Yehudah Hakohen Shkop, long may he live, among them great and famous rabbis, bestirred themselves to celebrate the jubilee of their master and teacher, an elder sitting in a yeshiva to spread [knowledge of] the Torah in public these past fifty years—from his youth in Telz to now in his old age in the Sha'arei Torah yeshiva in Grodno. In their letters and essays they elaborate on the stature, attitude, and character of the beloved *gaon*, Rabbi Simeon, long may he live. Although I know full well that in his pure, sensitive character and in his humility he will have unpleasant feelings and the praises to his face will prove to be burdensome—also the whole idea of a jubilee *to which venerable rabbis are unaccustomed*—for all that Rabbi Simeon Ha'emsoni [a pun on the name of a rabbi in the Talmud, here understood as 'the burdened one'], burdened in his holy task of carrying the load of the yeshiva, was compelled to give in and carry this burden as well for the sake of its purpose of bringing prosperity to the yeshiva, so to relieve him of the heavy burden and the yoke of the debts which press upon him without respite [emphasis mine]. (p. 11)

It was not only the celebration of a jubilee and the appearance of the jubilee volume that were unconventional among traditional rabbis, but also the contents of the volume, which include many biographical accounts and even the publication of a learned essay, quite in the modern style, by a former disciple of Rabbi Shkop, Professor Israel Davidson, in which a medieval poem on *shehitah* is transcribed from a manuscript copy, and furnished with elaborate footnotes. This essay could easily have appeared in a modern Festschrift. Incidentally, the volume contains a wealth of information regarding yeshiva life in pre-war Lithuania.

The *Sefer hayovel* set the precedent for the numerous volumes of a similar nature which appeared after the Second World War. The production of such volumes has now become something of an industry. Most of them are heavily subsidized by the families and affluent well-wishers of the honorands. The format is usually the same: a tribute or series of tributes; halakhic notes and essays by the departed or the living honorand; previously unpublished halakhic material by past masters; and studies by contemporaries. The emphasis in all these volumes is on theoretical halakhah, though generally some space is also given to questions of practical halakhah. I find myself fascinated by this material. It all reminds me of the years I spent in the yeshiva, and there are insights of value even for those who prefer to engage in modern scholarship. Yet real historical critical questions are rarely discussed. One never finds the slightest departure from the *haredi* pattern in this kind of work. Whenever I visit Jerusalem, I try to discover one of these volumes for sale in Me'ah She'arim. So far I have quite a number of them in my library, but shall refer here only to two in memory of rabbis whom I knew personally and who were involved more or less directly in the 'Jacobs Affair', taking their stand, naturally, with Chief Rabbi Brodie.

The first I shall consider is the *Sefer hazikaron* for Rabbi Yehezkel Abramsky,[12] the former head of the London Beth Din where, largely due to his influence, the United Synagogue began to lean much more heavily towards the *haredi* approach. On his retirement Rabbi Abramsky taught in various yeshivas in Israel, especially in the Slobodka yeshiva, whose authorities published another memorial volume, *Kovets zikaron*, in his honour.[13] I note some of the contents of the former volume. In addition to a number of biographical essays, halakhic comments by Rabbi Abramsky, and hitherto unpublished articles by famous rabbis of the past, there is a section on exegetical innovations (*hidushim*) by contemporary rabbis belonging to the Lithuanian school. Even though this volume contains discussions of practical questions, the thrust, even when discussing these, is on the purely theoretical aspects. There are essays on the following (I give only the topics discussed with brief notes on their nature):

Whether mourning on the first day over the death of a near relative is biblical or rabbinic (mourning on the other days is stated clearly to be rabbinic); on doubtful benedictions; on the law that mixed seeds in a vineyard and fruit grown during the first three years of planting have to be buried; on the search for leaven before Passover; on whether a foetus is a person in Jewish law; whether it is permitted to accept donations from Reform Jews for an Orthodox synagogue (this last response is by the former Sephardi chief rabbi of Israel, Ovadiyah Yosef; he states that strictly speaking it is permitted, but that one should certainly not canvass donations from Reformers); on the divisions of the priests in Temple times; on the law of wounding a Canaanite slave; on donations offered to the Temple in error (this could only apply in Temple times); on whether gelatin is kosher.

Rabbi Yitshak Ya'akov Weiss was the head of the Manchester Beth Din at the time of the 'Jacobs Affair'. He said at the time that if I were appointed principal of Jews' College he would proclaim a public fast! Since I was not appointed I missed the honour. On his retirement from the Manchester position, Rabbi Weiss became the head of the *beit din* of the Edah Haredit, the ultra-Orthodox community in Jerusalem. He was the author of the ten volumes of responsa (in the Hungarian style) entitled *Minhat yitshak*. These were very well received in the *haredi* world. The memorial volume for Rabbi Weiss, *Sefer hazikaron*, edited by members of the Edah Haredit,[14] consists of essays and responsa in

[12] Ed. J. Bucksbaum (Jerusalem, 1978).   [13] Benei Berak, 1977.   [14] Jerusalem, 1990.

matters of both theoretical and practical halakhah, but here the emphasis is on the practical.

In addition to Festschriften and memorial volumes there has been a spate of *ḥaredi* responsa, generally dealing with problems raised by the conditions of modern life but with a strong emphasis on decidedly premodern opinions. Some examples typical of the Hungarian or Polish, as opposed to the Lithuanian, schools can be cited. There is a curious blend of up-to-dateness and medieval attitudes throughout, so that a modernist Jew is able to applaud the former while taking issue strongly with the latter. The responsa collection *Shevet hakehati* by Rabbi S. K. Gross[15] discusses (no. 263) the question of whether a man under 40 years of age may render decisions in Jewish law. From the Talmud it might appear that he cannot, but the author, himself under 40, is at pains to conclude that he may. No. 332 discusses when people are entitled to object to others smoking in their vicinity. Nos. 348–53 all deal with the law against withholding the wages of a workman for even a single day. No. 359 examines whether the prohibition on treating a widow harshly applies even if she has now remarried and is no longer a widow. No. 364 states that though the Talmud frowns on scholars studying on their own, this prohibition does not apply nowadays, when so many books have been published, since the authors of the books are 'our study-companions'. No. 379 discusses whether the tenth commandment, 'Thou shalt not covet', means that one must not even say 'I, too, would like to have a wife like X's', or whether it only applies when one says 'I would like to have X's wife'. No. 383 is on jumping queues.

The responsa collection *Shevet halevi* by Rabbi S. Wosner[16] is among the best-known responsa collections used by *ḥaredi* rabbis. Among the responsa discussed are the following: 1. 35. The benediction to be recited on seeing a monarch applies to a queen and not only to a king. 1. 43. A *kohen* whose car ran over a pedestrian is not thereby disqualified from reciting the priestly blessing. 2. 56. Streamers and the like manufactured for use at Christmas may still be used to decorate a sukkah. 2. 58. Since 'the law of the land is law' a tax-inspector who reports to the authorities that a man has evaded his taxes is not an 'informer'. 2. 127. The case of a man who left a large sum of money to be distributed among the descendants of a hasidic *tsadik* who died over a hundred years ago—which of the

[15] Jerusalem, 1967.
[16] 2nd edn., vols. i–v (New York, 1981–4); vol. vi (Benei Berak, 1986).

descendants are entitled to receive a share? 4. 124. It is not an infringement of the fifth commandment when a young man marries the young woman of his choice despite parental opposition to the match. 6. 241. Compensation for the killing of a prowling dog which looked wild but had not actually attacked anyone.

The above are samples taken at random of the kind of problem discussed in *ḥaredi* responsa. Many more examples could be given, but that would take us beyond the scope of this book. Enough has been quoted to show how rabbis of a Hungarian or Polish background have their own approach to Orthodox life in the modern world. In point of fact, what has happened in *ḥaredi* life is that the rabbis no longer render decisions for the whole community, but know full well that they are addressing only their fellow *ḥaredim* who are ready enough to 'buy' whatever the rabbis decide, so that a kind of *ḥaredi* halakhah is produced. Even in a work on the talmudic tractate *Makkot—Birkot shamayim*,[17] by Rabbi Raphael Blum—the author has a lengthy introduction which has nothing to do with his learned commentary on the tractate, but in which he castigates those who depart from the *ḥaredi* lifestyle.

Rabbi Blum adopts an extreme conservative stance. He observes that in western European Jewish communities, where the Haskalah movement was rampant, it was hardly possible to find a city or village in which there was a Jew (*sic*), so great was the rate of intermarriage in those countries. It all began through changes in comparatively minor customs, but then the rot set in to encourage a wholesale abandonment of Judaism. Jews substituted secular studies for the traditional study of the Torah. In America, too, the desire to copy the mores of non-Jewish citizens prevailed, and the whole pattern of Jewish life changed, to the extent that Reform and Conservative Judaism became substitutes for Orthodoxy. Blum tells of a friend who asked an American rabbi why he did not castigate his congregation for their lack of Jewish observance, and asked how he would meet his Maker in the next world. The rabbi replied that he was only appointed by his congregants to make speeches and tell jokes and to be a social worker (Blum gives these words in transliterated English). Now, however, with the arrival on American shores of great rabbis from eastern Europe, the situation has improved. These rabbis have returned to traditional norms. They have built *mikva'ot*,

---

[17] New York, 1971.

arranged for proper supervision of kosher food, built synagogues in the old style, and transplanted onto American soil the institutions of the past. Old-world rabbis now have 'the image of God' in the New World, i.e. they wear long beards. Naturally, Blum has nothing good to say about the Haskalah. Mendelssohn and his cohorts were the disciples not of our father Abraham but of the wicked heathen prophet Balaam. This opinion would not deserve a mention were it not typical of the present *ḥaredi* exclusivist approach. Blum cannot forgo the opportunity of taking a massive swipe at modernism of all kinds, even Modern Orthodoxy, and even in a work devoted to pure talmudic commentary.

This exclusivist attitude made inroads into Modern Orthodoxy, a movement that still manages successfully to produce works of a high standard in the modern vein in English as well as in Hebrew. But when it comes to works on the philosophy of the movement one cannot help noticing a constant skirting of such issues as the relationship of historical critical scholarship to piety, the kind of issue with which this book is concerned. The great hero of Modern Orthodoxy is still Samson Raphael Hirsch, whose works have been translated into English and whose nineteenth-century, completely unhistorical approach is hailed as the only kosher attempt at coping with the problems of Judaism in Western society. I have referred earlier to the debate between Hirsch and Frankel on the question of the legitimacy of historical criticism. Modern Orthodoxy, without exception so far as I am aware, always sides with Hirsch, or rather generally ignores what Frankel and his followers have had to say. On the Pentateuch, Dr Hertz's *The Pentateuch and Haftorahs*[18] is still the last word for Modern Orthodoxy with all its cavalier attitude towards pentateuchal criticism.

In the Modern Orthodox journal *Tradition* there are numerous learned articles on the problems of Judaism in the modern world, but hardly any of them consider the problems to which the historical critical methodology gives rise, as can be seen by the otherwise excellent *A Treasury of Tradition* (a selection of the best essays in the journal).[19]

J. David Bleich is an outstanding halakhist of the Modern Orthodox school. Bleich's four large volumes, *Contemporary Halakhic Problems*,[20] are among the best summaries of the subject in any language, but are

[18] London, 1950.
[19] Ed. Norman Lamm and Walter S. Wurzburger (New York, 1967).
[20] New York 1977–95.

vitiated by his total rejection of the notion that sociological factors have had a say in the development of the halakhah. Bleich, in fact, denies that there has ever been any development in the halakhah. Typically, Bleich's *With Perfect Faith*,[21] a treatment of Maimonides' thirteen principles of the faith, is largely an anthology of what the medieval thinkers have had to say on the principles, with not the slightest attempt to evaluate the principles themselves in the light of new knowledge. For Bleich the question is always what Maimonides means, never whether Maimonides is right. I have come increasingly to realize that, for better or for worse, I and those who think like me occupy a different universe of discourse from that of both the *haredim* and the Modern Orthodox, at least so far as theological thinking is concerned.

In *haredi* districts nowadays one sees displayed in Jewish bookshop windows pious works of a kind somewhere mid-way between the *haredi* and Modern Orthodox worlds. These volumes are totally *haredi* in outlook but resemble Modern Orthodox works in that they are written in passable, often even in good, English, with the evident view of attracting modern Jews. Many of these works are biographies of famous contemporary or near-contemporary rabbis and hasidic *rebbes* of the old school. They are completely hagiographical in nature, their heroes portrayed as paragons of virtue whose devotion to the Torah amazes lesser mortals. It is impossible here to do more than glance at three typical works in this genre: *The Manchester Rosh Yeshivah: The Life and Ideals of HaGaon Rabbi Yehudah Zev Segal*;[22] *Reb Moshe: The Life and Ideals of HaGaon Rabbi Moshe Feinstein*;[23] and *Reb Yaakov: The Life and Times of HaGaon Rabbi Yaakov Kemenetsky*.[24]

I knew Rabbi Segal well. His father, whom he succeeded as head of the Manchester yeshiva, was one of my teachers. Reb Yudel, as he was called, was a truly saintly man, but the description of his personality in the introduction to his biography is in the over-the-top manner of which this kind of literature is so fond:

This book is by no means a definitive work. The full scope of the Rosh Yeshivah's greatness cannot be portrayed; we are light years away from the spiritual levels which he attained in all areas of *avodas Hashem* [divine worship]. Moreover, as

[21] New York, 1983.
[22] By Shimon Finkelman and Yosef Weiss (Brooklyn, NY, 1997).
[23] By Shimon Finkelman and Nossan Scherman (Brooklyn, NY, 1986).
[24] By Yonason Rosenblum (Brooklyn, NY, 1993).

a paragon of humility the Rosh Yeshivah strove to the best of his ability to conceal his character and his accomplishments. However, he could not conceal the fact that he studied the Torah with classic diligence all his long life and in so doing made its teachings a part of his very essence. As a disseminator of Torah for more than half a century, he taught the way of Torah—both regarding *mitzvos* between man and Hashem, and between man and his fellow—through word and by way of example.

The introduction to the Rabbi Feinstein volume states:

TOTAL IMMERSION IN TORAH—that was the Rosh Yeshivah's essence. The public is familiar with the legends that he finished Shas more than two hundred times and Shulchan Aruch more than six or eight hundred times. Those who knew him best insist that these are exaggerations; what truly matters is that learning was his life and that if it could be said of anyone that he was a living Torah, it was the Rosh Yeshivah.

Similarly, the introduction to the biography of Reb Yaakov observes:

Torah greatness is by its very nature incapable of precise description or quantification. No matter how one multiplies examples of a Torah scholar's insights into the Written Torah or his *chiddushim* (novellae) in the Oral Torah, it is impossible to capture the very essence of his brilliance—his overarching vision of the interconnectedness of every aspect of Torah, a vision which can only result from a complete command of the entirety of both the Written and Oral Torah. Even more importantly, these examples tell us nothing about the degree to which that vision has been integrated into the *talmid chacham* himself so that his personality can no longer be distinguished from his understanding of the Torah.

Why go on? There is surely much to admire in the great heroes of Orthodoxy, but how we would have liked to be told a little of their peccadilloes. How much more captivating would have been a 'warts and all' portrait. A larger-than-life picture tends to produce the sameness and narrowness shown in this kind of work that, far from rendering the Torah personality attractive, makes it remote and unbelievable. And it is all done in obedience to the monolithic approach in which only those 'greats' who conform to the supposed pattern qualify as such. Even many observant Jews will refuse to acknowledge that their religious faith does not allow them to cast a critical as well as a reverent eye on their champions, to say nothing of the fact that, as this book argues, criticism wedded to reverence is not out of place with regard to the Jewish tradition as a whole. For many of us it is not only that this literature usually leaves us cold. Its greater fault is that even when it is attractive it ultimately leaves us too warm.

SEVEN

REFORM

M Y OWN BACKGROUND was nominally Orthodox so far as my parents and family were concerned, but ultra-Orthodox during my studies in the yeshiva. In those days Reform possessed not the slightest allure. My parents, like the majority of Jews in Manchester, tended to view the Reform movement with complete indifference. They knew that there was a Reform synagogue in the city, frequented mainly by Anglicized Jews of German origin, but which they themselves would have had as little thought of joining as they would have of not keeping a kosher home. The teachers at the yeshiva hardly ever bothered even to attack Reform Judaism, which was never seen as presenting any kind of a challenge. This was in any event quite natural for a yeshiva on the Lithuanian pattern, since no Reform movement had arisen in Lithuania.

There was only one occasion when the *rosh yeshivah*, Rabbi Moshe Yitshak Segal, mentioned Reform Judaism to me. I had been engaged to preach in Southport over Yom Kippur. Preaching was new to me, so I asked the *rosh yeshivah* to give me a suitable topic on which to talk. He referred me to the talmudic passage (*Ḥullin* 91a) which deals with the mysterious visitor who wrestled with Jacob (Gen. 32: 25). This 'man', the Talmud opines, was none other than the guardian angel of Esau. There are two opinions as to the form the angel took when he fought with Jacob, raising dust which reached to Heaven. According to one opinion the angel appeared to Jacob in the guise of a heathen, but according to another opinion, he appeared in the guise of a scholar, a *talmid ḥakham*. The *rosh yeshivah* interpreted the raising of the dust to Heaven to mean that when a Jew wrestles with angelic forces the outcome of the struggle has an effect on his progress in heavenly matters. At times these forces appear as 'heathens', as those totally opposed to Judaism, and these are easily vanquished since a sincere Jew will always refuse to be diverted from a clearly perceived truth. The danger is present when these forces appear in the guise of talmudic scholars, when, as with Reform Judaism, they seek to persuade the loyal Jew that Judaism is best served when modernist tendencies are seen part of the faith's demands in the contemporary world. In a rather mild manner the *rosh yeshivah* said that there was no harm in introducing a polemic against Reform to the Orthodox community in Southport, implying that such temptations needed to be preached against to people of weaker faith, but that no yeshiva man would ever consider becoming Reform, and that in the yeshiva no real struggle for Orthodoxy was ever required.

The result was that even when I felt obliged to give up fundamentalist Orthodoxy, I was never tempted to go over to Reform. I found no real difficulty with Orthodox practices. It was only the theory behind fundamentalist Orthodoxy that I could no longer accept. I soon discovered that this kind of distinction between theory and practice—the one largely a matter of history, of how it all came to be, the other a matter of living religion—goes back, as stated earlier in this book, to Zechariah Frankel and the Breslau school, and is the driving force of Conservative Judaism in the USA, a movement with which I identified, while appreciating that what was suitable for American Jews was not necessarily entirely suitable for Jews in the UK. I later read fairly widely on the history of Reform Judaism from its beginnings in nineteenth-century Germany. The three most prominent Reform thinkers were Frankel, Abraham Geiger, and Samuel Holdheim (1806–60). Frankel, originally a Reformer like the other two, eventually moved to the right so that, in effect, he gave up the classical Reform position and is rightly regarded as the forerunner of Conservative Judaism, which, as I have said, appealed to people like me with no desire to abandon traditional Judaism, but who found the views of both Geiger and Holdheim far too extreme.

What was the real issue? Professor Louis Finkelstein, speaking of the need for a Conservative approach, used to say that an intelligent Jew is called upon today to have a Jewish heart and a modern mind. Reform Jews certainly have a modern mind. Their intellectual integrity in facing up to the challenge of modernity is apparent. Their refusal to accept untenable theories about the history of Judaism is only to be admired. If it is acknowledged that Modern Orthodoxy, Conservative Judaism, and Reform all share essentially the same aim of preserving the past while being open to the demands of the present and the future, the differences between the three groups lies mainly in how far one should go in this worthy endeavour, though, as noted in Chapter 6 of this book, Modern Orthodoxy does not allow any departure from what I have called the fundamentalist position. The parameters beyond which the Modern Orthodox cannot stir have been set entirely by the tradition, although, naturally, with a greater degree of flexibility than *ḥaredi* Jews would allow. Conservative Judaism conceives of the tradition itself in dynamic terms, while Reform is even less bound by the tradition by the very fact that it believes the tradition can be reformed. Ultimately it is a question of degree. I came to believe, like so many Jews observant in practice but open with regard to theory, that, since its inception, Reform, for us, has gone too far in its accommodation to the *Zeitgeist*.

Geiger was one of the outstanding scholars in the Wissenschaft des Judentums movement, but he also, like Rapoport in Galicia, had a distinguished career as a traditional rabbi. This has to be stressed. Geiger tried to work out a theological position for the Jewish community as a whole. He believed that the historical studies to which he himself made a real contribution did present very serious problems for traditional Judaism, but he would have liked to have seen these problems dealt with within the tradition itself. This is why Geiger could serve as the second rabbi of the Breslau community, officiating together with Rabbi Abraham Tiktin (1764–1820) in all traditional observances, even to the extent of drawing up bills of divorce in a completely traditional way. Such co-operation between an ultra-Orthodox rabbi and an arch-Reformer would be unthinkable nowadays. But it should be appreciated that the Tiktin–Geiger community itself contained many laymen with strong Reform leanings. In other words, Geiger believed, initially though not in the later period of his rabbinic career, that it was possible for a modern scholar to be a traditional halakhist. On the face of it, this was the view held by Rapoport and Frankel, but Rapoport was far less committed to biblical criticism than Geiger, and Frankel did not eventually agree to the programme of a Reformist party. Geiger's attempt failed; when a Reform congregation was established in Berlin, he was invited to become its spiritual head but refused. In Geiger's theology, some of the particularistic elements of the past should be dispensed with, but not those elements which make for group cohesion—hence Geiger's concern with the *get*. This area of communal cohesion continues to be an obstacle to radical Reform. It is all very well to introduce such things as changes in the synagogue service, even radical changes. That is no one else's business. But to remarry a woman without a *get* or to accept as a convert to Judaism one who has not undergone the correct conversion procedures, including immersion in the *mikveh*, is to create a barrier between Reform and Orthodox Jews.

Holdheim's Reform was more radical than Geiger's in this and in other areas. For Geiger, Jewish history shows that there has always been change in Judaism and that such change is demanded if the Jew is to live in the modern age. For Holdheim, there has to be a radical break with the past. In Holdheim's view the whole development of Judaism after the destruction of the Temple was an error. The whole of the Talmud and the legal systems based on the Talmud took a wrong turn by stressing the legal aspects of the Pentateuch instead of the other element of ethical monotheism. The ceremonial laws were connected with the ancient Jewish state, Holdheim maintained, and, instead of perpetuating them, the talmudic rabbis should have abolished them. It was the eternal truths of the Torah that modern Jews should maintain, not the unessential trimmings. In his view, ancient Jewish marriage laws belonged to civil not religious law and there was thus no need for a *get* to dissolve a marriage, no matter what the Talmud says. In a famous, or infamous, saying Holdheim declared, 'The Talmud was right in its day and I am right in my day.' This attempt to go it alone, even in matters of concern to the whole Jewish people, has befogged Reform Judaism to this day. Holdheim's messianism was in terms of the advance of Western civilization, with its invitation for all people to participate in the new life of freedom, tolerance, and social justice. Ceremonies which kept Jews apart from their fellow citizens should be abandoned. The irony of the situation lies in the fact that Holdheim was himself a product of yeshiva learning. This universalist had been an Orthodox rabbi, and a good one at that. He certainly knew perfectly well what he was rejecting. Holdheim's enemies said of him that the only Jewish thing about him was the way he spoke German.

German-speaking rabbis in the USA developed the Reform movement there with 'platforms', at first very radical but later more subdued. The Reform rabbis responsible for drawing up the Pittsburgh Platform in 1885 declared, among other things:

We recognize in the Mosaic legislation a system of training the Jewish people for its national life in Palestine, and to-day we accept as binding only the moral laws and maintain only such ceremonies as elevate and sanctify our lives, but reject all such as are not adapted to the views and habits of modern civilization . . . We hold that all such Mosaic and Rabbinical laws as regulate diet, priestly purity and dress originated in ages and under the influence of ideas altogether foreign to our present mental and spiritual state. They fail to impress the modern Jew with a spirit of priestly holiness; their observance in our day is apt rather to obstruct than to further modern spiritual elevation.[1]

Compare this with the declaration of the Columbus Platform in 1937:

The Torah, both written and oral, enshrines Israel's ever-growing consciousness of God and of the moral law. It preserves the historical precedents, sanctions and norms of Jewish life, and seeks to mould it in the patterns of goodness and of holiness. Being products of historical processes, certain of its laws have lost their binding force with the passing of the conditions that called them forth. But as a depository of permanent spiritual ideals, the Torah remains the dynamic source of the life of Israel. Each age has the obligation to adapt the teachings of the Torah to its basic needs in consonance with the genius of Judaism.[2]

The Columbus Platform is obviously less radical than the Pittsburgh Platform—note, especially, the substitution of 'the Torah, both written and oral' for 'Mosaic legislation', an insipid term, as Mordecai Kaplan remarked. Both platforms lay great stress on the moral and spiritual values of Judaism, but do not seem to have been fully aware that values as well as ceremonials often change from age to age.

The real organizer of Reform in America was Isaac Mayer Wise (1819–1900). Thanks largely to his efforts, the Hebrew Union College was established in Cincinnati, Ohio, in 1875 for the training of Reform rabbis. And then came the '*terefah* banquet'. At a banquet to celebrate the ordination of the college's first graduates there appeared among the items on the menu little black clams, soft-shell crabs, shrimp salad, frogs' legs, roast beef followed by cheese—all forbidden by the dietary laws. That *terefah* food should be served at a banquet to celebrate the ordination of rabbis caused traditional rabbis and laymen to recoil in horror, leading indirectly to the founding of the Conservative movement and the establishment of the Jewish Theological Seminary for the training of Conservative rabbis.

In Hungary, the Jewish community became divided into the Neologs (as the Reformers were called), the Orthodox (who formed themselves into a separate community), and the status quo congregations, those

---

[1] W. Gunther Plaut, *The Growth of Reform Judaism* (New York, 1965), 33–4.
[2] Ibid. 96–100.

who continued in the older tradition of a united community, comprising both Orthodox and Reform. Even the Neologs observed the laws which governed personal relations so that, for example, they issued bills of divorce in accordance with halakhah which were recognized by the Orthodox. Some Orthodox rabbis were tolerant of what they naturally considered to be the Reform heresy. Others were far less tolerant. I have surveyed some of the attitudes of Hungarian Orthodoxy to Reform in my book *Theology in the Responsa*.[3] Here I shall merely mention Rabbi Hayim Kittsee's attack on the Brunswick Reform Conference held in June 1844. Kittsee argued that the participants in the conference claimed to be rabbis but, in reality, were ignorant of rabbinic law, denied the Oral Torah (this is a constant refrain in Orthodox polemics) and other basic principles of the Jewish faith, and were heretics whose intention was to mislead ordinary folk. Nothing should be done to suggest for one moment that these men, who rejected the authority of the Talmud, could be considered as representatives of rabbinic Judaism.

At this comparatively early stage, the Reform rabbis were vehemently attacked, but it was really still a matter of like versus like. As the Reform movement developed, however, the suggestion by Kittsee and other Orthodox rabbis in Hungary that Reform rabbis are not real rabbis at all became more and more acceptable, with the result that many of the Orthodox today, even in the USA and England, to say nothing of the State of Israel, have acquired a monopoly over the rabbinate. Even those who do not favour a complete severance between Orthodoxy and Reform still refuse to use the title rabbi of a Reformer, even if he is skilled in rabbinic law. In the USA the Yiddish press, nominally Orthodox, either uses for a Reform rabbi the term *ra bi* ('baddy'), or puts the word rabbi in inverted commas as 'rabbi'. Others refer to a 'real' rabbi by the Hebrew term *harav* to distinguish such a one even from a Modern Orthodox rabbi. Throughout the history of Orthodox polemics against Reform the question prevails of whether to create a complete separation between the two groups, or whether to work together with the Reformers on matters of mutual Jewish concern. Cries are heard periodically for greater unity among Jews, but it has to be realized that where dogma is stressed exclusivism is bound to be the result. Truth can have no truck with error. This is still the usual Orthodox view. Samson Raphael Hirsch

[3] London, 1973.

went so far as to compare Orthodoxy to Roman Catholicism and Reform to Protestantism in the Christian community. For Hirsch, Orthodoxy and Reform, far from being two voices in Judaism, are two different religions. One or two Reform rabbis in the USA in the twentieth century accepted this notion that Reform Judaism is a new and different Judaism from that which obtained in the past. The majority of Jews after the Holocaust refuse to tread this path. Hitler, it is now frequently said, did not ask a Jew whether he was Orthodox or Reform. Moreover, sects like the Karaites voluntarily severed their connection with rabbinic Judaism, whereas the Reformers rightly look upon themselves as religious Jews who pay respect to the traditions of the Jewish people and acknowledge, if not the authority of the talmudic rabbis, at least their capability in teaching the ideals and values of the faith.

The Reform movement in Britain began with a meeting in 1840 of nineteen Sephardim and five Ashkenazim, who signed a declaration in which they expressed their dissatisfaction with the prevailing mode in the London congregations from which they had decided to secede.[4] The West London Synagogue of British Jews was consecrated in 1842. The attitude of these early Reformers was scripture-oriented. They believed that the Bible was the word of God but, while respecting the Oral Torah, denied that it had a divine origin. For example, they refused to recite the benediction 'Who has sanctified us with His commandments and has commanded us' over practices such as the kindling of the Hanukah lights, since these were not *commanded* in the Bible but were ordained by the talmudic rabbis. Rabbi Salomon Hirschell, chief rabbi of the Ashkenazim, and the Reverend David Meldola, together with representatives of the Board of Deputies, prepared a warning against the establishment of the new congregation and in 1842 this was issued as a *ḥerem* (ban) to be read in all synagogues in the country. The *ḥerem* reads: 'Any person or persons publicly declaring that he, or they, reject or do not believe in the authority of the Oral Law, cannot be permitted to have any communion with us Israelites in any religious rites or sacred act.' There began a fierce debate on the question of whether such a *ḥerem* was binding and some congregations took no notice of it. When Nathan Marcus Adler was appointed chief rabbi in 1845 he was persuaded

[4] The story of Reform Judaism in Britain is told in Anne J. Kershen and Jonathan A. Romain, *Tradition and Change: A History of Reform Judaism in Britain 1840–1995* (London, 1995).

to abolish the right of all future incumbents of the office to impose a *ḥerem*. Yet medievalism in the form of the *ḥerem* lingered on, in theory at least. It was brought to my attention by Dr Israel Feldman that his father told him that when Dr Bernard Drachman of the USA was being considered as a candidate for the office of chief rabbi, he declared that if appointed he would not sign away his right to impose a *ḥerem*, though in practice he would not dream of exercising the right.

Philosophical or theological considerations were hardly in the forefront of the severely practical Reformers in London, but the Reform congregations in Bradford and Manchester had close contact with the Reformers in Germany and were strongly influenced by their ideas. It is very interesting that before the London congregation appointed David Wolf Marks to be its minister in 1841, Isaac Marcus Jost was asked to secure a suitable candidate for the position of reader and lecturer. Jost approached Zechariah Frankel, then rabbi of Dresden, who refused on the grounds that the London Reformers had 'no sufficient principle of reform'. It is intriguing to speculate that, had Frankel gone to London, he might have developed his 'Conservative' approach there. Also intriguing is the fact that one of the candidates for the chief rabbinate, together with Dr Adler, was Samson Raphael Hirsch, Frankel's chief opponent. From it all there emerges clearly the 'modern' nature of the debate on both sides. Adler, Hirsch, and Frankel were all imbued with the spirit of Western culture, which each tried in his own way to accommodate within traditional Judaism.

In my home town, Manchester, the Reform congregation was founded by a number of German Jewish textile merchants, attracted to the city by its growing economy. At first those with Reformist leanings in Manchester sought to work within the general Jewish community, but when such a move was frustrated by Chief Rabbi Adler, a separate Reform congregation was established. The Manchester Reform congregation, growing out of an original Orthodox congregation, was in some ways more traditional in practice than those in London. The second day of the festivals, for instance, was still retained, even though it is of rabbinic origin. When the London minister, David Wolf Marks, wrote to Dr Schiller-Szinessy, rabbi of the Manchester Reform synagogue, on the question of the Oral Torah, Schiller-Szinessy replied:

In the congregation over which I am appointed to preside, the Second Days of Festivals will be kept, but such observances in no manner contravene the principle already admitted inasmuch as they will be observed, not as Mosaic and Biblical ordinance but purely and professedly as ancient institutions [upon] which many of our members look with a feeling of reverence.[5]

A number of Reform congregations were later established in the UK and are now amalgamated as the Reform Synagogues of Great Britain. In 1902 C. G. Montefiore founded a more radical Reform organization, the Jewish Religious Union, which led to the establishment of the Liberal Jewish Synagogue in 1911. Other Liberal congregations were established later. Liberal Judaism in Great Britain is akin to Reform Judaism in the United States, while the more traditional Reform is akin to Conservative Judaism in the States. There is now a Masorti movement in Britain which has adopted the middle-of-the-way position I am trying to advocate in this book. The Orthodox rabbinate tends to lump all 'progressives', including Masorti, together as those who deny the doctrine of *Torah min hashamayim*. The truth of the matter is that the Masorti movement differs from Liberal Judaism and even from the more traditionalist Reform in that it accepts halakhic norms, even though, like the Conservative movement in America and the Masorti movement in Israel, it is prepared to be flexible in the halakhic process. Thus Masorti finds severe fault with Reform's apparent indifference to some of the laws governing marriage and conversion, which sometimes prevents Orthodox Jews marrying Reform Jews. On the question of women participating in Jewish religious life, the Masorti movement, at least in one or two congregations, permits women to read the Torah and, with the exception of the New London Synagogue, there is mixed seating. The Reform congregation in London did not have mixed seating until quite late in its history. While I think I have some acquaintance with Reform Judaism in the United States, I am not really competent to discuss current trends there. In what follows, while I try to be fair to the facts, I am being rather impressionistic and, possibly, more governed by emotion than by reason.

I find myself, and I am sure many traditional Jews have similar feelings, applauding Reform and Liberal positions on many issues in theory, but unable to accept them in practice, partly because of the Orthodox tradition in which I have been raised, partly because they do not have any real appeal from a Jewish point of view. The services of Reform and

---

[5] Kershen and Romain, *Tradition and Change*, 65.

Liberal synagogues are based on an honest attempt at giving expression only to what the worshippers actually believe, and yet practices such as responses in English in the Protestant mode, an organ even on the sabbath, women rabbis and cantors, and the reading of only part of the *sidrah* (Torah portion) of the week, generally without cantillation, all remain foreign to me and others who dismiss such services as too 'churchy'. To the classical Reform fondness for occidental religion Schechter retorted: 'Since when has religion come from the West?' Religion is oriental by nature. No hard and fast rules can be given—after all, many Reform modes are now the norm in traditional synagogues as well—but it is not so much a question of rules and regulations as of mood. While the Orthodox simply get on with it, the Reformers are often so concerned with refining the religion from all they consider to be dross that services become more a series of theological statements than devotional exercises.

Reform is generally far better than Orthodoxy in the cultivation of the ethical and universal aspects of Judaism. Yet to refer to current Reform and Liberal attitudes, the standard by which innovations are measured is too insubstantial and too much influenced by the contemporary *Zeitgeist*, with the result that all too often the opinions voiced in the general progressive media become *the* Jewish view. These opinions are adopted wholeheartedly and then, and only then, are the classical Jewish sources examined in order to buttress them. For example, it is often now taken for granted in the secular Western world that homosexual relationships are made 'kosher' because the two persons concerned love one another. But according to Jewish values not every ethical question can be decided on the basis of love. Unless one is to shelve two thousand years of Jewish thought, there have to be rules governing a relationship for it to be a marriage. Of course, within a Jewish marriage it is essential for husband and wife to love one another; the talmudic rabbis forbid a man to betroth a woman by proxy, since when the couple meet they may not love one another, and it will then be too late. No liberal-minded person today would wish to make homosexual relations between consenting adults a criminal offence, nor will he fail to respect minorities in society. But it is hard to see how homosexual 'marriages' can be condoned if Jewish values are taken into consideration. When I asked a prominent Liberal rabbi whether C. G. Montefiore would have accepted homosexual behaviour as an alternative lifestyle, his answer was 'Of course not but, then, he was a Victorian, and if he were alive today, he would have different standards.' If Jewish standards depend on what is considered to be ethical in each particular age, this can only mean that there are no fixed Jewish ethical standards.

The problem of how far to go is certainly acute. Reform has made a highly significant contribution to modern Jewish thought by stressing the ethical and universalistic aspects of Judaism, setting aside the more unethical and particularistic statements found in the sources. One does not have to be an Eisenmenger[6] to be horrified at some of the statements in the Talmud on gentiles as an inferior breed, which no amount of apologetics can succeed in explaining away. Yet, in the process, Reform has had to grapple with the notion of the Chosen People, a particularistic and, some would say, an unethical doctrine, if ever there was one. The early Reform leader Abraham Geiger tried to cope with the problem by postulating a special religious endowment of the Jewish soul, a kind of feeling for religious truth, itself responsible for the emergence of ethical monotheism. Other Reform thinkers stressed the idea that Israel was chosen by God to be a 'light to the nations', the very particularism becoming a vehicle for spreading the word of God to all peoples. With few exceptions such as Stephen Wise and Abba Hillel Silver, Reform was not very enthusiastic about the Zionist dream but, after the Holocaust and the establishment of the State of Israel, the movement, true to its doctrine of progressive revelation, now sees support of the State of Israel as much as a divine imperative as do the Orthodox and the Conservatives. Reform rabbis have long been in the forefront of movements working for greater equality among all human beings and for the amelioration of social ills. Nowadays, Reform idealism is extended to cover ecological concerns, the protection of species, and the planet as a whole. (In this connection, it might perhaps be argued that to give too much weight, in the name of Judaism, to ecological concerns sometimes comes close to playing God.) All these are worthy aims and, though they can and do stand on their own, much is gained for Jews when it is shown that they were anticipated by our ancient teachers or, at least, implied in their teachings. The trouble is

---

[6] Johann Andreas Eisenmenger (1654–1704) was a notorious, if learned, Christian opponent of Judaism who collected rabbinic texts that he considered absurd in his *Entdecktes Judenthums* ('Judaism Unmasked'). The work has been widely used by antisemites.

that these concerns tend to relegate the practical *mitsvot* of Judaism to a secondary place. It is not, of course, that Reform does not know of practical *mitsvot* but, by constantly calling attention to the human values inherent in them there is a tendency to obscure the whole idea of divine commands. Although I wholeheartedly accept the non-fundamentalist approach and consequently have difficulties with the notion of the *mitsvot* as divine commands, I still differ from the Reform view in seeing the halakhah as essentially binding, albeit in a much more flexible way than Orthodoxy would allow. I have tried to address the question of a non-fundamentalist halakhah in my book *A Tree of Life*. In the introduction to the new edition of this book,[7] I call attention to the interesting new work done by a number of Reform rabbis on the possibility of a 'Liberal halakhah'.

For several years I taught Talmud at Leo Baeck College, the seminary for the training of Reform and Liberal rabbis, and for a shorter period I was chairman of the Education Board of the college. I do not think that by so doing I was 'selling out' to Reform. First, my role was purely academic. I neither tried nor was I expected to comment on the theological position of Reform. To make this clear, I adopted the habit of not wearing a *yarmulke* at the college, even though many of the students did wear one. I was declaring, and probably overdoing it, that my teaching role was the purely objective, academic one that I adopted when teaching Jewish subjects at the university. Secondly, the college, on paper at least, was itself a kind of general institution catering for Orthodox as well as Reform students, though, naturally, none of the Orthodox would really entertain for one moment the prospect of studying in what, after all, was a college for the training of Reform and Liberal rabbis. I stilled whatever qualms I may have had by the reassurance that, in any event, I had long moved away from the Orthodox extreme reluctance to acknowledge that the Reform and Liberal movements had any legitimacy whatsoever. In other words, I believed, and still do, that it is possible to pursue the objective study of Judaism without this having implications either way for one's personal attitude in the Orthodox versus Reform question or, to put it in another way, I could no longer accept that Orthodoxy possessed the whole of the truth and Reform none. My objection to Reform or Progressive Judaism was partly emotional and partly aesthetic. Given my Orthodox background, I found that Reform attitudes simply

[7] Forthcoming (London, 1999).

did not jell. It was all very honest, ethical, and universalistic but lacking, for me, the warm, uncomplicated form of worship typical of Orthodoxy. What would have satisfied both mind and heart was a modernist movement within Orthodoxy but, alas, no such thing existed then and none exists now.

I ought to mention another significant factor that prevented me from any close identification with Reform. Perhaps influenced by Protestantism, the British Reform movement, in its early days, under the guidance of David Wolf Marks, its first minister, was biblical in orientation, as mentioned earlier. The Talmud tended to be seen as a departure from the pristine purity of the biblical, prophetic message. In my youth I met one or two old ladies belonging to the Reform movement who indignantly refused to recite the blessing. 'Who has commanded' over the Hanukah lights, which they did light on the festival, just as they recited many of the traditional prayers; they could see no point in treating any command not mentioned specifically in the Bible as a divine command. Many early Reform Jews in England did keep some of the dietary laws, but limited their observance to refraining from eating animals whose meat was expressly forbidden in Leviticus and Deuteronomy. Eventually, this kind of Karaism gave way to a more historical approach in which the talmudic rabbis did have a voice, though only a secondary one. Yet, while the older view was abandoned, a certain distance from rabbinic Judaism and the halakhah still prevailed. The result was that, while I was pleased to have been invited to lecture on the Talmud at Leo Baeck College, I had to acknowledge that my talmudic background prevented me from too close an association with Reform rabbis who, by training and disposition, tended to relegate talmudic learning and practices based on it to a secondary place.

I have read practically everything that C. G. Montefiore has written and have found many insights in these works but, as an erstwhile yeshiva man, have been irritated by Montefiore's attitude to the talmudic rabbis. I have discussed the matter in my Claude Montefiore Lecture, delivered at the Liberal Synagogue in 1962, entitled *Montefiore and Loewe on the Rabbis*. The subject of the lecture was *A Rabbinic Anthology* by Montefiore and Herbert Loewe,[8] a work in which extracts are given from the aggadic literature on which the authors give their comments, Montefiore from the Liberal point of view and Loewe from the Orthodox. I

[8] London, 1938.

repeat here some of my observations in this lecture, by which I still stand. Montefiore adopts a somewhat condescending attitude to the rabbis. On page 609 of the *Anthology*, in a remarkable note in which he criticizes those Christian theologians who use the term 'Jewish' in a pejorative sense, Montefiore writes:

It is agreed [nowadays] that in AD 28 there were doubtless many black sheep among them [the rabbis], but it is also allowed that there were many white ones, as well as a large number of mixtures—grey sheep, not wholly white, but by no means completely black. Such a view of these old gentlemen is, I am convinced, much nearer to history and truth.

I have no doubt that Montefiore saw no great harm in referring to the rabbis as 'these old gentlemen', but there are hundreds of thousands of Jews today who spend their lives in talmudic and rabbinic studies who would find this grossly offensive.

A fundamentalist Orthodox Jew tends to view the talmudic rabbis as infallible, spiritual supermen, gifted with the holy spirit, who were, in some mysterious way, as much, or almost as much, the recipients of a kind of direct revelation from on high as the biblical authors. A non-fundamentalist Jew would certainly not see the rabbis in this way. But this attitude of Montefiore, many echoes of which are constantly heard in Reform writings, is simply unintelligible. The talmudic rabbis, infallible or not, are still the teachers of rabbinic Judaism and deserve far more than a gentle pat on the head. It might be mentioned that the majority of the talmudic rabbis were too young, so far as we can tell, to be dubbed 'old gentlemen' in any event. Having studied Talmud and halakhah for years, I could never contemplate joining a movement in which such a condescending attitude is adopted towards my heroes, the talmudic rabbis and the great halakhists, men, only human to be sure, with the greatest minds Judaism has produced. I confess, as I have tried to argue in this book, that the modern application of historical critical methodology to the Bible and the Talmud prevents me from ignoring the problems it raises. But I am still too much a product of the yeshiva world not to shudder at statements like those of Montefiore.

A further point should be made in this connection. Montefiore, for all his keen understanding of the nature of rabbinic thought, does suggest that the rabbis were ancient philosophers, but not particularly good philosophers: 'They [the rabbis] had no training in philosophy. How enormously they might have benefited if, under competent teachers,

they had been put through a course of Greek philosophy and literature.'
The mind boggles at the thought of Rabbi Akiva and Rabbi Joshua taking
courses in Greek philosophy. It is, in fact, a complete misunderstanding
of the nature of the rabbis' thinking even in the aggadah, to say nothing
of their most important sphere of interest, the halakhah. There was no
systematic thinking in Judaism, except for Philo, until the Middle Ages,
when Maimonides and others came under the influence of Greek philosophy in its Arabic garb. They were as little successful in reading good
philosophy into the rabbis as Montefiore was in reading bad philosophy.
The rabbis, in the halakhah, were lawyers; in the aggadah they were religious poets. Would a lawyer be a better lawyer if he had studied philosophy, or would a Shakespeare have been a better poet or dramatist?

Explaining why the *Anthology* deals almost entirely with aggadah and
not with the halakhah of the rabbis, Montefiore says:

The total omission of Halakah from my book, though unavoidable, must, I
fear, tend to give a false, because one-sided, impression of the Rabbinic religion,
and more certainly, of Rabbinic life. For all these legal discussions, all this
'study of the Law', all these elaborations and minutiae, were to the Rabbis the
breath of their nostrils, their greatest joy and the finest portion of their lives.
And yet to *most of us*, it has almost all become distant and obsolete: to most of
us the larger part of it seems a waste of mental energy and of time [emphasis
mine].[9]

How could anyone at all familiar with talmudic learning allow himself to
be included in that 'most of us'? In so far as this kind of attitude is shared
by Reform, and it seems to be in some measure, it is an additional reason
why Reform has never been and is not now a viable option, for me at
least.

[9] Montefiore and Loewe, *A Rabbinic Anthology*, pp. xvi–xvii.

EIGHT

SECULAR JUDAISM

AS A RESULT OF THE CHALLENGES to theistic belief in the nine-teenth and twentieth centuries—science versus Genesis, Marxism, Freud, biblical criticism, atheistic philosophy in general, and the Holo-caust and other terrible evils on an unprecedented scale—some Euro-pean Jews gave up Judaism entirely, preferring complete assimilation. These Jews were either indifferent to Jewish life or positively antag-onistic to it. Other Jews, however, though they had lost belief in the exis-tence of God, had a feeling of attachment to Jewish behaviour patterns and refused to abandon what they called the Jewish way of life. There thus developed the notion of a secular Judaism, in which some of the religious practices such as bar mitzvah and circumcision were still maintained, and even occasional visits to the synagogue were thought admirable, but all was seen in terms of emotional satisfaction, much as some people might celebrate Christmas as a holiday period even though they reject Christian dogma. Of 'secular Christians' Chesterton argued, why not have the fun if you do not have the faith? Secular Jews would retort that the Jewish way is 'fun' which they see no reason at all to give up.

It ought to occasion no surprise that some people have held, and some still hold, that religion is possible without belief in God. In ancient times Theravadic Buddhism, which by any definition deserves to be considered as a religion, was atheistic or, at least, taught that the God idea was irrelevant to its aim of overcoming human suffering.

In the early nineteenth century, Auguste Comte founded the religion of Positivism, the religion of humanity and the full harmony of life, with its Bible and sacraments and a religious calendar, but with mankind in the place of God. More recently, Julian Huxley propagated a 'religion without revelation' in which man can express his sense of awe and wonder without invoking a personal God. Huxley writes:

For my own part, the sense of spiritual relief which comes from rejecting the hypothesis of God as a supernatural being is enormous. I see no other way of bridging the gap between the religious and the scientific approach to reality. But if this rejection is once accomplished the abyss has disappeared in the twinkling of an eye, and yet all the vital realities of both sides are preserved.[1]

If religion in general can be advocated without belief in God, it is not so strange that a religion like Judaism, with its strong emphasis on action rather than dogma (though such a distinction has been overplayed by modernists), can be adhered to quite sincerely by people whose faith in God is either very weak or totally non-existent. At the beginning of the twentieth century, Ahad Ha'am sang the praises of the Jewish ethic and way of life as completely justifying themselves without recourse to any belief in the supernatural. Ahad Ha'am had a great influence on Mordecai Kaplan's religious naturalism. Kaplan, however, would rightly have repudiated vehemently the accusation that he did not believe in God, but the God around whom all of Kaplan's meditation revolves is a God conceived of in entirely functional terms. What matters for Kaplan is the way in which the God concept 'makes for salvation', its power to enrich and ennoble Jewish life. However, it simply will not do to classify Kaplan under the heading of secular Judaism. True, in Kaplan's Reconstructionism, Judaism is best described as a civilization rather than a religion in the narrower sense, but it is a *religious* civilization and knows of the concept of the *mitsvah* as a religious obligation.

Two Jews of great fame in the twentieth century, Albert Einstein and Isaiah Berlin, would not have described themselves, so far as I know, as adherents of secular Judaism, but neither seems to have believed in the personal God of traditional Judaism. In 1940, a symposium calling together scientists, philosophers, and religious leaders was held at the Jewish Theological Seminary in New York. Einstein wrote a paper for it in which he said: 'teachers of religion must have the stature to give up the doctrine of a personal God, that is give up that source of fear and hope which in the past placed such vast power in the hands of the priests'. When Professor Finkelstein, the head of the seminary, read these words he expressed his surprise that Einstein 'should give such an absolute judgment in a field that was philosophical and theological in character'. Einstein, he said, 'should realize that he must speak with as much reserve in these fields as he habitually does in his own field of natural science'.[2]

[1] *Religion without Revelation* (London, 1957), 24.
[2] Robert N. Goldman, *Einstein's God: Albert Einstein's Quest as a Scientist and as a Jew to Replace a Forsaken God* (Northvale, NJ, 1997), 3.

Sir Isaiah Berlin, distinguished exponent of the history of ideas and a leading British sage and philosopher, belonged to an Orthodox synagogue and was regarded as a key figure whose advice was sought by Israeli and Anglo-Jewish leaders. He rarely spoke in public about his views on religion, but a few months before he died in 1998, in an interview broadcast on television immediately after his death, this kindly man of complete integrity felt himself obliged to state that, while it would be nice for him to live on after the death of his body he did not believe that he would, since he had evidence neither of personal survival nor of a personal God. When Isaiah Berlin's father lay dying he asked whether Isaiah thought there was an afterlife and Isaiah said he did. Isaiah later confessed that he saw this as a justifiable lie in order to set the old man's mind at rest. And yet Isaiah was intensely proud of his Jewishness. He once boasted to me that he possessed the tefillin of his ancestor, Rabbi Dov Baer, the *mitteler rebbe* of Lubavitch, though he did not say that he actually wore them. One Rosh Hashanah Isaiah Berlin worshipped with us in the New London Synagogue, where I caught him, if that is the right word, reciting the prayers with what certainly seemed to be devotion. I think I even glimpsed a tear in his eye. Why not? After all, attachment to Judaism and even to prayer is possible for a secular Jew, although a believer would say that this is due to what Lubavitcher hasidim call *dos pintele yid*, 'the inner point of Jewishness in the Jewish soul' through which God is acknowledged in the heart of those who in the mind doubt His existence.

As stated, the horrors of the Holocaust have moved some Jewish thinkers to deny the reality of God, while continuing to affirm Jewish values as especially significant in an age which desperately needs balance, stability, and the means of dealing adequately with life's problems. Richard Rubenstein is prominent among Jewish thinkers who speak in glowing terms of the value of the life of the Torah while believing, in Rubenstein's words, that 'in the final analysis, omnipotent Nothingness is Lord of all creation'.[3]

One can certainly understand how Judaism can have an appeal, even a powerful appeal, without God, yet that is not to say that such an approach is a valid interpretation of the Jewish religion. From biblical times onwards, for all the variety of ways in which the faith was ex-

[3] *The Condition of Jewish Belief: A Symposium Compiled by the Editors of 'Commentary' Magazine* (repr. Northvale, NJ, 1989), 20.

pressed, belief in God was its vital heart. God was more real to the biblical authors than the members of their own family, than the very air they breathed. His glory filled the universe. Sun, moon, and stars did His bidding. His voice was heard in the storm and in the promptings of the human conscience (the biblical authors themselves would have said 'the human heart'). Before Him all the inhabitants of earth were as naught and the gods of the nations were sheer illusion, at least in the later biblical passages.

Jewish teachers throughout the ages, and, for that matter, ordinary Jews in their homes and synagogues, did not normally question, and certainly never doubted, even in times of bitter anguish, that God is real. The refined concepts of Sa'adya and Maimonides differed profoundly from that of the dynamic Godhead as taught by the kabbalists. But the belief in God's existence was a constant, even for those who stressed His utter incomprehensibility. Classical Reform departed radically from the tradition in a number of areas, but never faltered in reciting the Shema. And what sense can one make of Jewish institutions when that which gives them their spiritual power has been banished? What, except banality, remains of the sublime concept of the *mitsvah* as a divine command, when the whole concept of One who commands has been surrendered? Prayer without the God who hears our prayers becomes, at best, the calling of attention to certain values which are somehow 'there'. The sabbath becomes an exercise in celebrating human creativity and in the periodic refreshment required if it is to be engaged in successfully—worthy ideals to be sure, but quite different from the glorious affirmation week by week that this world did not just happen but was brought into being by a benevolent Creator.

The synagogue itself loses all its numinous quality. Instead of a place in which the Jew meets his Maker, it becomes either an instrument of Jewish survival or a facility for social exchange, a club rather than a sanctuary.

With God, the tragic dimensions of life are real. Some of the loftiest religious souls have cried out to God against life's injustices, seeing the complaint itself as somehow God-inspired. Without God, in a world where chance rules all, the tragic is reduced to the pathetic, men crying out in pain and huddling together for comfort but knowing all too well in their heart of hearts that there is nothing to be done and that there is none to listen. Dark the world is even with God. Without Him, dark

and light both lose their ultimate meaning. The Holocaust has indeed
burned itself deep into our being. Anyone who tries to justify it or even
to explain it is a heartless clod. But the awesome fact remains that many
of those who perished went into the jaws of death singing 'I believe in
perfect faith'.

What, it might be asked, of intellectual integrity? Can a modern man
believe in God? No serious-minded theist would urge others to believe
that which they know to be false. No one can believe that which they
know to be impossible, and we are too much aware of the 'opium for the
people' slogan even to try. But what is there in modern thought at its
best which makes it dishonest to believe in God? What new knowledge
has accrued to make faith in God untenable? Of course, the theistic
faiths have received a battering in the nineteenth and twentieth centuries, but theists have learned to grapple with the new problems.
Certain ideas have had to go, but this is seen by conscientious theists not
as a reduction of faith, but as its enlargement and evidence of its vitality.
If revelation has to be understood differently from the way in which it
was understood in the Middle Ages, this hardly means that we must
conclude that there is no One to reveal Himself. And if, as we are now
increasingly aware, men have often been guilty of talking nonsense
when speaking of God, what can be more absurd than the spectacle of
men using the forms and language of worship if there is no Object of
worship?

As stated earlier in this book, the question has sometimes been put to
me: If you admit that there is a human element in the Torah, why stop at
that? Why affirm the divine element? Why not say that the Torah is a
marvellous, purely human, construction from which Jews are entitled to
select those ideas and practices which enrich their lives as Jews? For
those of us who do believe in God there is only one answer. We are not
secular Jews because God really *is*, even though, as history shows, He has
chosen to co-operate with humans in the development of His Torah.
For us our religion is not a secondary item, with which one can readily
dispense, but ultimate truth, so that secular Judaism is a contradiction in
terms. While the non-fundamentalist Jew will keep, say, the dietary
laws, even though he has an open mind on their origin, he will still see
his observance of these laws as an act of obedience to a divine command,
for him at least, albeit the command is mediated through the experiences of the Jewish people. For the secular Jew there are no such com-

mands because there is no Commander. He may choose, on occasion at least, to refrain from eating *terefah* food and may never eat pork, but only because he wishes to promote Jewish life, or because kosher food is tastier, or because it links him to his people. This explains the fondness in some circles for kosher-style food, i.e. traditional Jewish dishes that are not necessarily kosher.

It should be asked whether advocates of secular Judaism have always arrived at their position by profound thought on religious problems and difficulties, or whether they are reacting not to religion itself but to the extremes of Orthodoxy and, especially, to its often judgemental attitude. Secular Judaism is hardly a significant movement. It is represented chiefly by a small group of Yiddish-speaking Jews in the USA, Yiddish-speaking presumably to emphasize the folksy aspects of Judaism. 'Secular' Jews (*ḥilonim*) in Israel are only so called in contradistinction to the Orthodox, or *datiyim*, and no philosophy of secular *Judaism* has emerged, though recently attempts have been made to create such a philosophy in Israel with faint echoes in Anglo-Jewry—very faint, it has to be said. One hears from advocates of secular Judaism that the vast majority of Jews do not believe in God, with the implication that it is good to save Judaism from a position that hardly anyone accepts. This is simply not true. Who can dare to tell the many millions of Jews who fast and pray on Yom Kippur that they do not believe in God? Like, I would imagine, the majority of Jews, observant or otherwise, I frankly find the whole notion of a secular Judaism so bizarre that even to attack it is to give it a credence it does not deserve. The aside to which I devote this chapter is because, at times, I have myself been accused of entertaining such a notion or, at least, have been invited to choose between fundamentalist Orthodoxy and secular Judaism, a choice I find ridiculous.

While it is simply untrue to say that that most Jews do not believe in God, there is some evidence that the ethnic aspects of Judaism tend to be stressed over the religious aspects, as witness the popularity of hasidic tales and other tales of life in the *shtetl*; happy-clappy services in the synagogue; ostentatious wearing of a *yarmulke* as a badge of identification; the adoption of the quaint late kabbalistic practice of the bride walking seven times round the groom at a wedding; the singing of Zionist or Israeli songs at Hebrew classes. Through all this it is unfortunately implied that a religious approach to Jewish life will never succeed in winning young people to Judaism, whereas the opposite is true. Sensitive young men and women, and, for that matter, older men and women as well, tend to be put off by an attitude that Judaism is not really true but can be exciting as a Jewish pursuit. What is exciting about Judaism is its affirmation not just of an attractive way of life but of the truth that alone can satisfy the soul.

The Afterlife

In contrast to secular Judaism, where the doctrine of the Hereafter obviously has no place, this doctrine seems to me to be at the heart of a religious approach to Judaism. Despite current downplaying of the whole idea of the afterlife, and despite the often-heard claim that Judaism is a this-worldly religion, it has always seemed to me that a Judaism without the belief in the survival of the soul after the death of the body is as unintelligible as a Judaism without God. True, like the Torah itself, Jewish eschatology has had a history, but for well over two thousand years belief in some form of the individual soul's immortality has been an essential feature of the Jewish religion just as it is an essential feature of Christianity and Islam, which took over the belief from Judaism. In this area, too, I have been unable to accept the view of secular Judaism that there is no God who guarantees that what we do with our lives has eternal significance. It simply will not do for a non-fundamentalist to conclude that since the whole doctrine of the Hereafter has developed gradually from perhaps primitive notions, there is little or no truth in it, any more than he can allow himself to believe that, since the idea of Torah and *mitsvot* has evolved, they are not true. There is no middle way here. Either human life is unbearably bleak or it is the gateway to eternal bliss in the presence of God.[4]

The Italian Jewish religious genius, Moses Hayim Luzzatto (1707–47), wrote his *Mesilat yesharim* ('Path of the Upright') as a guide to the living of the good life as conceived of in the rabbinic Judaism of his day. Although Luzzatto's thought, strongly influenced by Kabbalah, is essentially pre-modern, his style of writing is in 'modern' Hebrew, of which he is sometimes held to be the founder. Rabbinic ideas on the afterlife are given expression in a surprisingly new form, no doubt influenced by the general religious thought of post-Renaissance Italy. At the beginning of the first chapter of his book Luzzatto writes:

[4] On this subject, see Neil Gillman, *The Death of Death* (Woodstock, Vt., 1997).

The ultimate foundation of piety and the root of perfect worship is that it be clear and true for a man to know what is his duty in life and to what it is essential for him to direct his gaze and aim in everything in which he toils all the days of his life. Now that which our Sages of blessed memory have taught us is that man was created for no other purpose than to find delight in the Lord and to bask in the radiance of His Shekhinah [divine presence], which is true delight and the greatest of all possible pleasures. The place of such delight is the world to come, for this has been created for this essential purpose. But the way for the attainment of this desirable end is through this world. This is why the rabbis say that this world is like a vestibule to the world to come. The means which bring man to this purpose are the *mitsvot* which the Lord, blessed be He, has commanded us, and it is only in this world that the *mitsvot* can be carried out. Therefore, man has first been put into this world in order that he may attain, by these means, to the place prepared for him, namely, the world to come, to sate himself in the good which he has acquired for himself through these means ... The Holy One, blessed be He, has put man in a place where there are many things which tend to distance him from God. These are worldly desires. If he allows himself to be drawn after these he becomes increasingly remote from that which is truly good.

Luzzatto continues in this vein throughout his book. In his picture, this life is seen as a preparation for heavenly bliss, but a careful reading of the book shows that he does not decry worldly things in themselves. On the contrary, they are the essential means for man to come closer to God through his struggle with temptation. It is only when worldly things are seen as an end in themselves instead of as a means to the sublime end of nearness to God that they become a hindrance instead of a help.

I recall very vividly how, when I first read these words of Luzzatto, I was carried away in youthful naïvety to promise myself that I would try to follow Luzzatto's scheme. Naturally, I soon grew out of this ridiculous, uncomplicated posture, realizing that it is absurd for a young man to delude himself into believing that he can really live with an otherworldly stance. Later still, having obtained some knowledge of Luzzatto's own struggles, I began to question whether this great mystic was quite as saintly as he appears to be from his writings. For all that, when I wrote *We Have Reason to Believe*, I did believe, and still do, that a Judaism without some idea of an afterlife is a distortion.

I see no reason, in fact, for not standing by the position I adopted in *We Have Reason to Believe* and in my other theological works, that Judaism teaches that our life is a pilgrimage to eternity, while being aware of the difficulty of conceiving the nature of eternal bliss. We can have no adequate conception of an existence beyond space and time any more than we can have a conception of God Himself. Suffice it to say in this chapter that a secular Judaism without a belief in God and the afterlife holds no attraction for me.

Of relevance to the question of the afterlife is a doctrine I would like to examine here—that of the 'bread of shame', which I shall try to trace from its origins. Many years ago in Gateshead and Manchester I sat at the feet of the renowned teacher of *musar*, Rabbi E. E. Dessler (1881–1954) and, together with other youthful enthusiasts, would uncritically swallow whole the master's very erudite and eloquent discourses, in which there was a blend of *musar*, Kabbalah, and hasidism, with an added spice of caustic humour as well as an occasional reference to the theories of Freud and Einstein—the whole constituting a heady mixture that could not fail to intoxicate highly impressionable young men. (Dessler did give talks to young women but never to men and women at the same time.) Some of his disciples remained in the *musar* camp, others, myself included, became disenchanted with Dessler's attempt to reconcile the irreconcilable, and, to some extent, with the whole *musar* stance. Yet many of Dessler's ideas, especially those regarding this world as a preparation or school for life in the next, found a permanent home in our hearts and minds to influence our religious lives, tending at times to produce a mood of severe introspection, often resulting in disillusionment with the world and its glittering prizes. As Dessler himself was fond of saying, 'Anyone who has studied seriously in a yeshiva may or may not have a large share in the world to come. One thing is certain, however, he will never enjoy fully the joys of this world.' Prominent among Dessler's other-worldly themes was that of *nahama dikesufa* ('bread of shame'), a doctrine I have mulled over repeatedly and shall here try to investigate rather more thoroughly from both the historical and theological points of view.

The doctrine is offered as an explanation of why God has ordained that human beings undergo a probationary period on earth in order for them to merit eternal bliss in the Hereafter. Why did He not create from the outset incorporeal beings with the capacity to enjoy His nearness for ever? The rabbinic tradition does anticipate Keats that this world is a vale of soul-making, but the rabbis do not explain why humans have to 'make' their souls when God could have given them souls ready-made, so to speak. Basically, the answer is that God wished to create humans with a stern independence by which they spurn unearned gifts, even the tremendous spiritual gifts bestowed by God Himself. By making the good their own by godly living in the world out of their own free choice, humans earn the good that alone resembles God's authentic goodness. Being God-like by making the good their own is in itself the sole means human beings have of resembling their Maker, whose goodness is self-authenticating. A poor man of independent spirit will prefer his own, earned morsel of bread rather than enjoy the unearned delicacies offered to him as an act of benevolence at a rich man's table. When he is obliged due to circumstances to accept charity, the food, as 'bread of shame', becomes bitter in his mouth.[5]

Does the doctrine of the 'bread of shame' have any significance for Jewish theological thinking today? Obviously it has none in a naturalistic philosophy of Judaism or in a theism that has no use for the entire concept of a Hereafter. I find it quite alarming that among so many Jewish thinkers today, the doctrine, common to all the great theistic religions, is nowadays either abandoned completely or reinterpreted in terms of the individual living on in his works, or in his children, or in the lives he has influenced. It is hard, to say the least, for a committed theist to believe that God has created the marvellous individual personality only to 'waste it', in the language of the contemporary thriller. If belief in the Hereafter is affirmed, then the doctrine of the 'bread of shame' fits in very well with the rightful modern affirmation of human independence, as well as providing a powerful response to the Marxist critique of religion as 'pie in the sky when you die'. According to this doctrine the 'pie' has been baked, so to speak, by the individual himself. God's grace is still at work but, by that very grace, eternal bliss is earned by the person who strives to approximate to it in this life. And there is still the wider hope that, as the Jewish mystics affirm, no soul will be permanently lost but, according to this view, those souls will perforce be obliged, through their own free choice, to enjoy that immeasurable bliss as the 'bread of shame'. The mystery remains of course. In this area everything must obviously be left to God. Yet it is not too far-fetched to read the

[5] Dessler used to refer frequently to the doctrine in his discourses, but the only direct reference is in his *Mikhtav me'eliyahu*, ed. Aryeh Carmel, 4 vols. (Jerusalem, 1983), iv. 8 ff. Here he discusses the question in connection with the angels who have no free choice, yet the theme is implicit throughout the work.

doctrine into the typically Jewish affirmation of both this world and the next in the famous statement of the second-century *tanna*, Rabbi Jacob, who is reported to have said, 'One hour of repentance and good deeds in this world is better than the whole life of the world to come; and one hour of bliss in the world to come is better than the whole life of this world' (*Pirkei avot* 4: 17).

NINE

MYSTICISM

M Y FASCINATION with Jewish mysticism began when my *rebbe* in the yeshiva, Rabbi Yitshak Dubov, a prominent Lubavitcher hasid, took me and another boy, on sabbath afternoons, through the intricacies of Habad thought, and sang the Habad melodies full of mystical yearning at the communal meal on these afternoons in the yeshiva. Although, officially, Manchester Yeshiva was a Lithuanian-type yeshiva, looking somewhat askance on mystical fervour,[1] Rabbi Dubov's extra-curricular activities were tolerated. I personally found these activities to be more than a welcome relief from the yeshiva's emphasis on matter-of-fact talmudics. It all came as a breath of fresh air to an impressionable youngster.

My mystical inclinations, whether real or imaginary, were fortified when Rabbi Dubov invited some of the students to his home to meet Rabbi Yitshak Horowitz, known as Reb Yitshak Masmid (*masmid* is the Ashkenazi Hebrew term used of someone who constantly studies Torah), a leading exponent of mystical theology in the Habad vein. This emaciated figure seemed to us youngsters a typical ascetic (none of us had actually known of this term) whose head reached to the heavens. Reb Yitshak Masmid ate very little but drank heavily in the belief that alcohol could act as a stimulant to the deeper longings of the soul. I recall Reb Yitshak addressing the yeshiva students one night immediately after we had carried out the traditional ceremony of the benediction over the moon (*kidush levanah*), a mystical rite if ever there was one. In this ceremony, carried out preferably in the open, at the beginning of the month, a benediction is recited in which God is praised for the creation of the moon and the other heavenly bodies. There follows the declaration, recited three times while standing on tip-toe, 'Just as I dance towards thee [the moon] but cannot reach thee, so may none of my

---

[1] See the pioneering study by Allan Nadler, *The Faith of the Mithnagdim* (Baltimore, Md., 1997).

enemies be able to approach me for evil.' A biblical verse is then recited three times: 'Terror and dread fall upon them; by the greatness of Thine arm they are as still as a stone' (Exod. 15: 16). This verse is then recited backwards three times. Then follows the thrice-repeated declaration 'David, King of Israel, is alive and enduring', after which one turns to three different persons, saying to each, 'Peace upon you', to which the response is 'Upon you be peace'. There follows the prayer, also recited three times, 'Let there be a good sign and a good fortune for us and for all Israel. Amen.' After a number of further declamations, the rite ends with the prayer: 'May it be Thy will, O Lord my God and God of my fathers, to fill the flaw of the moon, that there be no diminution in it. May the light of the moon be like the light of the sun and like the light of the seven days of creation, as it was before it was diminished, as it is said "the two great luminaries" [Gen. 1: 16]. And may there be fulfilled for us the verse that is written: "They shall seek the Lord, their God, and David, their king" [Hos. 3: 5]. Amen.' This is the ceremony as recorded in the old prayerbooks; more recent prayerbooks omit the more magical passages. The whole is an amalgam of various ideas found especially in Kabbalah. In kabbalistic thought the moon represents the Shekhinah, the female aspect of Deity, which like the moon, waxes and wanes, so to speak. In non-kabbalistic language, the waxing moon represents God's indwelling Presence, which is withheld from its fullest manifestation until the advent of the Messiah. When we yeshiva students went out into the cold night, bathed in the light of the moon, and performed the rite, we would have had little inclination to engage in demythologizing even if we had known of this concept. We were attracted by the sheer mystery of the rite, including, or perhaps one should say especially, the magical elements: the threefold repetitions, the dancing towards the moon (a hangover from ancient moon worship the sceptic would no doubt say), and the greetings to one another as if we had just returned from a long journey, as, indeed, we had.

Reb Yitshak Masmid reminded us on that occasion that the very stones cry out to be trodden on by a student of God's word as contained in the Torah. We sensed, at least at that awesome moment, that the 'flaw' in the moon, referred to in the prayer of *kidush levanah*, truly represented the flaw in the Shekhinah that endures as long as the world remains in its unredeemed state. Reb Yitshak returned to Europe, where he was murdered by the Nazis, but none of us remained the same after his visit. When, later on at the Gateshead *kolel*, I heard the discourses of Rabbi Dessler, a representative of the *musar* school mentioned earlier, I learned that this Lithuanian charismatic figure had also studied with Reb Yitshak Masmid during the latter's visit to England.

Kabbalah

Young though I was, I did have at that time an inkling of the saying of the kabbalists that nothing should be allowed to stand in the way of one whose soul moves him to study Kabbalah. I have no doubt now that there was a strong element of spiritual pride in the desire to belong to the élite, to those who were privileged to pierce the veil, a prurient desire to enter into the mysteries denied to lesser folk. The relationship between mysticism and sex has often been discussed by psychiatrists. This element, too, was bound to be present in full-blooded adolescents leading a life of study with no contact with women outside the confines of their own families. I must add that while talmudics as taught in a rather unimaginative way in the yeshiva could be dry and uninspiring, once I had begun to study on my own and later on with advanced students in Gateshead I found the study of the Talmud a thoroughly absorbing and exciting activity. This study, consisting of acute, analytical reasoning, as described in the chapter on Orthodoxy, kept my feet on the ground and prevented me from any absurd dream that I could become a mystic adept. Yet for a long time afterwards, even when I came to recognize the questionable aspects of kabbalism, there still lurked at the back of my mind the notion that somehow Kabbalah contained the key with which the door to the divine was to be opened. My immature dreams were only finally shattered when I began my studies at University College.

I was advised to read Gershom Scholem's classical work, *Major Trends in Jewish Mysticism*,[2] by my teacher at University College, Dr Siegfried Stein. Scholem's historical approach came like a shocking and at the same time invigorating cold shower. Scholem and his school showed that Kabbalah arose in Provence in the twelfth century and was a series of purely human speculations rather than, as I had innocently assumed in my yeshiva days, a series of communications by God regarding His true nature. Here, once again, I came to see that when the historical critical methodology was applied, while it did not necessarily create havoc for

[2] 3rd edn. (London, 1955).

faith, any theological position on the role of mysticism in Jewish life could not ignore the results of scholarly research into its origins.

In kabbalistic thought, the *sefirot* (the powers or potencies or energies in the Godhead) are conceived after a human pattern. Indeed, for the kabbalists the human will, wisdom, and emotions and the very organs of the human body mirror the realities of the sefirotic world. The kabbalistic solution to the problem of biblical anthropomorphism is that there does actually exist, in the world of the *sefirot*, a reality, a spiritual entity, known, for instance, as the hand of God, of which the human hand in the form it assumes in the finite, material world is a pale reflection. Since man is mightily formed on the pattern of the *sefirot*, he is at the end of a great chain of being which reaches back to them and hence—and here is the basic thrust of Kabbalah—human deeds have a cosmic effect. When human beings are virtuous they send beneficent impulses on high to promote the harmony of the *sefirot* and cause the flow of the divine grace. When humans are vicious they send baneful impulses on high to disturb the harmony of the *sefirot* so that the flow of divine grace is impeded. The importance of man in the kabbalistic scheme is probably the reason why Kabbalah came to be seen as a significant doctrine in Judaism, despite such strange features as the dynamic Godhead and the existence of male and female principles, ideas which are highly unconventional, to say the least, in Jewish thought. In normative Judaism the role of man in God's plan is highly significant.

This is the kabbalistic system upon which is based the great kabbalistic work, the Zohar, which first saw light towards the end of the thirteenth century in Spain. A further elaboration was introduced by the famed kabbalist of sixteenth-century Safed, Isaac Luria, known as the Ari, 'the Lion'. The Lurianic version of Kabbalah seeks to answer the question of how the finite world, containing evil, falsehood, multiplicity, and imperfection, can have emerged from the perfect, infinite God. Lurianic Kabbalah is concerned not only with the sefirotic processes but also with that which preceded them—at least at the stage when the *sefirot* begin to emerge as differentiated entities from the recesses of Ein Sof ('the Limitless', God as He is in Himself). This step in the process is one of withdrawal or contraction—*tsimtsum*. In order to make room, as it were, for the *sefirot*, the Ein Sof 'withdrew from Himself into Himself' to leave an 'empty space', the primordial space into which there eventually emerged space and time as we know them.

According to the kabbalists there are two aspects to the Torah, one concealed, the other revealed. The revealed aspect consists of the surface meaning as understood by the tradition. The concealed or hidden aspect consists of the kabbalistic doctrines, which are said to be the real inner meaning known only to the mystical adepts who handed this down from master to disciple. The very word Kabbalah (from the root *kibel*, 'to receive') means the received tradition. How do the kabbalists know about this hidden meaning? They reply that it was revealed to the second-century CE teacher Rabbi Simeon bar Yohai, who, according to the Talmud (*Shabbat* 33*b*), hid in a cave, together with his son, Rabbi Eleazar, in fear of persecution by the Roman authorities. There the two teachers received various revelations and these were known to the kabbalists. Towards the end of the thirteenth century, the Spanish kabbalist Moses de Leon presented what he claimed were the revelations vouchsafed to Rabbi Simeon bar Yohai in the Book of the Zohar. Luria, during his stay on an island in Egypt, claimed to have been visited by the prophet Elijah, from whom he received further illuminations. When Luria settled in Safed, he gathered around him a small circle of disciples, prominent among them Hayim Vital, who recorded Luria's teachings. Despite opposition at first, the Zohar became the third canonical work for many Jews, the other two being the Bible and the Talmud. Thus, for many, the three works came to be seen as 'the Torah', that is, not three separate works but a single Torah, the essential teachings of which were given to Moses at Sinai during the forty days and nights he stayed on the mount. Just as the Talmud is the depository of the Oral Torah, the Zohar (and the Lurianic writings, according to the majority of the later kabbalists) contains the inner Oral Torah. It is true that many Orthodox Jews believe that you do not have to believe in the Zohar and Kabbalah in order to qualify as an Orthodox Jew, and there is considerable discussion on the actual ruling in cases where the halakhah is in conflict with Kabbalah, yet very few Orthodox Jews today deny that the Zohar is a sacred book in a category of its own. The Zohar is frequently quoted in Orthodox works as an authoritative text.

To give an illustration of how it all works, we can refer to the Zoharic comment on the first verse of the Bible. In the Hebrew the verse reads *bereshit bara elohim et hashamayim ve'et ha'arets*, usually translated as 'In the beginning God created the heavens and the earth.' The verb *bara*, in the plain meaning 'He created', has the word *elohim* ('God') as its subject, i.e. 'God created'. The word *bereshit* can be translated not as 'In the beginning' but as 'with a beginning', which is how the Zohar understands this word. Moreover, the subject of *bara* is 'hidden' and does not occur in the verse. The hidden subject is the Ein Sof and the first of the *sefirot*, Keter, 'the Crown'. Keter is conceived of as a will to will, not, as yet, a will to create. The real beginning of the sefirotic process is represented by the *sefirah* Hokhmah ('Wisdom'), the stage at which all the details of creation are contained *in potentia* in the divine Mind. The realization of the full details in that Mind is in Binah ('Understanding'), from which emanate Tiferet, the male principle in the *sefirot*, known as 'Heaven', and the female principle, Malkhut, known as 'Earth'. Thus the Zohar reads the verse as describing the emergence of the *sefirot* from the Ein Sof. In its Zoharic interpretation the verse reads, 'With a beginning [by means of Hokhmah] [He, Ein Sof, the hidden subject not actually mentioned in the verse since it is beyond any verbal expression, almost like X or Y as a symbol] created [i.e. caused to be emanated] *elohim* [God, but here the divine name represents Binah; and from Binah] the heavens and the earth [the male and female principles in the Godhead together with the other lower *sefirot*].'

The 'death of the kings' in Genesis 36 provides another example of mystical interpretation. It is based on the Zohar, but receives its full elaboration in the Lurianic scheme. For the kabbalists it is inconceivable that the Torah would waste time in telling us about Edomite kings. They consequently interpreted this and similar apparently irrelevant material in the Bible as referring, in the inner meaning, not to humans at all but to processes in the divine unfolding.

The Historical View

Attracted though I was, and to some extent still am, to the mystical approach to Judaism, thanks to Scholem and his school I could no longer swallow Kabbalah whole or even partially. If fundamentalism is untenable with regard to the Bible and the rabbinic literature, it is hardly an option when it comes to the Zohar and Kabbalah in general. Historically considered, the kabbalistic picture of how it all came to be is simply wrong. However it all happened, the kabbalistic account is completely unhistorical.

For anyone with even the faintest historical sense, the Zoharic exposition of Genesis 1: 1 and the Lurianic account of the 'death of the kings' are quite impossible as biblical exegesis. The kabbalistic doctrines originated in the circle of Isaac the Blind in Provence in the twelfth century. Even though many of the ideas found in Kabbalah may well go back to ancient times, there is no reference to the system either in the Bible or in the talmudic literature. Many kabbalistic ideas are obviously the result of speculation on the relationship between God and creation, and the influence of medieval Jewish philosophy is evident throughout. The Zohar seems to be aware of the anachronism involved, since it consciously avoids much direct reference to the term *sefirot*, for that would give the game away. It is not suggested that the Zoharic authors did not believe that the idea contained in the verse is its true meaning, but they seem to acknowledge that terms like *sefirot* and Ein Sof were of a much later coinage.

The role of Moses de Leon in the composition of the Zohar was a subject of debate from the day this mysterious book first appeared. How could it be the work of the second-century teacher, Rabbi Simeon bar Yohai, when it attributes to this sage references to the Crusades and gives a mystical interpretation of the Portuguese word *esnoga* referring to the synagogue? Orthodox kabbalists retort that Rabbi Simeon foresaw that the Crusades would occur, just as he foresaw the names of Babylonian teachers who appear in the Zohar but lived long after Rabbi Simeon's death. The passage on the word *esnoga* may be a later interpolation. If the latter principle is relied upon it means that so much of the Zohar is of a really late date that it is hard to distinguish these passages from the 'authentic' words of Rabbi Simeon bar Yohai. The whole discussion is treated adequately by Isaiah Tishby in his *The Wisdom of the Zohar*,[3] and there is no need to repeat it all here. The consensus of scholars today is that Moses de Leon was the actual author of the Zohar, with other authors adding parts at a later date, and they have detected differences and even contradictions between these later sections and the Zohar proper. Once it is recognized that the Zohar is a human work, there is, naturally, no guarantee that its teachings are necessarily sound and true. Of course, to say this is not to deny that the Zohar does contain many wondrous teachings, but the appeal of these lies in the effect they have on the religious mind and heart. Nowadays, we are entitled to marvel at some of the kabbalistic insights, but we can no longer declare,

[3] Oxford, 1989.

as did the kabbalists themselves, that there really are *sefirot* and that God really did hint at the sefirotic doctrine when He 'dictated' Genesis and the passage regarding the death of the Edomite kings to Moses. Moderns cannot accept that God 'dictated' the book of Genesis to Moses even in its plain meaning. We are back to King David and Psalm 137. Our newly acquired sense of history simply does not allow us to see King David as the author of this psalm or Simeon bar Yohai as the author of the Zohar. The same historical critical method is employed in rejecting both these conclusions.

Furthermore, the doctrine in which the world is governed by the ten *sefirot* was attacked by early Jewish sages as a breach of Jewish monotheism, 'worse' than Christianity, it was protested, in its idea of ten in one rather than three in one. Again, Kabbalah itself, while undoubtedly the fruit of intense mystical thought and experience, does not constitute a form of Jewish mystical theology. The hearts of the mystically inclined may still leap with rapture at kabbalistic exuberances, but such a leap is quite different from reflection on mysteries conveyed by God Himself. The element of sheer poetry in Kabbalah is captivating; the Zohar is full of exquisite religious poetry, much of which was never intended to be taken literally. When Jewish practices are based on Kabbalah, as some of them are, it is banal to reject them simply on the grounds that their origin is incorrectly understood by the kabbalists. If the biblical precepts have become binding, in the Masorti view, irrespective of origin, there is no logic in rejecting practices based on Kabbalah because of their allegedly base or superstitious origin. Value, not origins, is the issue. In other words, whatever value is inherent in kabbalistic practices, it is this value that should be sought, not the mere fact that it is in Kabbalah. There is the further point that the very fact of its acceptance by the tradition itself endows Kabbalah with a certain significance. We may not accept, for instance, the kabbalistic interpretation of the rite of staying up all night on the eve of Shavuot to study the Torah, yet this pious habit has acquired, by way of Kabbalah, an entrance into Jewish life, even among many Reform Jews, and surely it is a practice worthy to be followed as valuable in itself. The practice of singing the *Lekhah dodi* hymn composed by the kabbalist Solomon Alkabets to welcome the Sabbath Bride is universally followed today even though, in the original hymn, the reference to the Sabbath Bride is not only to the sabbath here below but to the Shekhinah united with Her Spouse on high. Of course, a good deal depends both on whether a particular practice has been adopted by the community of Israel and on whether it is seen as being of religious value.

A demythologizing process is possible in which the values of kabbalistic ideas can be seen to behind the actual formulations. Take the mystical treatise *Tomer devorah* ('The Palm Tree of Deborah') by the Safed kabbalist Rabbi Moses Cordovero (1522–70). In this treatise it is shown how the mystical adept can imitate the various qualities of the *sefirot* in order to become closer to God and affect the cosmos by stirring up these qualities. At the stage of Keter, Cordovero comments, there is only complete mercy and love, the *sefirot* of Hesed and Gevurah (Lovingkindness and Power) not having emerged as yet. So, too, in the saintly life, there is a stage in which only mercy and compassion should prevail. With regard to Hokhmah, man should appreciate that the divine wisdom extends in its merciful providence to all creatures, and man should imitate this aspect of the sefirotic realm. As Cordovero puts it:

Furthermore, his mercy should extend to all creatures, neither destroying nor despising any of them. For the Supernal Wisdom is extended to all created things—minerals, plants, animals, and humans. This is the reason for the rabbis warning us against despising food. In this way man's pity should be extended to all the works of the Blessed One just as the Supernal Wisdom despises no created thing, for they are all created from that source, as it is written [Ps. 104: 24]: 'In wisdom Thou hast made them all' . . . In this way he should despise no created thing, for they were all created in Wisdom. He should not uproot anything which grows, unless it is necessary, nor kill any living thing unless it is necessary . . . To sum up, to have pity on all things and not to hurt them depends on Wisdom, unless it be to elevate them higher and higher, from plant to animal and from animal to human. For then it is permitted to uproot the plant and to kill the beast, to bring merit out of demerit.[4]

One need not accept the kabbalistic scheme in order to appreciate Cordovero's sublime ideas of human co-operation with God in preserving the universe He has created. The mystical notion of an earth crammed with heaven speaks to those with ears to hear even if they do not believe in the dynamic Godhead of Kabbalah.

Or take the statement of Hayim Vital, Luria's disciple, on *tsimtsum*:

Know that before there was any emanation and before any creatures were created, a simple higher light filled everything. There was no empty space in the form of

---

[4] *The Palm Tree of Deborah*, trans. Louis Jacobs (London, 1960), 83–5.

a vacuum but all was filled with that simple infinite light. This infinite light had nothing in it of beginning or end and was all one simple, equally distributed light. This is known as 'the light of Ein Sof'. There arose in His simple will the will to create worlds and produce emanations in order to realize His perfect acts, His names, and His attributes. This was the purpose for which the worlds were created. Ein Sof then concentrated His being in the middle point, which was at the very centre, and He withdrew that light, removing it in every direction away from that centre point. There then remained around the very centre point an empty space, a vacuum. This withdrawal was equidistant around that central empty space, so that the space left empty was completely circular. It was not in the form of a square with right angles. For Ein Sof withdrew Himself in circular fashion, equidistant in all directions. The reason for this was that since the light of Ein Sof is equally spaced out it follows by necessity that His withdrawal should be equidistant in all directions, and that He could not have withdrawn Himself in one direction rather than in any other. It is well known in the science of mathematics that there is no figure more equal than the circle. It is otherwise with the figure of the square, which has protruding right angles, or with a triangle or with any other figure.[5]

Vital continues that into this empty space the *sefirot* emerged, followed eventually by four worlds, one beneath the other. Vital concludes:

Before the emergence of these four worlds Ein Sof was One and His name One in a wondrous, mystical unity of a kind beyond the comprehension even of those angels nearest to Him. For the mind of no creature can comprehend Him, since He has neither place nor limit nor name.

Stripping this astonishing statement of its kabbalistic details, we are not being too imaginative to find in it acute speculation on the great mystery of creation, though expressed in a numinous manner. This is part of the appeal of Kabbalah. It dares to speak the unspeakable, to allow man to think great thoughts on the way finite creatures can have emerged from the Infinite. While Kabbalah is not entirely rational, it certainly cannot be dismissed as nonsensical. If one tries to get behind Kabbalah, if one tries to discover not what the kabbalists are actually saying but what lies beneath the surface, Kabbalah can find a response at least in the hearts of the mystically inclined.

What of direct mystical experience as opposed to kabbalistic speculation? In my book *Jewish Mystical Testimonies*,[6] I have translated from the Hebrew some descriptions of such experiences—of the Riders of the Chariot, for example, who employed certain techniques in order to

---

[5] *Mevo she'arim*, ed. J. L. Ashlag (Tel Aviv, 1961), i.   [6] New edn. (New York, 1996).

embark on a psychic journey to the heavenly halls. It has to be said that the Jewish mystics were normally very reticent about their personal experiences, so that most of us cannot follow them in any clear way. We do not know how to proceed and have no way of testing whether their encounters were authentic, and whether they really met God. Against this is the evidence of mystical adepts in all religions. It would certainly be rash to dismiss it all as sheer delusion. Reference should also be made to Max Kadushin's 'normal mysticism'.[7] According to this great exponent of rabbinic Judaism, mystical experience in the Jewish religion is not a kind of flight into a higher world but a daily affair, experienced whenever the Jew recites a benediction in which he addresses God directly for example. Rabbi Aryeh Kaplan has written a number of works on Jewish meditation in which he draws on the kind of material contained in my *Jewish Mystical Testimonies*. The problem with Kaplan's approach is whether moderns with a very different psychic make-up from the saints and mystics of former ages can really follow them in their mystic quest.

Hasidism

As for so-called practical Kabbalah, in which the kabbalist tries to use the mysteries in order to change nature, this does smack heavily of magic and superstition. Of course, if one believes in Kabbalah as revealed truth, one may believe that it is possible to coerce the *sefirot*. But how many moderns can accept such a position? Recently, there has been a surge of interest in Kabbalah, an interest which all too frequently borders on the occult, the nonsensical, and the magical. Current 'pop' Kabbalah, on which there has been a spate of works, some of them attractively presented, often gets it wrong and also tends to become a substitute for traditional Judaism, a kind of Jewish Yoga or Zen, all under the heading of 'spirituality'. And so we turn to hasidism, also currently enjoying a massive resurgence and attracting, as fellow-travellers, many modern Jews who do not consider themselves to be Orthodox. It is not hard to discover the appeal of hasidism to religious Jews. This colourful, warm, spiritually sensitive movement offers, as has often been said, mysticism for the masses. Many young Jews, disillusioned by conventional religion, believe that in hasidism they can find the greater

[7] Max Kadushin, 'Normal Mysticism', in id., *The Rabbinic Mind* (New York, 1965), 194–272.

inwardness they crave. Why go to Hare Krishna or the Moonies, they are told by those concerned to win them over to traditional Judaism, when you can get the soulfulness for which you long from this thoroughly Jewish movement? It is notoriously difficult to detect the Jewishness of a movement. The *mitnagedim*, the eighteenth-century opponents of hasidism, roundly declared that hasidism is far from being thoroughly Jewish and, in its panentheistic theology (the doctrine that all things are contained in God) and its excessive veneration of the *rebbe*, is not Jewish at all. Modernist Jews cannot accept hasidism as their philosophy of Judaism because, like Kabbalah upon which the movement is based, its conclusions are derived from fundamentalist premisses. Martin Buber may have been responsible for a neo-hasidic movement, one with very few followers in the modern world, but to be a real hasid you have to accept the following propositions: that Kabbalah is the result of a divine communication, and that the hasidic *tsadik* or *rebbe* is so spiritually endowed that he can influence nature, perform miracles, and act as an infallible guide to his followers. One cannot rule out *a priori* that God has bestowed supernatural powers on certain holy men, but how could we know in each particular case that He has done so? In point of fact, a would-be hasid has to choose as his master a particular *rebbe*. Usually, there is no real choice; the master is the one who has served as such for the hasid's family. After the destruction of European Jewry, links with the past were largely severed, but a few hasidic dynasties have survived and are today often more active than ever before, and in greater numbers, in Israel, the USA, and other countries.

Basically, all hasidic literature consists of counsel for the attainment of *ḥasidut* (saintliness), although much of the literature is ambiguous on the question as to whether the way in all its fullness is reserved for the *tsadik* or is intended to apply to every sincere hasid. Even the tales of the *tsadikim*, a prominent feature of hasidic life, were partly intended to provide examples of saintly conduct for emulation by the hasid or, where emulation was considered inappropriate, for the hasid to draw lessons from them for his own, admittedly inferior, strivings. The classic hasidic texts, the hasidic Torah, amount to a vast library of spiritual guidance. It should also be said that the hasidic masters tend to be suspicious of a hasid attempting flights of soul that are not for him. Rabbi Tsevi Elimelekh of Dynów (1785–1841), for example, in his *Derekh pikudeikha* holds that it is wrong for a man consciously to desire a high degree of spiritual elevation.[8] This master comments as follows on the verse 'Neither shalt thou go up by steps unto my altar, that thy nakedness be not uncovered thereon' (Exod. 20: 23):

To my mind there is a hint in this precept that a man should not [consciously] seek elevation and lofty stages even in God's service, namely, to wish to attain to the holy spirit or to wish Elijah to appear to him and the like. If God does honour him with some elevated stage, he should give thanks to the Lord, Who is good, but he himself should not seek great things. Rather should he serve the Lord in love and fear and simplicity, like a son who strives on behalf of a father he loves more than himself. But if the idea comes into his mind that he is worthy to attain to elevated stages, then, God forbid, he will be scrutinized and his shame uncovered. Consequently, let a man not seek consciously for this but hope in the Lord and do good, namely, that which the Torah commands us to do. It is otherwise with regard to the attainment of the holy spirit and the appearance of Elijah and such like. We are not commanded concerning these in the Torah, yet when a man is honoured in this manner from Heaven he is then obliged to give thanks to the Lord for His gracious and free gifts. This is the meaning of 'Neither shalt thou go up by steps', namely, your shame will be revealed that you do not really care to serve God for His own sake, like a son who strives etc., you seek only your own greatness. Understand this well.

Judging by contemporary hasidic attitudes, hasidim today would question whether this author's admonition could conceivably be addressed to them. They would in all probability refuse to entertain for one moment the thought that they could possibly reach the elevated stages of which he speaks. That is best left to the *tsadik*.

It might be worthwhile, at this stage, to consider some examples of hasidic 'Torah' on the theme of Jacob's dream:

And he dreamed, and behold a ladder set up on the earth, and the top of it reached to heaven: and behold the angels of God ascending and descending on it. (Gen. 28: 12)

This dream of Jacob has received many varied interpretations in the history of Jewish exegesis.[9] The hasidic masters read their own interpretations into the narrative, obviously fascinating to them, of a ladder linking heaven and earth. Here I shall examine three typical interpretations found in the hasidic classics.

[8] [Lemberg, 1851] (Jerusalem, n.d.), 172–5.
[9] A useful summary of midrashic and medieval comments on Jacob's ladder is given by Nehama Leibowitz in her *Studies in the Book of Genesis* (Jerusalem, 1972), 298–304.

Rabbi Jacob Joseph of Polonnoye (d. *c*.1784)

In the writings of this seminal hasidic author[10] the dream of Jacob receives various interpretations. Like most hasidic authors, Rabbi Jacob Joseph presents no systematic treatment of a theme but rather comments as the spirit moves him. In one passage in his *Toledot ya'akov yosef* he interprets the dream as symbolic of the *tsadik* at a low stage (*madregah*) of his spiritual ascent.[11] At this stage the *tsadik* is 'set up on the earth'; he is earthbound and comparatively remote from God. Yet precisely because he is aware of his lowly stage and is distressed at his descent from holiness, he is moved to rise higher; his head reaches heavenward. The more a man perceives himself to be remote from God, the more God, who dwells with the contrite of spirit, is with him to help him rise higher. The *malakhim* ('angels' but here understood as 'those who are sent') are the members of the Jewish people who have been sent into the world in order to perfect their souls by living the life of holiness as ordained by the Torah. There are a number of groups (*kitot*; R. Jacob Joseph possibly uses this word because the *mitnagedim* dubbed the hasidim as belonging to a *kat*, a 'sect'). There are those who cleave to the *tsadik* (*ledabek et atsmam*, referring to the ideal of *devekut*, attachment to God through attachment to the *tsadik*) even when they perceive that he is lowly of spirit. They descend with the *tsadik* and are not put off by the fact that he is at an inferior stage, because they know that he will rise much higher and take them with him in his ascent. The word *bo*, usually translated 'on it', is taken to mean 'because of him'. Those sent into the world who attach themselves to the *tsadik* rise through him from their descent. Others (an obvious dig at the *mitnagedim*), however, ignore the *tsadik* and certainly have no desire to become attached to him. On the contrary, they exalt themselves over him and feel greatly superior to him. When the *tsadik* rises these people cannot rise with him since there is no cure for one who despises a *talmid ḥakham*.[12] In the

[10] On R. Jacob Joseph and his doctrine of the *tsadik*, see Samuel H. Dresner, *The Zaddik* (New York, 1960).

[11] [Koretz, 1780] (repr. Jerusalem, 1966), *Vayetse, 22a*.

[12] *Shabbat* 119*b*. It is well known that the hasidim intentionally reinterpreted talmudic passages which refer to the *talmid ḥakham* to refer to the *tsadik*; see Joseph Perl's preface to his satire on hasidism, *Megaleh temirin* (Vienna, 1819), n. 1: 'Even the name *talmid ḥakham*, which, at first glance, does refer to scholars [*lomedim*], as the *lomedim* say for our many sins, applies to the *tsadikim*.'

next verse it says, 'Behold the Lord stood over him', that is to say, the Shekhinah is with the *tsadik* even when he is at his lowly stage.

Rabbi Moshe Hayim Ephraim of Sudylkow (d. 1800)

Rabbi Moshe Hayim Ephraim, grandson of the Ba'al Shem Tov, was the author of *Degel maḥaneh efrayim*, after which he is known by the hasidim as 'the Degel'. The work was first published by the author's son in Korets in 1810.[13] The Degel's comment on Jacob's dream opens with a reference to a statement of his grandfather, the Ba'al Shem Tov. The Degel writes:

Contained in this passage [of the dream] is the mystery of greatness and small-ness [of soul]. The saying of my master, my grandfather, his soul is in Eden, his memory is for a blessing, is well known, that 'the living creatures run to and fro' [Ezek. 1: 14], and it is impossible for a man to remain always at the same stage, but he is obliged to ascend and descend. His descent is for the purpose of fur-ther ascent. For when a man becomes aware that he is in the state of smallness he prays to the Lord, as it is said: 'But from thence ye will seek the Lord thy God, and thou shalt find Him' [Deut. 4: 29]. The meaning of 'from thence' is, from whichever place you find yourself, as my master, my grandfather, his soul is in Eden, his memory is for a blessing, has said.

The mystic's 'dark night of the soul' is described by the Degel, using kabbalistic terminology, as 'smallness' (*katnut*), while enlargement of soul is described as 'greatness', *gadlut*. The application of the verse in Ezekiel about running to and fro was first made by Cordovero,[14] but this famous sixteenth-century mystic applies the idea to human cog-nizance of God. Cordovero remarks that when man engages in worship he cannot help having a picture of God in his mind, but whatever he de-picts is totally inadequate since God is beyond all comprehension. Man must, therefore, run to and fro in his mind, running to affirm God's ex-istence and then immediately recoiling from the mental picture he is bound to have. In the saying of the Ba'al Shem Tov quoted by the Degel, this running to and fro is applied not to cognitive awareness but to the states of *katnut* and *gadlut*. There is an ebb and flow in the mysti-cal life. The typical hasidic doctrine of *devekut* depicts a state which, as Rabbi Jacob Joseph also observed, is impossible for man to maintain all the time. When his mystical experience is intense, when his soul is

---

[13] (Jerusalem, 1963), 40–1. I discuss this passage in my *Hasidic Thought* (New York, 1976), 44–7.   [14] *Elimah rabati* (Brody, 1881), ch. 1, section 10, 2*b*.

completely absorbed in contemplation of God, he is said to be in the
state of *gadlut*. But when he is remote from *devekut* he is in the state of
katnut. The word for 'living creatures' in the Ezekiel verse is *ḥayot*, but
this is pointed in hasidic interpretation to read *ḥiyut*, 'vitality'. Man's
spirit soars in rapture and is full of vitality when he is in the *gadlut* state,
but becomes weak when he is the *katnut* state. Yet the state of *katnut*
must not be despised. On the contrary, once the mystic appreciates that
he is in that state and is severely distressed at the diminution of his spiritual vitality, clear evidence that he has become remote from God, this
very fact is a spur for him to rise higher. The very descent is the spur to a
greater ascent. The descent is in order to ascend and is not a descent at
all but an ascent, just as one who climbs a ladder may need to step down
a rung or two in order to rest and then continue the ascent with renewed energy. 'From there' in the verse quoted by the Ba'al Shem Tov
means from wherever the mystic finds himself, even the *katnut* stage.
Indeed, the Ba'al Shem Tov implies, he can only seek his God from that
stage.

The phase used by the Degel, 'a descent for the purpose of ascent'
(*yeridah letsorekh aliyah*), is taken from the Talmud (*Makkot 7b*). There
are cases of accidental homicide for which a person is culpable and has to
go in exile to one of the refuge cities (Deut. 19: 1–15), but there are other
cases where he is not held culpable. If a man going down a ladder falls
off the ladder onto someone beneath him and kills the man upon whom
he falls, he is held to be culpable. But if he falls while climbing up the
ladder he is not culpable. The Talmud discusses whether he would be
held culpable if he fell while descending, but with his intention for the
descent being for the purpose of an ascent. This legal terminology is
employed by the Degel and in other hasidic works for the spiritual descent of the *tsadik*. This is not really a descent at all since it is for the purpose of the ascent.

The Degel continues that Jacob's ladder set up on the earth sym-
bolizes the mystic's descent. The top of the ladder reaches to heaven
since the *tsadik*'s soul soars higher precisely because the feet of the
ladder, in the ascent of which he obtains the fresh vitality by which to
rise, are on the earth, close to earthly things. In a passage from Jacob
Joseph of Polonnoye's *Toledot ya'akov yosef*, it is claimed that the descent of the *tsadik* is made chiefly so that he may raise his followers
to greater heights. In the Degel's analysis the *tsadik* himself needs to

descend to the state of *katnut* without which he can never attain the state of *gadlut*.

Rabbi Shelomo Zalman of Koputs (1830–1900)

Rabbi Shelomo Zalman's *Magen avot*[15] is a late hasidic work in the Habad line and can serve as a summary of Habad treatment of the ideas said to be implicit in Jacob's dream. Rabbi Shelomo Zalman's exposition is, however, shot through with kabbalistic terminology, all according to the particular Habad understanding. It is consequently impossible to reproduce all the technicalities in English. I shall give no more than a brief paraphrase which, it is hoped, manages to capture at least the gist of the argument.

In the Habad understanding of Lurianic Kabbalah the 'light' of Ein Sof pervades all to the extent that, from God's point of view, as it were, there is no universe and no creatures. But the infinite light of Ein Sof had to be screened and partly removed, as it were, to leave room for the *sefirot* and, ultimately, the finite creatures on earth to emerge. There are four worlds, one higher than the other. These are the worlds of Atsilut ('Emanation'), the highest of the four, the stage of the sefirotic realm; Beriyah ('Creation'); Yetsirah ('Formation'); and Asiyah ('Action', the source of this world on high and including this world itself). These four are abbreviated as ABYA. The *sefirot* of each world are present in the world immediately beneath but in a fainter form, so to speak, since each lower world is more remote from Ein Sof. Thus the Hokhmah ('Wisdom') of Beriyah descends from the Malkhut of Atsilut and so on down to the lowest of the *sefirot* of Asiyah. This whole process is known as *hishtalshelut ha'olamot*, the evolution of the worlds. But there is a paradox here. If the Ein Sof is all, how can there be four worlds or, indeed, anything at all? The answer is that, from our point of view, the worlds are real enough, but that it is God who keeps them in being, renewing them at every moment.

When the Jew recites the Shema, affirming the unity of God, his mind should embrace the whole process of the evolution of the worlds. He should trace back all the different forces through world after world until he reaches the Ein Sof. He should then, when he prays, retrace the whole process and so bring down God's blessing, since cosmic energy is required to keep the universe in being at every moment.

[15] (Berditchev, 1902), 22*a*–23*b*.

This is the meaning of the ladder. The ladder represents the ascent of all worlds to Ein Sof, which the mystic contemplates when he recites the Shema and by so doing assists the process. This ascent of the righteous helps the angels to sing their songs of glory, as a result of which divine grace flows freely throughout creation in glorious melody. But for the unification to be achieved the mystic has to sacrifice himself to God, that is to say, to become lost to himself as his mind dwells on the glorious scheme.

Rabbi Shelomo Zalman adds that there are, in fact, two ladders, the holy one he has described and the unholy one, in which the demonic powers also draw down their sustenance from the Ein Sof. The letters of the word *sulam*, when transposed, form the word *semel*, an image, since the unholy is a perverse image of the holy. This unholy ladder also reaches from earth to heaven and is influenced by human deeds, but in the opposite way to the holy ladder. The angels of God ascend the unholy ladder through man's evil deeds. The more the mystic's thought is on the holy ladder, the less the power of the unholy ladder. The more the angels descend the unholy ladder, the greater the ascent of the angels on the holy ladder, and all through human deeds.

The interpretation of Jacob's ladder was widespread among all hasidic groups, but each master tried to introduce his own original ideas. We simply do not have sufficient information to enable us to know how such ideas passed from master to master and hasid to hasid, although once the major hasidic works had been published it was the book that was responsible for the spread of the ideas. Yet each master seems to have believed that he, too, could make his own individual contribution, since the Torah has many facets. However, in later hasidic works there is comparatively little on Jacob's ladder, perhaps because the later masters believed the subject to have been exhausted.

All this provides an illustration of how, in hasidism, texts are used not as exegesis but in order to read hasidic ideas into them. No doubt the hasidic masters did believe that scriptural verses contained the hidden meaning read into them, a view hardly acceptable to a liberal supernaturalist. Yet a modernist, whose liberal stance cannot allow him to agree with the hasidic masters that what they are saying is the true hidden 'Torah', can still avail himself, albeit with reservations, of the insights provided for his own religious strivings. In this book, this distinction between the original meaning of a text and the insights that can be seen to be implied in that text is applied to Scripture and rabbinic literature as a whole.

Hasidism is, then, a captivating movement, with many attractive features. Leaving aside the hasidic mystical theology considered above, many devout Jews without any mystical pretensions love the hasidic way of life. But a modernist finds in hasidism features that are either superstitious or off-putting in other ways—the very secondary role of women, the *rebbe* blessing his followers after they present their petitions to him to pray on their behalf, the intolerance of some groups, and the equally upsetting patronizing attitude of others, to say nothing of the inability of moderns to accept the kabbalistic doctrines upon which hasidism is ultimately based. There is much to admire in hasidism, but there is also much to create barriers.

As an illustration of both the strengths and weaknesses of hasidism today we might examine the Lubavitch movement. The Lubavitch dynasty, guided by the seventh *rebbe*, Rabbi Menahem Mendel Schneersohn, set up a world-wide network of educational institutions, publishing translations of the Habad classics, the discourses of the *rebbe*, and other educational material, and sending emissaries to distant parts of the globe. Lubavitch '*mitsvah* tanks'—trucks manned by young men who drive around Jewish neighbourhoods and urge people to perform *mitsvot*—tour the streets with tefillin which they urge Jewish passers-by to put on in order to carry out the precept. In Soviet Russia, at great risk to life, Lubavitchers taught the Torah and saved many Jews for the faith. It is notorious, however, that the Lubavitchers believed that the *rebbe* was, in reality, the longed-for Messiah, waiting patiently to reveal himself as such. Even after the *rebbe*'s departure from the world, many faithful followers still believe that he is the Messiah who will return to earth to fulfil the messianic role of bringing mankind back to God. This in itself is sufficient reason to reject the Lubavitch doctrine. When was it ever heard in Judaism that the Messiah would die and come to life again? Apart from this, the movement is pre-modern, not chronologically but ideologically. Lubavitch is a town in White Russia, the traditions and way of life of which the Lubavitch movement seeks to preserve. Although today the movement uses modern technology for the furtherance of its aims, these aims are based on totally pre-modern premisses. A liberal supernaturalist can only become a Lubavitcher hasid by surrendering any sense of intellectual integrity he happens to possess.

The same applies to the other hasidic dynasties—Ger, Satmar, Vishnitz, Belz, Bobov, and so forth—their very names implying that traditional Judaism means for their adherents a Judaism that belongs to a previous age.

To sum up, for what it is worth, my own attitude: I have written books and articles on Kabbalah and hasidism, but personally accept only what they have to offer to those who wish to pursue the mystic quest. I can as little entertain personally my becoming a kabbalist or a hasid as I can be a fundamentalist.

TEN

MODERNISM AND INTERPRETATION

A S NOTED IN THE EARLIER CHAPTERS of this book, the contribution of the historical school has been to enable us to see the
classical sources of Judaism against their background. Anyone who tries
to study theology cannot afford to ignore the findings of the historian
but must erect his constructions on the results of their findings. He
may, of course, feel obliged to take issue with the historians on this or
that matter, but must then do so by employing the historical critical
methodology, and when he does this he is a historian himself. What a
theologian, *qua* theologian, is doing is asking not what actually happened in the past—that is the job of the historian—but rather how what
happened in the past is relevant to belief in the present; or, to put it rather
differently, how eternal truths expressed in a particular time can be
extrapolated from their time-bound expression, a notoriously difficult
task.

In this chapter I want to try to wed the theological approach to the
historical critical one by considering three significant Jewish themes:
the purpose of creation, 'enjoyment of life', and the doctrine of *imitatio
dei*.

In this very tentative exercise I examine the history of these themes in
Jewish thought with a view to showing how precarious is the position of
moderns, to be so convinced both that their new ideas are valuable and
that the sources anticipate these that they become guilty of anachronism
in their interpretations. It is this problem that is the main concern of this
chapter, yet since this is, after all, a book on theology, the three themes
are also considered on their own merits. In a sense I have been trying
to engage in this kind of exercise in the book as a whole. For all that,
it might be useful to have a special chapter on how theology can rely
on history while pursuing its own line. Since the wider question is

discussed, the chapter is entitled 'Modernism and Interpretation' rather than 'A Modernist Interpretation'.

The Purpose of Creation

In his famous, stimulating, but admittedly one-sided, essay *Ish haha-lakhah*,[1] Rabbi Joseph B. Soloveitchik observes that Rabbi Simhah Zelig, the disciple and colleague of Rabbi Hayim Soloveitchik (Rabbi Joseph's grandfather), told him the following story. Rabbi Hayim and Rabbi Simhah Zelig once paid a visit to someone's house in Vilna. While the two were waiting for their host to appear, they glanced at some books lying on the table, by Habad hasidim. They noticed that the books contained a debate on whether God created the world for the sake of His goodness or for the sake of His love. Rabbi Hayim remarked to Rabbi Simhah Zelig, 'Both views are in error. God created the world neither for the sake of His goodness nor for the sake of His love but for the sake of His will.'[2] This story is told by Soloveitchik to support his thesis that for 'halakhic man' the halakhah is of supreme importance because it constitutes the will of God, by which the world was created. Soloveitchik adds:

This view, set down by Maimonides as a firm principle in the *Guide*[3] and prevalent in many forms in voluntaristic religious and metaphysical systems—e.g. that of Solomon ibn Gabirol in *Mekor ḥayyim* ['Fountain of Life'] and that of Duns Scotus (who was influenced by the former)—is the very seal of halakhic man. The word was created in accordance with the will of God, who wills to contract His Divine Presence in it. Therefore, we are called to act and to arrange our lives in accordance with this fundamental idea.

In point of fact, other Jewish thinkers disagree with Maimonides' 'voluntaristic' view and, in any event, it by no means follows from the idea

[1] *Ish hahalakhah* (Jerusalem, 1979), 52–3; English trans. by Lawrence Kaplan, *Halakhic Man* (Philadelphia, Pa., 1983), 52–3.

[2] In a footnote, however, Soloveitchik points to statements in Habad literature which speak of Keter, the Will, as the divine ultimate, i.e. when Keter emerges from its concealment in Ein Sof. According to Kabbalah it is at this stage only a will to will, not, as yet, a will to create.

[3] *Guide of the Perplexed*, trans. M. Friedlander (London, 1881), iii. 13; trans. S. Pines (Chicago, Ill., 1963), i. 123–8; new trans. into Hebrew by J. Kapah (Jerusalem, 1971), 83–9. See also Isserles, *Torat ha'olah* (Königsberg, 1854), part 3, 47 end. Isserles says of Maimonides' view that the creation was due solely to God's will that 'there is no greater folly than this in his [Maimonides'] wisdom'.

that God created the world by His will that the halakhah is to be followed because it is the expression of that will. The truth is that the whole question of the purpose of creation has received different answers in the history of Jewish thought.

Sa'adya Gaon concludes the chapter on 'creation' in his *Sefer ha'emunot vehade'ot* ('Book of Beliefs and Opinions') with a reply to one who wonders for what purpose God created all creatures.[4] Sa'adya first suggests that God, being God, does not, like a human being, need a motive for what He does and may not have had any motive in creating the world. This seems to differ from the view that God created the world because He so willed. Sa'adya seems to be saying that arbitrary acts are possible for God, although, presumably, Sa'adya would qualify this by postulating that terms like 'will' and 'arbitrariness', taken as they are from human speech, are irrelevant to discourse on God. Yet, evidently dissatisfied with such an approach, Sa'adya suggests two reasons why God created all things. The first is to make known His wisdom to human beings. The second is to benefit human beings by their use of all these things so that they might obey Him. Thus, for Sa'adya, if the question 'What was the purpose of God?' is logically coherent, God created the world and its creatures for the sake of human beings, both so that they might know the wonders He performs and so that they might enjoy the goods that will lead them to obey Him. Sa'adya leaves the question open why God should wish humans to know Him and obey Him. Ultimately, it would seem, Sa'adya's view is not so different from that of Maimonides, who writes, 'Thus we are obliged to believe that all that exists was intended by Him, may He be exalted, according to His volition.' Maimonides quotes the verse 'The Lord hath made everything *lema'anehu*' (Prov. 16: 4). The word *lema'anehu* can mean 'for its own sake', i.e. of each creature, or it can mean 'for His sake', that is, for the sake of His will. Maimonides quotes in this connection the verse 'Everything that is called by My name and that I have created for My glory, I have formed it, yea, I have made it' (Isa. 43: 7). Maimonides equates 'for My glory' with 'for My will' because, as he states earlier in the same chapter, one can always ask why God needs mankind to worship Him, so that even this aim cannot be the ultimate one.

Naturally, in the 'organic' thinking of the ancient rabbis one looks in vain for anything approaching the systematic thinking of the medieval

---

[4] *Sefer ha'emunot*, part 1, ch. 4.

philosophers on the purpose of Creation.⁵ Probably the most-quoted rabbinic text in this connection is the *baraita* (an extra-mishnaic source that dates from the period of the Mishnah in the second century CE) found in the conclusion to *Pirkei avot* (6: 11):

Whatsoever the Holy One, blessed be He, created in His world, He created it only for His glory, as it is written, 'Everything that is called by My name and that I have created for My glory, I have formed it, yea, I have made it' [Isa. 43: 7]. And it says, 'The Lord shall reign for ever and ever' [Exod. 15: 18].

In *Midrash tanḥuma* (*Vayikra*, ed. Buber, p. 6*b*) the other verse mentioned by Maimonides is quoted: 'God says, "All creatures have been created to praise Me", as it is said, "Everything the Lord hath made for His own sake".' It is reasonable to conclude that 'for His glory' in the *Pirkei avot* passage means in order for His creatures to praise Him, as in the *Tanḥuma*. The reference in these two passages is only to human beings praising God. But in the ancient text *Perek shirah* all creatures sing, each voicing its particular praise to the glory of God. Rabbi Moses di Trani (1500–85), known as the Mabit, in his commentary on *Perek shirah* gives an interpretation of this hymn according to which its purpose is to remind man that all things were created for his benefit, so that, by reflection on this, he will be led to God.⁶

It would be difficult to find anywhere in Jewish or, for that matter, non-Jewish religious literature, a more startling, not to say outrageous, view on why God created the world than in the work *Kol sakhal* ('Voice of the Fool'). This book, an attack on the rabbinic tradition, was produced by the strange Italian genius Leon da Modena (1571–1648), who attributed the work to a Spanish Jew of the sixteenth century and provided a reply under the title *Sha'agat aryeh* ('Roar of the Lion'). Both works were published with an introduction and notes by I. S. Reggio in Gorizia in 1852. Reggio believed (the issue is still discussed by scholars⁷) that da Modena was himself the author of the *Kol sakhal*. Be that as it may, chapter 3 of the *Kol sakhal* is entitled 'The Purpose of the Creation'.

---

⁵ In general it is implied in rabbinic literature that God's purpose in creating the world was for the sake of the Torah; see the famous passage in Rashi on Gen. 1: 1.

⁶ *Perek shirah* was first published as an appendix to Moses di Trani (Mabit), *Beit elohim* [Venice, 1576] (Warsaw, 1872).

⁷ See Talia Fishman, *Shaking the Pillars: 'Voice of a Fool', an Early Modern Jewish Critique of Rabbinic Culture* (Stanford, Ca., 1977).

In it, after first stating that, while it is improper for man to speculate on God's intention it is just as improper to believe that His deeds are pointless, the author puts forward his own view. This is that God has created all creatures to serve man so that He may obtain pleasure from man's ups and downs in his struggles against adversity, much as a human king (the bizarre illustration is the author's) takes particular delight in the antics of his favourite dog, bird, horse, or monkey!

Reggio cannot refrain from protesting in the strongest terms against such a perverse view:

This view, original with da Modena, that all creatures have been created for their Creator's pleasure, has never even been contemplated either by the earlier or by the more recent thinkers. Apart from the fact that it is a false novelty invented only by him it is odd in the extreme and is obviously erroneous for many reasons, so that every truly God-fearing man, concerned with the honour of his Maker, will guard himself from stumbling over it and will keep it far distant from his boundary.[8]

In support of his view, da Modena quotes the verse 'Everything that is called by My name and that I have created for My glory', but, says Reggio, the plain meaning of the verse is quite different. (Reggio probably understands, according to the plain meaning, that the word *kol*, 'all', in the verse refers to the sons and daughters mentioned in the previous verse and not to all things in creation.) Reggio, no blind admirer of everything in the Talmud, says that he knows that someone will quote in da Modena's defence the *baraita* in *Pirkei avot*, which does quote the verse as a proof-text for the view that God has created everything for His glory, but no matter how many *baraitot* are found, they cannot succeed in suggesting any departure from the plain meaning of a scriptural verse.[9] As for da Modena's quote from Plato, 'Man is the plaything of God',[10] shall we construct our religion on the view of the Greek philosopher who denies the very cornerstone of our religion, that man is free to choose the good and reject evil? In reply to the question 'What is the purpose of the Creation?', Reggio remarks that, according to the teachings of our Torah, since God is all-good His goodness had to emerge from the potential to the actual, so that He created the world to benefit

[8] Reggio's n. 3, pp. 90–3.
[9] In this note Reggio takes Maimonides to task for departing from the plain meaning of Scripture.
[10] *Laws* VII, ed. R. G. Bury (Cambridge, Mass., 1926), 803.

His creatures, quoting the verse; 'For the Lord is good; His mercy endureth for ever' (Ps. 100: 5).

Another Italian author, very different from both da Modena and Reggio, the kabbalist Immanuel Hai Ricchi (1688–1743), deals with the question in his *Mishnat ḥasidim*.[11] At the very beginning of the work, Ricchi states that God created the world 'in order to show forth His perfection and to bestow of His goodness'. In the commentary *Ta'am etso* by Rabbi Pinhas Elijah Hurwitz (1765–1821) of Vilna, author of *Sefer haberit*, this is understood to mean that there are two reasons why God created the world: (1) to show forth His perfection; (2) to bestow of His goodness. Hurwitz remarks that the meaning of the first reason is that God wished to show forth His perfection in order to boast of it (*sic*). For a human being to boast of his achievements is unworthy, but there can be no objection to God doing so, says Hurwitz, any more than it can be said to be unfitting for Him to be proud, as the Scriptures declare. There are other reasons, too, why God created the world, continues Hurwitz, but these are the two main ones. Moreover, the first is the more significant, with the other being secondary. When the rabbis say that God only created the world for His glory they do not mean to negate the other reasons, but intend to point to this as the main reason. Consequently, Moses Hayim Luzzatto is greatly in error, avers Hurwitz, when he gives the second as the only reason at the beginning of two of his works. The rabbis give the reason that it was for His glory, and in the benediction recited at a wedding the wording is 'He created everything for His glory'.

With the exception of Hurwitz, these authors were Italians. The influence of the Italian Renaissance on Jewish thought can hardly be ignored, especially with regard to its universalism and humanism. The religious humanism of the Italian Renaissance found expression in Pico della Mirandola's support for it in Kabbalah.[12] Jewish thinkers such as Azariah

---

[11] [Cracow, 1889] (Jerusalem, 1982), 1*a*.

[12] Pico della Mirandola (1463–94) was an Italian nobleman who acquired a sound knowledge of Kabbalah, which he interpreted in accordance with his own religion, Christianity. He was followed by other Christians, who developed a Christian kabbalah. See Lewis W. Spitz, 'Humanism', in Mircea Eliade (ed.), *Encyclopaedia of Religion* (New York, 1987), vi. 513; Chaim Wardi, 'Pico della Mirandola, Giovanni', *Encyclopaedia Judaica* (Jerusalem, 1972), xiii. 500–1; and Robert Bonfil, *Rabbis and Jewish Communities in Renaissance Italy* (London, 1993), 280 for the attempt by Italian authors to combine philosophy with Kabbalah.

dei Rossi and Judah Moscato reflect the influence of Renaissance thinking.[13] Reggio tried to reconcile Torah and philosophy (the title of one of
his works).[14] It is hardly surprising, therefore, that the thinkers mentioned here should have considered the typically Renaissance theme of
the purpose of creation.

As noted previously, it is futile to look for this kind of abstract discussion in the concrete, unsystematic thought of the talmudic rabbis. It is
necessary, nonetheless, to look at a passage in the Babylonian Talmud
(*Eruvin* 13*b*) in which some scholars have detected a consideration of
our theme. The passage reads:

Our rabbis taught: For two and a half years the House of Shammai and the
House of Hillel engaged in a debate. These say: It would have been better for
man if he had not been created than if he had been created, while the others
say: It is better for man to have been created than if he had not been created.
They put it to the count and concluded: It would have been better for man if he
had not been created than if he had been created, but now that he has been
created let him scrutinize (*yefashfesh*) his deeds. Others say: Let him examine
(*yemashmesh*) his deeds.

This passage has no parallel in other early rabbinic sources and is found
only here in the Babylonian Talmud. The opening words 'Our rabbis
taught' denote that the passage is tannaitic, that is, that it dates no later
than the end of the second century CE. The *baraita* purports to record
the debate between the two Houses, but it does not necessarily follow
that we have an actual debate. This depends on the whole question of
attribution of debates between such early authorities as the two Houses,
a question to which attention has been called by Jacob Neusner and
others.[15] Obviously, the words 'Our rabbis taught', the usual introduction to a tannaitic source, are late and may be the words of the
editors of the Babylonian Talmud, possibly as late as the end of the fifth
century CE. This applies *a fortiori* to the addition 'Others say', and it is

[13] See Cecil Roth, *The Jews of Italy* (Philadelphia, Pa., 1946), 193–215; Alexander
Altmann, '*Ars Rhetorica* as Reflected in Some Italian Jewish Figures of the Italian
Renaissance', in id., *Essays in Jewish Intellectual History* (Hanover, NH, 1981), 97–118;
on Moscata, see Israel Bettan, *Studies in Jewish Preaching: Middle Ages* (Cincinnati,
Oh., 1939), 192–226.

[14] See Roth, *Jews of Italy*, 497–8.

[15] See for instance Jacob Neusner, *The Rabbinic Traditions about the Pharisees Before
70* (Leiden, 1971), part 3, 320–66, and David Goodblatt, *Rabbinic Instruction in
Sassanian Babylon* (Leiden, 1975).

possible that the words 'but now that he has been created . . .' are also a later addition to the original *baraita*.

The passage, discussed earlier in a different context,[16] must be considered in relation to a passage which is found on the same page in the Talmud. Before the Talmud quotes our *baraita* it quotes the saying of Rav Abba in the name of Samuel: 'For three years the House of Hillel and the House of Shammai engaged in a debate. These say: The law follows our rulings but the others say: The law follows our rulings. A *bat kol* [heavenly voice] proceeded to declare: Both these and these are the words of the living God but the law follows the rulings of the House of Hillel.' The homily is then introduced, explaining that the reason why the *bat kol* decided in favour of the House of Hillel is that its members were more modest than those of the House of Shammai.

The passage is acknowledged to be late. Samuel was an early third-century *amora*,[17] and yet the formulation is exactly the same as in the *baraita*. It would seem, too, that just as there is a legendary element in the Samuel narrative so is there in the *baraita*. In the Samuel narrative the two Houses engage in debate for three years, a nice round number implying completion. Why do they debate the matter for two and a half years in the *baraita* narrative?[18] The reason may be that since the debate here was eventually decided by vote it was said to have endured for an incomplete number of years, whereas in the Samuel narrative the debate would have continued were it not for the intervention of the *bat kol*.

Rashi explains *yefashfesh* as referring to man's past deeds and *yemash-mesh* as referring to his future deeds.[19] Moses Hayim Luzzatto, however, in his *Mesilat yesharim*, understands *yefashfesh* as referring to man's deeds in general, of which he should reject the bad, and *yemashmesh* as referring to a close investigation into the good deeds to see if they are pure and undertaken without ulterior motives.[20] The whole tenor of Luzzatto's work is, in fact, in what might be termed a post-Renaissance

[16] See above, Ch. 3, 'The Human Element in Rabbinic Literature'.
[17] Abba bar Samuel in the Munich Codex, but the date is barely affected.
[18] But see Raphael Rabbinovicz, *Dikdukei soferim* (Brooklyn, NY, 1875) for the variant reading here, too, of three years.
[19] See marginal note in the Vilna edition of the Talmud that the *Arukh* understands this quite differently from Rashi, and see Ritba.
[20] *Mesilat yesharim*, ch. 3, beginning; for the English translation, see *The Path of the Upright*, ed. M. M. Kaplan (Philadelphia, Pa., 1936), 23.

vein. Luzzatto, it might be mentioned, wrote a Hebrew drama in the style of the Italian dramatists.

The Tosafists (the medieval French scholars who compiled glosses to the Talmud)[21] detect an apparent contradiction between our passage and the passage in the Babylonian Talmud, *Avodah zarah* (5a), where a saying of the third-century Palestinian *amora* Resh Lakish is discussed: 'Come, let us be grateful to our ancestors, for if they had not sinned [by worshipping the golden calf] we would not have come into the world.' If we are grateful for being born does this not show, contrary to the final vote in the *baraita*, that life is good? The Tosafists give two replies. One is that the Talmud ultimately understands Resh Lakish as saying not that if the ancestors had not sinned we would not have been born, but only that if they had not sinned they would have been immortal and, being with us in the same world, their excellence would have been such as to reduce us to insignificance. It would have been as if we had not been born. The other reply of the Tosafists is that our *baraita* refers to the wicked, whereas Resh Lakish is speaking of the righteous.

Modern scholars have discussed the *baraita* from various angles. George Foot Moore refers to the *baraita* as typical of the kind of problem discussed in the apocalypses, problems of suffering which became even more acute after the destruction of the Temple.[22] Moore thus takes it for granted that the account of the debate is historical, a position that is more than a little dubious.

Claude Montefiore remarks:

This passage has been quoted as an example of the fundamental pessimism of Rabbinic attitudes towards life. This is absurd. The passage is clearly a record of some famous dialectical discussion, without any true bearing on the arguers' *real* views about actual life. The Rabbis were prevailingly optimists, and whenever circumstances allowed it, they enjoyed life. Their *manner* of enjoyment may not be ours, but that does not make *their* enjoyment less. (emphasis Montefiore's)[23]

Montefiore is correct that the passage is academic, but is wrong in invoking the totally different question of the enjoyment of life and the question of pessimism versus optimism. Neither of these questions is discussed in Montefiore's terms in the rabbinic literature and certainly

[21] See Tosafot s.v. *noah lo*, and Tosafot on the passage in *Avoda zarah*.
[22] *Judaism*, 3 vols. (Cambridge, Mass., 1958), ii. 285 n. 2.
[23] Montefiore and Loewe, *A Rabbinic Anthology*, 529.

not in our *baraita*, which, theoretical though it is, has to do with man's duties in life. Moreover, it is impermissible to lump all the 'rabbis' together as if their views were monolithic and uttered in the same period.

Ephraim E. Urbach similarly argues that it is a common error to read the *baraita* as evidence for the 'pessimistic' attitudes of the rabbis, with parallels in Greek and Latin authors.[24] But Urbach, too, connects the *baraita* with such passages as those dealing with procreation to show that 'the rabbis' believed life to be good. However, the *baraita* is not discussing whether life, now that we have it, is good. Obviously it is, since God created life. The *baraita* is dealing with the very different question of whether ultimately the bad outweighs the good.

All these authors fail to see the anthropological nature of the *baraita*. It is not asking what was God's purpose in creating the world, or whether the world was created solely for man's benefit. The statement that it would have been better for man if he had not been created is logically flawed if taken literally. How could it have been better for man not to have been created, since if he had not been created he would not have been there for it to have been better for him? Obviously, the whole statement is an example of rabbinic hyperbole, denoting something like, 'the human predicament is fraught with risk, so man had better take care'. This fits in very well with numerous rabbinic teachings that this life is a school of training for the afterlife. The debate between the Houses is very different from the debate between Sa'adya and Maimonides on whether the Creation was solely for man's benefit.

Dean Matthews in *The Purpose of God*, after presenting a profound defence of the teleological argument, reminds us of how easily talk of design can result in a narrow vision according to which everything God has created is solely for man.[25] Modern Jewish theologians would do well to ponder on Matthews' fine ending:

The universe is, when all is said, full of darkness and tragedy. It has profound abysses of being which the plummet of reason cannot sound. It is not only the 'vale of soul making', it is not only the home of man, it is not even only the training ground for his home beyond, nor only the sphere where human values are realised—it is all these things, but it is much more. It is the work of a sublime Artist who expresses Himself in its majesty and its beauty; and its sublimity is part of its justification.

[24] *Ḥazal* (Jerusalem, 1969), 224–6; English trans. *The Sages: Their Concepts and Beliefs* (Jerusalem, 1979).
[25] W. E. Matthews, *The Purpose of God* (London, 1935), 177.

Enjoyment of Life

The enjoyment of life and its pleasures, material as well as spiritual, is rarely seen, nowadays, as incompatible with a religious outlook, but this was not always so. The saying of Rabbi Jose Hakohen, 'Let all thy deeds be for the sake of Heaven' (*Pirkei avot* 2: 12), has been interpreted in Jewish thought in two different ways. Does the maxim mean, as it is often understood to mean, that the physical appetites—eating, drinking, sex—should be gratified ideally with neither pleasure nor passion but solely for the sake of God? Or does it mean that since God has created human beings with physical appetites, it is the will of God that these be enjoyed, the enjoyment constituting in itself worship for the sake of Heaven? It is, of course, all a matter of where the emphasis is to be placed. It is hardly likely that the saintly followers of the first view never enjoyed their food, nor that the followers of the second view never had their minds solely on God. Obviously there were severe tensions in the lives of the few hardy souls who tried to adopt Rabbi Jose's ideal. Rabbi Jose is, in fact, described as a 'saint' (*ḥasid*) in the preceding passage in *Pirkei avot*, implying that his advice was originally intended for the few God-seekers rather than the mass of people. Modernist Jewish authors who call attention to the so-called sane attitude of Judaism on the question of the enjoyment of life fail to note the rich variety of Jewish attitudes which makes any generalization extremely precarious.

Our investigation can profitably begin with Abba Hillel Silver's cogently argued but one-sided treatment in his *Where Judaism Differed*.[26] Silver suggests that Judaism differed from other religions on the proposition 'That Men Should Not Enjoy Life'.[27] After citing illustrations from the classics of other religious philosophies in which the needs of the body are viewed with indifference or even with abhorrence, Silver points to what he considers to be the different attitude of Judaism. He remarks:

Rab, who together with Samuel established the leading academies in Babylonia and made it a center of Rabbinic studies, is quoted as saying: 'A man will some day have to give an account to God for all the good things which his eyes beheld and of which he refused to partake'. He also said to his disciple R. Hamnuna, 'My son, according to your ability do good to yourself, for there is no enjoyment in the netherworld, nor will death be long in coming.'[28]

[26] New York, 1956.   [27] Ibid. 212–62.   [28] Ibid. 261.

Silver, in referring to the importance of Rab, evidently seeks to anticipate the objection that such a modern-sounding sentiment is atypical. It
is typical, Silver implies, because who could be more typical of ancient
rabbinic thought than the teacher who, together with his colleague,
established the leading Babylonian academies?

Let us see what the first passage actually says (Jerusalem Talmud,
Kiddushin 4: 12, 66*d*, not, as in Silver, 2: 65*d*). The saying occurs in a
passage in which it is first said that it is forbidden to reside in a town
which has no doctor, no bathhouse, and no court of law, to which was
added, a town which has no vegetable garden. The passage continues:

Rabbi Hezekiah [and] R. Kohen [say] in the name of Rab, 'A man will in the
future have to render an account, and a reckoning for everything his eyes saw and
he refrained from eating. Rabbi Lezer took this saying into consideration, and he
would save his pennies so as to spend them on each kind of food once a year.

The reference to 'in the future' means 'in the world to come' on judgment day, not, as Silver renders it more innocuously, 'some day'. And
there is nothing in the passage about refusing to partake of 'all the good
things'. The reference throughout the whole passage is to food, and in
the context, to healthy food. Thus the meaning is simply that a man
must look after his health and not deny himself wholesome food. Rabbi
Lezer's practice, as a poor man, probably means the same: that he tried
to enjoy a little of each kind of healthy food at least once a year. It is even
possible that the standard commentators are right in connecting Rabbi
Lezer's practice with the need to recite the benediction 'Who has kept
us alive' (*sheheheyanu*) when enjoying new fruit for the first time in the
year. Is it conceivable that, according to Rab, every rabbinic ascetic
would be called to judgment for every permissible pleasure he denied
himself? As the questioner puts it in the responsa of the Sephardi rabbi
Joseph Mashash,[29] the statement that a man will be obliged to render an
account and a reckoning for everything his eyes saw which he refrained
from eating is contrary to what all the moralists say when they warn
against over-indulgence in food, and to their dictum that if a man has a
desire for a certain dish and he refrains from eating it, it is accounted to
him as if he had fasted that day. Mashash agrees with his questioner and
explains the passage in the Jerusalem Talmud as referring to the benediction of 'Who has kept us alive'. As is evident from his responsa,

[29] *Mayim hayim*, 2 vols. (Jerusalem, 1985), ii, no. 104: 4, pp. 63–4.

Mashash, for a rabbi of the old school, was something of a modernist. But his historical sense was sufficiently acute not to allow him to read modern ideas into the sayings of the ancient rabbis.

Rab's advice in the second passage (BT *Eruvin* 54*a*) is a quotation from the book of Ecclesiasticus, chapter 14, in which 'doing good to thyself' means giving the Lord his due offering (verse 11) and doing good 'unto thy friend' (verse 13). Moreover, even if the Greek-inspired book of Ecclesiasticus does refer to making the most of worldly opportunities, it is clear from the talmudic context, in which there are sayings on learning as much Torah as possible, that Rab has adapted the saying to refer to the accumulation of learning while there is still time. Rab was hardly saying to Rabbi Hamnuna, 'Enjoy yourself as much as you can while you have time, since time is fleeting', as if he were an ancient Robert Herrick urging his disciple to 'Gather ye rosebuds while ye may'.

The misappropriation of Rab's saying in the Jerusalem Talmud is by no means peculiar to Silver. Emil G. Hirsch writes, 'The most beautiful [*sic*] saying of the rabbis about Asceticism is: "Man will have to give account in the future for every lawful enjoyment offered to him which he has ungratefully refused" .'[30] In his *Jewish Theology* Kaufmann Kohler has this to say:

Neither does Judaism begrudge man the joy of life which is the fruit of industry, nor rob it of its moral value. On the contrary, that ascetic spirit which encourages self-mortification and rigid renunciation of all pleasure is declared sinful. Instead, we are told that in the world to come man shall have to give account for every enjoyment offered him in this life whether he used it gratefully or rejected it in ingratitude.[31]

Both Hirsch and Kohler give as their source the passage in the Jerusalem Talmud, *Kiddushin*, and both introduce the idea of gratitude, which does not appear anywhere in the passage. Hirsch and Kohler were radical Reformers, but even the more moderate Morris Joseph can use the passage in the Jerusalem Talmud to support his argument:

Even the senses, then, have their rights. The physical life cannot be sustained save by their gratification. Nor is the pleasure yielded by their gratification to be looked at askance as something on the borderland of sin. It is legitimate, seeing that it is the fulfilment of God's plainly-declared will. By making the satisfaction of bodily needs pleasurable He has set the seal of His approval upon it . . .

---

[30] 'Asceticism', *Jewish Encyclopaedia* (New York, 1901), ii. 167.
[31] New edn. (New York, 1968), 318.

'In the hereafter', the Rabbins [*sic*] boldly affirm, 'every man will be called to account for the earthly pleasures he has rejected'.[32]

Among other modernist Jewish thinkers the litany of 'life is to be enjoyed' is repeated as if this is the view of Rab in the Jerusalem Talmud. A. E. Sufrin writes, 'Rab went so far as to say that in the Great Judgement Day man would have to give an account for every lawful pleasure he refused.'[33] Pinhas Peli claims, 'In this spirit is also the saying of Rav: A man will have to give account on the judgment day of every good permissible thing which he might have enjoyed and did not.'[34] And, *mea culpa*, I unthinkingly followed the same line in my book, *The Jewish Religion: A Companion*.[35]

It almost seems as if modernist Jewish theologians, in their failure to find an ally in ancient rabbinic sources, are obliged to fall back in desperation on the supposed teaching of Rab, which is then presented as the normative Jewish view, so different from the excesses of Christianity. It cannot, of course, be denied that there is a trend in pre-modern Jewish thought fully in accord with the 'modernist' position. The passage in the apocryphal book of Ecclesiasticus has been noted above. And even the canonical book of Ecclesiastes states, 'Rejoice, O young man, in thy youth; and let thy heart cheer thee in the days of thy youth. And walk in the ways of thine heart, and in the sight of thine eyes; but know thou, that for all these things God will bring thee into judgment' (11: 9). Yet the final clause of this verse sounds a warning against indulgence in the enjoyment of the good things of life. Certainly that is the rabbinic view. The Babylonian Talmud (*Shabbat* 63*b*) remarks that the first part of the verse contains the words of the evil inclination, and the final clause the words of the good inclination. The apparent contradiction is noted, too, in the Midrash (*Ecclesiastes rabbah* on this verse), where it is said that, on the face of it, the words of Solomon seem to contradict the teaching of Moses: 'That ye go not about after your own heart' (Num. 15: 39). For this reason the sages wanted to hide away the book of Ecclesiastes (i.e. not to admit it into the canon of Sacred Writ). Finally, however, the Midrash states, Solomon himself, in the final clause of the verse, sounded the warning, and so the sages were able to say, 'Solomon has spoken

[32] *Judaism as Life and Creed* (London, 1903), 369.
[33] 'Asceticism, Jewish', in James Hastings (ed.), *Encyclopaedia of Religion and Ethics* (Edinburgh, 1908), ii, 97–9.
[34] 'Asceticism', *Encyclopaedia Judaica* (Jerusalem, 1972), iii. 680.
[35] (Oxford, 1995), 35.

well'. The Midrash, in fact, applies 'rejoicing in thy youth' to the study of the Torah, i.e. 'be glad to be able to study the Torah in your youth'.

In his popular volume on the study of the Torah, *Rejoice O Youth!* Rabbi Avigdor Miller, not always historically minded, comes near to the thought of the ancient rabbis when he concludes his work:

And now, back to the place of happiness, the Yeshiva. 'Rejoice O Youth in your boyhood, and let your mind make you happy in the days of your young-manhood' (Koheles 11: 9). 'Resh Lakish said: This refers to the Torah-study' (Shabbos 63*b*) 'Rejoice in your studies; learn with joy and a happy mind' (Rashi, ibid.). You are the wealthiest of men, for you possess many years of great Opportunity. And now, to your Torah-studies; and on to your goal of glorious Achievement.[36]

At the opposite extreme from the modernists is the extremely austere formulation in the *Shulḥan arukh*:

The Sages say: 'Let all thy deeds be for the sake of Heaven', that even things permitted such as eating, drinking, sitting, rising, walking, lying down, sexual intercourse, speech, and all the needs of your body should all be for the worship of God or for that which brings about His worship. Even when he is thirsty and hungry, it is not praiseworthy if he eats and drinks for pleasure, but he should intend that he eats as much as he needs so as to be alive that he may serve his Creator. And so, too, even when he sits in the counsel of the upright and stands in the place of the righteous and walks by the advice of the whole-hearted, it is not praiseworthy if he does it for his own pleasure and to fulfil his own purposes and desires, unless he does it for the sake of Heaven. And so, too, when he lies down to sleep. It goes without saying that at a time which he can spend study-ing the Torah and carrying out the precepts, he should not indulge in sleep for his pleasure, but it is not praiseworthy if he sleeps for his pleasure even when it is at a time when he is obliged to rest from his labours. He should intend to give sleep to his eyes and rest to his body for the sake of his health, so that his mind will not be disturbed through lack of sleep when he studies the Torah. And so, too, with regard to sexual intercourse ordained by the Torah. It is disgraceful if he performs the act in order to slake his lust or for his bodily advantage. Nor is it praiseworthy if he does it in order to have children who will serve him and take his place. Rather he should intend to have children who will serve his Creator, or he should intend to fulfil the duty of *onah* [of satisfying his wife] like a man who pays his debts. And so, too, with regard to speech. Even when he speaks words of wisdom his intention should be for the purpose of serving the Creator or for that which will result in His service. The general principle is that a man should set his eyes and his mind upon his ways and weigh up all his

---

[36] *Rejoice O Youth!* (New York, 1962), 381.

deeds in the balance of his intellect, so that whenever he observes something that can result in the service of the Creator he should do it, otherwise he should not do it. And one who behaves in this way serves his Creator all the time.[37]

To be noted is the more negative attitude towards sexual pleasure in this stark statement, which goes back to the commentary of Rabbi Jonah Gerondi (d. 1263) in his commentary on the passage in *Pirkei avot* 2: 12. (I have discussed the evolution of this attitude in my book *A Jewish Theology*.[38]) Eating and drinking for pleasure is only said to be not praiseworthy, whereas sex for the husband's pleasure (though not for the wife's) is said to be disgraceful.

In hasidism, the doctrine of 'enjoyment' comes to have nuances of its own, particularly in the idea of 'serving God in corporeality', that is, engaging in bodily activities for the purpose of reclaiming the 'holy sparks' scattered in all things and imprisoned by the demonic powers.[39] The hasidic understanding of the doctrine is, otherwise, the same as that of Rabbi Jonah and the *Shulḥan arukh*, in which there is no room for any accommodation of the pleasure idea. And yet, in a number of hasidic sources,[40] it is reported in the name of the Seer of Lublin that the statement in the *Shulḥan arukh* that the sex act should be performed solely for the sake of heaven can only apply before the act is carried out. The act itself cannot but be attended with pleasure, otherwise it is impossible. Consequently, these authors hold, a man should give thanks to God afterwards for affording him this pleasure; a realistic reservation that is still very unusual in Jewish pietistic literature.

In the work *No'am elimelekh*,[41] the following statement of intention is provided, to be recited before eating a meal:

For the sake of the unification of the Holy One, blessed be He, and His Shekhinah. I do not eat, God forbid, for my bodily pleasure, but only that my

---

[37] *Oraḥ ḥayim* 231.

[38] (London, 1973), 168–73.

[39] See my article 'Eating as an Act of Worship in Hasidic Thought', in Siegfried Stein and Raphael Loewe (eds.), *Studies in Jewish Religious and Intellectual History Presented to Alexander Altmann on the Occasion of his Seventieth Birthday* (Birmingham, Ala., 1979), 157–66.

[40] For instance, in Tsevi Hirsch Eichenstein, *Sur mera va'aseh tov* [Lemberg, 1840] (Munkacz, 1901), trans. by Louis Jacobs as *Turn Aside from Evil and Do Good: An Introduction and a Way to the Tree of Life* (London, 1995), 21. See also Tsevi Elimelekh of Dynów, *Derekh pikudeikha*, part 1: *Ḥelek hadibur*, no. 5, p. 34.

[41] Elimelekh of Lyzhansk, *No'am elimelekh* [Lemberg, 1788], ed. G. Nigal, 2 vols. (Jerusalem, 1978), *Tsetl katan*, no. 15, p. 617.

body be strong for God's service. Let not any sin, transgression, evil thought, or physical pleasure prevent the unification of the Holy One, blessed be He, and His Shekhinah by means of the holy sparks in this food and drink.

Thus Rabbi Elimelekh does not suggest that all pleasure be suppressed when eating and drinking, only that the pleasure experienced should not outweigh the motive of 'for the sake of Heaven'. Rabbi Elimelekh continues, 'Whenever he eats or drinks anything, he should have in mind that the taste he experiences in his mouth when he swallows the food or sips the drink is the innermost part of the sacred entity and the holy sparks which reside in that food or drink . . .'. It is none too clear what Rabbi Elimelekh means by this unusual statement that the taste of the food and drink is the inward part of the holy. He probably means that the sense of taste is a pale reflection of its source in the sacred realms, the form in which the divine vitality inherent in all things makes itself felt. It would surely be going too far to read into Rabbi Elimelekh's strange saying that there is something holy and spiritual in the taste of the food and drink, even though the food and drink are in themselves grossly physical, much as a gourmet might say of a dish that it tastes divine. In any event, Rabbi Elimelekh, whatever reservations he may have with regard to food and drink, has no reservations regarding the negation of pleasure in the sex act. Both Rabbi Tsevi Hirsch Eichenstein and Rabbi Tsevi Elimelekh,[42] while advising that thanks be given for the pleasure in the sex act, quote Rabbi Elimelekh's statement that the reason that no benediction has been ordained to thank God for sex is because the act is impossible without the 'evil inclination'.[43] Similarly, Rabbi Elimelekh comments on the verse: 'As he was about to enter Egypt, he said to his wife Sarai, I know now what a beautiful woman you are' (Gen. 12: 11) that Abram only became aware that his wife was beautiful when he came in closer proximity to the lewd Egyptians.[44]

Another hasidic master, Rabbi Shneur Zalman of Lyady (1745–1813), in his *Tanya* claims that the average man (in the thought of this author the 'average man' is a saintly person who has, nevertheless, to struggle with his lower nature) is torn between his love for God and his love

---

[42] R. Tsevi Hirsch Eichenstein (1763–1833) and R. Tsevi Elimelekh of Dynów (1785–1841) were hasidic masters in Galicia. See the introduction to my translation of Eichenstein's work *Turn Aside from Evil and Do Good*, pp. xiii–xxxvii.

[43] Elimelekh of Lyzhansk, *No'am elimelekh*, 'Vayishlaḥ', 95.

[44] Ibid., 'Lekh lekha', 26.

of pleasure. The only way for him to succeed is by decrying worldly pleasures:

He must set aside periods to take counsel with his soul in order to abhor evil, as, for example, when our Sages of blessed memory advise [reflection on] a woman as a vessel full of filth, etc. and so forth. So do all delicacies and pleasures become vessels full of filth. And so, too, with regard to all the pleasures of the world, the wise man sees what will become of them, they will rot and become worms and rubbish.[45]

A more realistic hasidic view is found in the work *Ḥashavah letovah* by Rabbi Hanokh of Aleksandrow (1798–1870).[46] This hasidic master, in a comment on the verse 'In all thy ways acknowledge Him, and He will direct thy paths' (Prov. 3: 6), remarks that deep down a Jew wishes to eat for the sake of Heaven so that, even though he actually eats for his own enjoyment, God will be with him in that his eating will be for the sake of Heaven. While it is true that his assent for it to be for the sake of Heaven is involuntary and, strictly speaking, contrary to his real motive, i.e. to enjoy his food, yet even such contrary motivation is acceptable just as, in Jewish law, assent given under coercion counts as assent.

Before leaving hasidism, it is proper to refer to a remarkable passage in the work *Eglei tal*[47] by the late hasidic master, Abraham ben Ze'ev Nahum Bornstein of Sochaczew (1839–1910). In the introduction to this halakhic work the author argues, in contrast to some hasidim, that to enjoy the study of the Torah is not only permissible but highly desirable. Those hasidim are wrong, this author remarks, who believe that to study the Torah 'for the sake of Heaven' means to study purely as a duty without obtaining any pleasure from the study. Rabbi Abraham states that, on the contrary, here the pleasure principle is essential. A joyless mouthing of the words is not study at all. To be sure, a man who studies the Torah solely because he enjoys the intellectual stimulus is far removed from the ideal. But if a man does study the Torah because it is a religious obligation he is obliged to take pleasure in his studies.

Coming nearer to modern times, we find opinions divided in the nineteenth-century Lithuanian *musar* school. Rabbi S. J. Zevin quotes two opinions,[48] the first of which appears in the 1938 volume of *Keneset*

---

[45] *Likutei amarim: Tanya* (Vilna, 1930), ch. 14.
[46] [Piotrków, 1929] (Jerusalem, 1992), 77.
[47] [Pietrikow, 1905] (New York, 1968).
[48] *Sefarim vesoferim* ('Books and Authors'), 3 vols. (Tel Aviv, 1959), volume on Midrash etc, pp. 130–1.

yisrael, the journal of the Slobodka *musar* yeshiva. Rabbi Yitshak Schor considers the rabbinic idea of sabbath 'delight in the Lord' as expressed by eating good food and drinking fine wines. How can this be delighting in the Lord? Rabbi Schor replies that on the sabbath God invites man to be His guest and enjoy His world without having to work for it, as he has to do during the other six days of the week. Through this very delight man comes closer to God who gave the pleasurable experience to him, so that the enjoyment of the world is the means to delighting in the Lord. In the name of Rabbi Nathan Tsevi Finkel, the famous 'Old Man' of Slobodka mentioned in Chapter 6, Rabbi Schor continues:

From the teachings of our master [R. Nathan Tsevi] we learn that this is the way of human perfection all the rest of the year [and not only on the sabbath]. We have to take delight in Him in all our physical pleasures, through which a man becomes increasingly aware that he takes delight in God. This is man's service and his preparation in the vestibule [this world] for the purpose intended in the palace [the world to come], where he will take delight in the Lord directly from his holy Source without any other means [being required].

Similarly, another disciple of the 'Old Man', A. Z. Levanon, observes that it is quite erroneous to see the need for a benediction before enjoying worldly pleasures such as eating and drinking as a kind of tax one has to pay for enjoying the world.[49] On the contrary, the benediction is the essential means of bringing a man to God even while enjoying the world since, after all, it is God who provides the enjoyment. Reflection on this truth provided by the benediction brings man closer to his Creator. Rabbi Zevin notes the totally different view of another disciple of the 'Old Man', Rabbi Judah Laib Hasman: 'All this-worldly matters are solely for the purpose of testing whether man will skip over them. He should see with his eyes but not touch them. They are only as a delight to the eyes, but if he eats thereof he will suffer eternal death.'[50] The gloomy language employed—'he will suffer death'—referring to Adam's fall, is apparently intentional. What a difference between the two attitudes, one seeing worldly pleasures as the essential means to delight in God, the other seeing them as temptations to be overcome! Rabbi Hasman is firmly within the older moralistic tradition.

Another neo-modernist among the musarists is Rabbi Joseph Leib

---

[49] 'The Yoke of the Kingdom of Heaven' (Heb.), in D. Weinberger (ed.), *Hasaba mislabodka* (Brooklyn, NY, 1987), 65–8.

[50] *Or yahel* (Jerusalem, 1938), 24.

Bloch (1860–1930), *rosh yeshivah* of Telz. Very unusually for a tradition-alist, Rabbi Bloch interprets the verse 'Rejoice O youth' as not only allowing but positively advocating the enjoyment of life. In his *Shiurei da'at*,[51] his comments are headed: 'Weigh the circuit of thy feet' (Prov. 4: 26). Rabbi Bloch's basic contention is that each human being has his own path, his own circuit adapted to his needs, material as well as spiri-tual. It is futile to try to suppress or ignore these basic needs. On the contrary, provided the young man to whom the verse is addressed directs his ways ultimately towards the ethical and spiritual side of existence, his material desires and ambitions are good in themselves. Self-fulfilment and ambition and an appetite for good living, provided these are within a person's 'circuit', are good because without these a person would not be truly human.[52]

The moralists seem always to be on the watch for opportunities to decry pleasurable activity, like the Victorian nanny who said, 'Go and see what the children are doing and tell them not to.' A good example (or bad according to one's taste) is provided by the different comments on the talmudic saying 'Withdraw your hand from a meal you greatly enjoy' (*Gittin* 70a), which Rashi understands to mean 'Do not overeat because the food is so tasty', thus seeing the saying as a warning against unhealthy overeating. That this is the meaning can be seen from the context, which deals with various prescriptions for healthy living. But the sixteenth-century mystic, Elijah de Vidas, in his *Reshit ḥokhmah*[53] takes it to mean that one should not eat at all from a very tasty dish. It is to this that Mashash's questioner, mentioned above, refers. It is only right to note, however, that in the whole of this passage de Vidas is chiefly concerned with unhealthy indulgence in the pleasures of the table. He refers specifically to eating food that is harmful to the body. But de Vidas is certainly far removed from the attitudes of the mod-ernists. From our investigation it emerges clearly that the notion that life is to be enjoyed as a good in itself is a modern idea, one not found in this form in the classical sources. Rabbi Schor, the sole exception, may well have been influenced, unconsciously perhaps, by the Haskalah move-ment, a real threat to traditional rabbinism in the Lithuania of his day,

[51] 3 vols. (Tel Aviv, 1953), ii. 104–16.
[52] Bloch's original views are treated in greater detail in Dov Katz, *Tenuat hamusar*, 5 vols. (Tel Aviv, 1958), v. 17–109.
[53] [Amsterdam, 1708] (Jerusalem, 1984), ii. 15: 30 and 40, pp. 390–3.

moving him to declare, in so many words, 'anything you can do we can do better'. The attitude of the modernists is, in any event, not necessarily to be rejected on the grounds that it is untraditional, and many of us no doubt find such an attitude more attractive and, dare we say, less prone to the objection that religious people are deluding themselves when they imagine that their minds are on God rather than on the pleasures of the table and of sex. Be that as it may, what modernists are not entitled to do is to read modernism anachronistically into the ancient sources. This would be a betrayal of intellectual honesty.

The Doctrine of *Imitatio Dei*

An attempt is here made to trace the doctrine of emulating God (*imitatio dei*, in the Latin formulation) in Jewish thought. I use this phrase as convenient shorthand for a not atypical Jewish idea, but I have been unable to discover this particular term for the idea or its Hebrew equivalent in any of the classical Jewish sources. I do not know who first used the expression *imitatio dei* among modern Jewish thinkers, and I suspect that it was coined on the analogy of Thomas à Kempis's *Imitatio Christi*. Nevertheless, the idea is certainly found in Jewish sources and these are worthy of discussion, both for themselves and for the light they throw on the way Jewish ideas develop from age to age, and how a degree of unity is preserved amidst diversity.

Although this idea is found in pre-rabbinic Jewish thought,[54] it receives its fullest expression in the talmudic and midrashic sources. It is, however, incorrect to state, as is often done in modern works,[55] that the doctrine is 'the basis of Jewish ethics' for the ancient rabbis, since the rabbinic sources are limited to the effect of character on deeds rather than the deeds themselves. The latter, for the rabbis, come under the heading of the precepts of the Torah, which are to be followed because God has so commanded, not in order for man to emulate the divine. It is extremely dubious in any event to speak of rabbinic ethics, as if the rabbis ever thought of a formal system of ethics.

[54] Philo, *De specialibus legibus* 4. 73–5, quoted in David Winston, *Philo of Alexandria* (London, 1981), 239–40. Philo writes: 'For what one of the ancients aptly remarked is true, that in nothing does human behaviour more nearly resemble God than in showing kindness. For what greater joy could there be for the created than to imitate God eternal?'

[55] See e.g. Kohler, *Jewish Theology*, 479–80; Samuel S. Cohon, *Jewish Theology* (Assen, 1971), 167; Solomon Schechter, *Aspects of Rabbinic Theology* (New York, 1961), 199–201.

The Rabbis

The earliest reference to the doctrine in rabbinic thought is found in the *Sifre* on a verse which speaks of walking in all God's ways (Deut. 11: 22).[56] In the context the verse means to obey God's laws, the 'ways' being those God has ordained for man, the paths He has commanded men to walk in. The New English Bible rightly translates the phrase 'to walk in all His ways' as 'by conforming to his ways', i.e. the ways He has mapped out for man in which to walk. But in the *Sifre* the 'ways' are understood to mean the ways in which God Himself walks, so that the injunction is for man to walk in the ways in which God walks, that is, to copy God by behaving as He is said to behave. This passage in the *Sifre* should first be translated in order to determine what this source is actually saying:

'To walk in all His ways'. These are the ways of Hamakom ['The Place', a common rabbinic name for God], blessed be He, a God compassionate and gracious [Exod. 34: 6]. And it says: 'And it shall come to pass, that whosoever shall be called by the name of the Lord shall be delivered' [Joel 3: 5, the *Sifre* evidently reading the verse in this way]. How is it possible for man to be called by the name of Hamakom? But as Hamakom is called compassionate, you should also be compassionate. The Holy One, blessed be He, is called gracious; you should also be gracious, as it is said: 'The Lord is gracious and full of compassion' [Ps. 145: 8], and give freely [*ḥinam*, 'for nothing', a pun on *ḥanun*, 'gracious', in the verse]. Hamakom is called righteous, as it is said 'For the Lord is righteous, He loveth righteousness' [Ps. 11: 7]; you should also be righteous. Hamakom is called merciful, as it is said 'For I am merciful, saith the Lord' [Jer. 3: 12]; you should also be merciful. Hence it says: 'Whosoever shall be called by the name of the Lord shall be delivered'. And it says 'Everyone that is called by My name' [Isa. 43: 7] and it says: 'The Lord hath made every thing for His own purpose' [Prov. 16: 4].

There are variant readings in this passage in the *Sifre*, and there appears to be a collation of statements from other sources,[57] but the general thrust is clear. For man to walk in God's ways and be called by God's name, he should imitate the divine qualities of compassion, graciousness, righteousness, and mercy.

The *Mekhilta* commenting on the verse (Exod. 15: 2) 'This is my God *ve'anvehu*', quotes, among other interpretations of this word, the

[56] *Sifre*, ed. L. Finkelstein (New York, 1969), no. 49, p. 114.
[57] The *midrash* on the verse in Joel, for example, appears originally to have been a separate *midrash* later inserted here.

following in the name of the second-century *tanna* Abba Saul, 'Abba Saul says: [It means] We should resemble Him. Just as He is compassionate and gracious so should you be compassionate and gracious.'[58] In the *Mekhilta* version there is no indication of how Abba Saul derives his teaching from the word *ve'anvehu*, but the usual explanation, given by Rashi,[59] is that Abba Saul reads this word as *ani vahu*, meaning 'I and He', to yield the thought 'I should be like He'. Thus the doctrine of *imitatio dei* is stated here, but by a different process of derivation than that used in the *Sifre*. Thus far tannaitic sources. In the Babylonian Talmud, *Sotah* 14*a*, a far more comprehensive statement of the doctrine is given in the name of the third-century Palestinian *amora*, Rabbi Hama, son of Rabbi Hanina:

What is the meaning of the Scriptural verse 'Ye shall walk after the Lord your God' [Deut. 13: 5]? Is it then possible for man to walk after the Shekhinah, for has it not been said: 'For the Lord thy God is a devouring fire' [Deut. 4: 24]? But [the meaning is] to walk after the qualities [*midot*] of the Holy One, blessed be He. Just as He clothes the naked, as it is written: 'And the Lord God made for Adam and his wife coats of skin, and clothed them' [Gen. 3: 21]; so should you clothe the naked. The Holy One, blessed be He, visited the sick [Abraham after his circumcision], as it is written: 'And the Lord appeared unto him by the oaks of Mamre' [Gen. 18: 1]; so should you visit the sick. The Holy One, blessed be He, comforted mourners, as it is written: 'And it came to pass after the death of Abraham, that God blessed Isaac his son' [Gen. 25: 11]; so should you comfort mourners. The Holy One, blessed be He, buried the dead, as it is written: 'And He buried him in the valley' [Deut. 34: 6]; so should you bury the dead.

In this elaboration of Rabbi Hama, son of Rabbi Hanina, the principle of imitating God's benevolence is extended to imitating the deeds which follow from the benevolent character, yet here too the principle is not made into one of ethics in general, but only refers to the benevolent acts to which the benevolent disposition should give rise.

It is somewhat surprising that in none of the sources mentioned above is the doctrine derived from what, on the face of it, is an obvious source—the verse 'You shall be holy, for I, the Lord your God, am holy' (Lev. 19: 2). It is possible that some of the rabbis read this verse as meaning, 'You should not be holy because I am holy, but because I, being

---

[58] *Mekhilta*, ed. I. H. Weiss (Vienna, 1865), *Shirata*, 47.
[59] On *Shabbat* 133*b* on this statement of Abba Saul.

holy, command you to keep the laws which follow on the injunction'. It is also possible that some of the rabbis preferred not to use this verse to derive the concept of *imitatio dei*, since it is impossible for man to be like God in holiness. Nevertheless, in the following rabbinic sources this verse is used as a basis of derivation for the ideal of *imitatio dei*.

Sifra on this verse comments, 'Abba Saul says: [It can be compared to] a king's retinue. What should it do? It should copy [*mehaleh*] the king.'[60] A variant reading has 'It should wait [*mekhakeh*] for the king', i.e. to see which way he intends to go and then follow him. The reading 'copy' seems preferable since the saying is attributed to Abba Saul, but 'wait' is also possible, and it amounts to the same thing. The verse thus is taken to mean 'Be holy as I am holy'.

In the later *midrash*, *Leviticus rabbah* the doctrine of *imitatio dei* is explicitly stated to be derived from this verse: 'The Holy One, blessed be He, said to Moses: Go and say to the children of Israel: My children, just as I am separate [from unholiness] so should you be separate. Just as I am holy so should you be holy. *Ye shall be holy*.'[61] In another passage in *Leviticus rabbah*, however, this verse is treated with greater reserve: '*Ye shall be holy*: I might have supposed "like Me", therefore it says "I am the Lord". My holiness is superior to yours.'[62] This is elaborated on in the *Midrash hagadol*: "Ye shall be holy, for I, the Lord your God, am holy." Imitate [*tedamu*] My ways. Just as I am holy so should you be holy. It might have been supposed that His [holiness] is not greater, therefore the verse says *I am the Lord your God*. My holiness is superior to yours.'[63]

In all these rabbinic passages, their authors were evidently bothered by the fact that the ideal of *imitatio dei*, implying that man can resemble God in some manner, seems to be in conflict with the idea that God is so different from man that to speak of such imitation borders on blasphemy. The rabbinic solution is to introduce reservations and qualifications, as if to say, yes, it is good for man to resemble his Maker, but any suggestion that he do so fully is to be rejected. It is as if the rabbis were saying: 'Man can and should strive to be God-like, but he cannot really be like God.'

[60] *Sifra*, ed. I. H. Weiss (Vienna, 1862), *Kedoshim* on Lev. 19: 2, p. 86*b*.
[61] *Leviticus rabbah*, ed. M. Margulies (Jerusalem, 1972), 24: 4 on Lev. 19: 2, p. 556.
[62] *Leviticus rabbah* 24: 9, p. 565.
[63] *Midrash hagadol: Leviticus*, ed. A. Steinsaltz (Jerusalem, 1975), on Lev. 19: 2, p. 535.

Maimonides

Only Maimonides among the medieval Jewish thinkers devotes space in his writings to the doctrine of *imitatio dei*. Like other medieval authors, he gave halakhic form to the aggadic idea of 613 precepts,[64] listing which precepts are primary and which only secondary. In obedience to his scheme, Maimonides records the rabbinic *imitatio dei* as the authentic understanding of the biblical verses. In his *Sefer hamitsvot* Maimonides writes:

The eighth mitzvah is that He has commanded us to be like Him, may He be exalted, insofar as possible. This is His saying: 'And walk in His ways'. The explanation has been given [by the rabbis]: Just as the Holy One, blessed be He, is called gracious so should you be gracious. Just as the Holy One, blessed be He, is called compassionate so should you be compassionate. Just as the Holy One, blessed be He, is called merciful so should you be merciful. This idea has been repeated in clear words when it is said 'Walk after the Lord', which is explained as imitate His good deeds and the glorious qualities by which God, may He be exalted, is described as a parable for the One who is exalted with great elevation above all.[65]

Here, and in his other writings, Maimonides is very circumspect, concerned as he evidently is not to ascribe human qualities to the Deity. He stresses that God is elevated beyond all human thought. That He is 'called' gracious and compassionate is only a 'parable'. When the *Sifre* uses the expression 'called' it is only as a midrashic play on the verse 'called by the name of the Lord'. But Maimonides, in obedience to his doctrine of attributes, takes 'called' to mean 'so-called'.

In his *Mishneh torah* Maimonides departs still further from the rabbinic understanding in his identification of *imitatio dei* with his golden mean.[66] The ways of God, in which man is to walk, are the 'balanced' ways in which extremes are avoided. Samuel David Luzzatto was so critical of Maimonides' golden mean that he dubbed it 'Atticism', i.e. Greek and not Jewish thinking. The 'middle way' obviously owes more to Greek ideas about the harmonious life than to rabbinic teaching. As Maimonides puts it:

We are commanded to walk in these middle ways and they are the good and upright ways, as it is said: 'And walk in His ways'. And so did they [the rabbis]

[64] The original idea of 613 precepts is aggadic (see *Makkot* 23*b*), but was treated as serious halakhah in the Middle Ages; see my *A Tree of Life* (Oxford, 1984; rev. edn. forthcoming), 16–18.

[65] *Sefer hamitsvot*, positive commandment no. 8, p. 10 (Arabic numerals).

[66] *Mishneh torah*, *De'ot* 1: 5–6.

teach the meaning of this *mitsvah*. Just as He is called gracious, so should you be gracious. Just as He is called compassionate, so should you be compassionate. Just as He is called holy, so should you be holy. In this manner the prophets call God by all these attributes: long-suffering, great in mercy, righteous, upright, perfect, mighty, strong, and so forth, in order to make known that these are good and upright ways, and that man is obliged to conduct himself in them and to imitate Him so far as it lies within his capacity.

It can be seen that here Maimonides has departed further from the rabbis in referring to the sterner attributes of strength and might, whereas the rabbinic sources refer only to the gentler attributes of compassion and mercy. As Solomon Schechter rightly observes, 'It is to be remarked that this God-likeness is confined to his manifestations of mercy and righteousness, the Rabbis rarely desiring the Jew to take God as a model in his attributes of severity and rigid justice, though the Bible could have furnished them with many instances of the latter kind'.[67] Similarly, Abraham Cohen writes, 'The Rabbis, on the other hand, did not over-look that in the Bible qualities are attributed to God which should not be copied by men, such as jealousy and anger'.[68] While Schechter and Cohen are undoubtedly correct so far as the rabbis are concerned, Maimonides' logic compels him to postulate that man is obliged, at times, to emulate the sterner attributes as well. Since for Maimonides God is only 'called' by His attributes so that man should emulate them, and they are not descriptions of God as He is, it follows that when He is 'called' by the sterner attributes it must also be for the purpose of human emulation, at least in some circumstances—by a ruler, for example, in order to promote the well-being of society.

Maimonides states the matter explicitly in his *Guide*.[69] In his general scheme, there are two kinds of attribute: those of essence and those of action. The attributes of essence—that He exists, that He is one, that He is wise—can only be understood in a negative way, i.e. that he is not the opposite. Maimonides' doctrine of negative attributes is stated in a number of places in his *Guide*.[70] But the attributes of action do not refer to God's nature but to His deeds which, if performed by humans, would be governed by their feelings, rather than dispassionate. Indeed, according to Maimonides, human beings should occasionally emulate God's

[67] *Aspects of Rabbinic Theology*, 203–4.
[68] *Everyman's Talmud* (London, 1949), 211–12.
[69] *Guide of the Perplexed*, i. 54.   [70] Ibid. i. 52–3, 56–8.

sterner attributes in destroying evildoers, but being God-like here involves emulating Him in His dispassionate activity:

It behoves the governor of a city, if he is a prophet,[71] to acquire similarity to these attributes, so that these actions may proceed from him according to a determined measure and according to the deserts of the people who are affected by them and not merely because of his following a passion. He should not let loose the reins of his anger nor let passion gain mastery over him, for all passions are evil; but, on the contrary, he should guard against them as far as lies within the capacity of man. Sometimes, with regard to some people, he should be *merciful and gracious*, not out of mere compassion and pity, but in accordance with what is fitting. Sometimes, with regard to some people, he should be *keeping anger and jealous and avenging* in accordance with their deserts, not out of mere anger; so he may order an individual to be burned without being angry and incensed with him and without hating him, because he perceives the deserts of that individual and considers the great benefit that many people will derive from the accomplishment of the action in question.

It appears from this astonishing passage that the sterner attributes should also be emulated, but only by a wise governor, and only because it will eventually lead to the greater increase of goodness. Yet it is not only Samuel David Luzzatto who finds this ideal of the dispassionate ruler ordering the execution of one who deserves it cold and cruel. It requires no great feat of imagination to see that Maimonides here reflects not only his well-known principle, in the words of Ahad Ha'am, of 'the supremacy of reason', but also the social and political conditions of the times in which he lived when, before modern democracy had been thought of, stern and just government could only be found among men whose passions were always in danger of getting out of control, to the detriment of the people they governed.

The Mystics

Kabbalah, which arose in Provence in the twelfth century and found its fullest expression in the Zohar towards the end of the thirteenth century, has its own understanding of *imitatio dei*. The kabbalists, influenced by the philosophers in their avoidance of the attribution of human characteristics to the being of God, and yet ardent in their pursuit of the 'living

[71] Kapah in his translation of the *Guide* understands this to mean by a prophet, as an emergency measure, or by judicial processes of the court. Friedlander, in his English translation, i. 1, suggests that this is an error in the text, which should read 'noble' instead of 'prophet', i.e. a man of noble disposition.

God' of the Jewish tradition, developed the idea that there are two aspects of the Deity. God as He is in Himself, the Ein Sof ('Limitless') is utterly beyond all human apprehension, unknowable to the extent that one cannot even speak of it at all. The God of religion is Ein Sof as manifest in the *sefirot*, the ten powers or potencies in the Godhead. The kabbalists go beyond Maimonides in denying even negative attributes for Ein Sof. On the other hand, the kabbalists hold that even positive attributes are permitted when used of the *sefirot*. It follows that one cannot speak, according to the kabbalists, of emulating Ein Sof, since one cannot speak or even think of the Ein Sof aspect of Deity. The doctrine of *imitatio dei* is restricted to imitation of the *sefirot*. Indeed, since the *sefirot* are mirrored in man's very being, his task is precisely that, to resemble the various *sefirot* as he brings these into play, and by so doing to bestir them in order to bring down to earth the flow of divine grace. In the words of the Zohar,[72] the impulse from below brings about the impulse from above. In a sense man is not so much obliged to imitate the *sefirot* as to *be* the *sefirot*, in that his deeds have a cosmic effect. When man is virtuous he sends benevolent impulses on high and assists the harmony that should obtain in the sefirotic realm, and then the unarrested divine grace can flow throughout all creation. If, on the other hand, man is vicious, he sends baneful influences on high to disturb the harmony of the *sefirot* and so impede the flow of divine grace.

In the remarkable work *Tomer devorah* ('The Palm Tree of Deborah') by Moses Cordovero, this famous mystic of Safed, building on Zoharic ideas, describes in rich detail how the mystic should emulate the sefirotic realm in every aspect of his life.[73] Space does not permit a detailed analysis of Cordovero's scheme, but a few references to it will suffice for the consideration of how the mystics applied the doctrine of *imitatio dei*. The highest of the *sefirot* is Keter, 'Crown'. According to the Zohar,[74] Keter is the stage in the divine unfolding at which there is no judgment and sternness, but only pure mercy and the higher thirteen attributes mentioned in Micah 7: 18–20. The mystic should emulate Keter by bringing these purely merciful elements into play. Just as the higher mercy is extended to all, even to those who provoke God, so too should man have patience even with those who provoke him. No man could sin without

72 Zohar i. 86*b*, i. 84*a*, i. 235*a*, etc.
73 See my translation, *The Palm Tree of Deborah* (London, 1960).
74 See Zohar iii. 72*a* and 131*b*.

the vitality with which God endows him. God could have simply withdrawn that vitality, since man uses it to offend Him, and yet He continues to give life and strength to the sinner even while he uses the vitality given him for sin. Even when Cordovero describes the imitation of Gevurah, the *sefirah* of power and judgment, he, unlike Maimonides, does not argue that man should, in some circumstances, emulate God's sternness and judgment, but states that the divine power of judgment is bestirred by man's sins, and that these are the result of his evil inclination. The way to emulate power is thus to exercise self-control and keep the evil inclination in check, according to Cordovero.

When describing the emulation of Hesed, 'Lovingkindness', Cordovero states that it is possible to be 'kind' to God by being kind to other human beings, thus helping the fulfilment of the divine purpose. By visiting the sick, for example, and healing them, the mystic not only benefits creatures here below but helps restore the unity of the Shekhinah with Her spouse, the *sefirah* of Tiferet, the male principle in the Godhead, for whom She is lovesick. Even when burying the dead the mystic performs this kindness to the world on high, since ultimately all the *sefirot* are embraced by Ein Sof, so that to assist them in their ascent to Ein Sof is, in a sense, to bury them there, so as not to create division and disharmony in the supernal worlds.

Other kabbalistic authors follow Cordovero's pattern, affirming a two-way traffic in this matter. Man imitates the *sefirot* and, as a result, the *sefirot* imitate him. But some of the later mystics develop the doctrine in their own way without necessarily invoking the notion of the *sefirot*. The Moroccan kabbalist Hayim Ibn Atar (1696–1743), in his famed commentary *Or haḥayim*, discusses at length the verse: 'Ye shall be holy for I the Lord your God am holy' (Lev. 19: 2).[75] Ibn Atar argues that the words 'for I the Lord your God am holy' do not mean that this is the reason why holiness is enjoined, but mean that Israel is to resemble God in His holiness. But how can this be, since Israel is incapable of grasping the meaning of the many incomprehensible stages of the divine holiness? In reply Ibn Atar introduces the kabbalistic idea that when man sanctifies himself he adds, as it were, degrees of sanctity on high. Moreover, since the divine holiness is beyond all limits, man can resemble his Maker by coming ever closer to an approximation of that holiness, even though he can never fully approximate to it.

[75] (Jerusalem, n.d.), on Lev. 19: 2.

The Hasidim

There is surprisingly little on *imitatio dei* in the literature of hasidism, no doubt because the hasidic ideal is that of *bitul hayesh*, 'loss of self-hood', self-transcendence in the service of God. If too much attention is given to the idea of man imitating God, this tends to frustrate the ideal of man losing himself. In one of the very few passages in hasidic literature dealing with *imitatio dei*, by Dov Baer, the Maggid of Mezhirech (d. 1772), this nuance is clearly implied.[76] The Maggid is puzzled at the statement in the *midrash* (quoted above) that it might have been supposed that man should be as holy as God, and that therefore the verse says 'I am the Lord', i.e. My holiness is superior. How could it even be imagined that man can be as holy as God? And if it means that man should be God-like in following God's attributes, then, indeed, man has to imitate God's attributes. The Maggid gives a novel interpretation to the *midrash*. God's holiness is controlled, the infinite divine light cannot be revealed in all its fullness, otherwise finite creatures could not exist and would be absorbed in its glorious splendour. It might have been supposed that man's reaching out to God in holiness should be like God, in His holiness, reaching out to him. Man should control his holy striving in order to be God-like. Therefore the verse tells us that God's holiness should not be emulated in this respect, but that man's striving for holiness, his giving of himself, should be uncontrolled. However, it would appear that the Maggid had more than one comment on this *midrash*. Kalonymus Kalman Epstein of Cracow (d. 1829) records an interpretation of the final clause of the *midrash* which he claims he heard in his youth in the name of the Maggid.[77] This in Hebrew, *kedushati lema'alah mikedushatkhem*, literally, 'My holiness is superior to your holiness'. But this is read as *kedushati lema'alah— mikedushatkhem*, 'My holiness on high is from your holiness', i.e., in the typical kabbalistic understanding, God's holiness is the result of human striving for holiness. In the kabbalistic scheme God needs man to send benevolent impulses on high by means of his holy deeds so that, in a sense, there is no meaning to God's holiness apart from man. God as He

---

[76] *Magid devarav leya'akov*, ed. Rivka Schatz-Uffenheimer (Jerusalem, 1976), no. 189, pp. 289–93.

[77] *Maor vashemesh* (Tel Aviv, 1965), 'Kedoshim', 138–9. Cf. Levi Yitshak of Berditchev, *Kedushat levi* (Jerusalem, 1964), 198–9, on Lev. 19: 2.

is in Himself is beyond all human comprehension, so that it only makes sense to speak of God's holiness in His relationship to man.

The doctrine of *imitatio dei* has been traced from its appearance in the various rabbinic sources through the works of Maimonides, the kabbalists, and the hasidim. Throughout the tension is evident between the powerful idea that man can in some way imitate God and the idea that God is unknowable and hence cannot be imitated. The rabbis do not appear to have been bothered overmuch by all this. Their thinking is not in the nature of a systematic theology. Maimonides is troubled by the problem, and stresses that God is only 'called' by His attributes, and that this 'calling' is for man to imitate not God but those features by which God is 'called'. In Kabbalah it is the *sefirot* that have to be emulated. In hasidism there is very little on the whole question, but more emphasis is placed on the union of man and God than on man, apart from God, imitating Him.

If, as this chapter has sought to demonstrate, ideas about the purpose of creation, the enjoyment of life, and the imitation of God have undergone a variety of interpretations in the history of Judaism—and the same would apply to many other important theological issues—how does a liberal supernaturalist go about adopting such ideas with the degree of certainty which religious life seems to demand? The plain answer is that if he is convinced—through his reasoning and through the role these ideas have assumed in the tradition—that the basic ideas are significant, he need not fear that uncertainties in understanding will result in a go-as-you-please attitude. In the nature of the case, all theological thinking, which, after all, involves the colossal but inevitable chutzpah of trying to grasp the mind of God, is bound to be vastly tentative. And, as we have seen even for the fundamentalist, there are no perfectly clear, dogmatic statements about these themes which allow no room for personal decision.

I have chosen these three themes because they seem to me to be highly significant in Judaism, judging by discussions over many years with like-minded religious Jews and from reading the works of representative Jewish thinkers. And yet a liberal supernaturalist cannot simply invoke a series of sacred texts. On such complex matters, he must make up his own mind, a mind that has been shaped, in part, by modern thought. When thinking, for example, of whether life should be enjoyed, he will probably, as a supernaturalist, be sufficiently moved to accept as true and as the glorious end of religion the doctrine that there is a Hereafter in which God will be enjoyed for ever by those worthy of it, and yet, as a liberal, he will refuse to regard this-worldly matters as things to be engaged in only reluctantly. When thinking of the purpose of creation, he may side with Maimonides and the early kabbalists, that the whole idea of purpose, with its human associations, is totally inapplicable to God as He is in Himself, and yet refuse to deny that, so far as our human grasp is concerned, there is a divine purpose to human life. When thinking of the idea of *imitatio dei* he will see, as a supernaturalist, the tremendous, religious value in the extra dimension given to the ethical life by this doctrine, and yet, as a liberal, will probably feel, in contrast to Maimonides, that the gentle rather than the stern attributes of Deity are to be followed, since his liberalism has made him only too aware of how fanaticism can so easily gain entrance into the lives of those convinced that they are called upon to be God's policemen.

In this chapter, as well as in the rest of the book, I have tried to show that Judaism is not monolithic and that when Jewish thinkers speak of normative Judaism, they tend to affix the label to those aspects of the tradition to which they are personally attracted. There is liberation in the thought that there is no alternative for a religious Jew in his quest for the transcendent than to try, guided by the tradition, to think some things through for himself. He can be loyal to the Torah and observe the *mitsvot*, and yet have an open mind on the kind of theological issue considered in this chapter. In a word, he can, and should, be a liberal supernaturalist.

ELEVEN

CONCLUSION

A S A S E Q U E L, after forty years, to *We Have Reason to Believe*, this book has sought to defend the theological position of liberal supernaturalism which I had taken in the earlier book and tried to follow through in other theological works during the intervening period. I have tried, in this book, to show why I still have reason to believe in a personal God and in 'Torah from Heaven', provided that this latter doctrine is understood in a non-fundamentalist way. In the preceding chapters I have tried to demonstrate why, for moderns, the fundamentalist attitude, for all its power—it does have power, witness the large number of intelligent, sophisticated men and women who still adopt it—is untenable because it is contrary to the facts of history. Yet, I have argued, a rejection of fundamentalism need not and should not result in a repudiation of halakhah, the legal side of Judaism, provided halakhah is seen in dynamic rather than static terms.

I do not delude myself into imagining that I have arrived at my position by pure theological reflection, and doubt whether anyone else really arrives at his or her religious stance on these grounds. Other factors—emotional, sociological, experiential—than the cognitive are involved in religious belief. Most of us are creatures of habit and conformity in religious matters. Our pattern of life is largely determined by our parentage, the social group to which we belong, and our education, so that an Orthodox Jew, while he may question this or that aspect of his tradition, will not usually contemplate becoming a Reform Jew, and the latter, while finding features of Orthodoxy personally attractive, will usually decide that his religious destiny is with Reform. Jews, like other religious folk, simply get on with it. Given my own background—at first lukewarm, later fiery, Orthodoxy—I would no doubt have remained fully Orthodox in theory as well as practice, and would probably have spent all my days as an inhabitant of the yeshiva world, had I not been

introduced to the study of Jewish history. As Solomon Schechter remarked, the real problem for modern Jews is presented by the comparatively new discipline of history. I would have been content to subscribe
to the traditional view that King David was the author of the Psalms,
Moses of the Pentateuch, Rabbi Simeon bar Yohai of the Zohar—there
are enough quasi-sophisticated attempts to indicate that these traditions
are true—were it not that historical studies show that Psalm 137 was
written very much later than David, that the Pentateuch is a composite
work, with large parts, at least, much later than Moses, and that the
author of the Zohar was Moses de Leon.

To become convinced of the historical truth and revise in consequence
one's religious understanding is not to be compared to an Orthodox Jew
becoming Reform or a Reform Jew becoming Orthodox, since the practitioners of the historical critical method are not ideologues, putting forward a rival religious position to either Reform or Orthodoxy, but are
rather, at their best, simply trying to uncover the facts.

This is the grounds of my dissent from fundamentalist Orthodoxy:
that it is untrue to the facts. What is required is not conversion, in the religious sense, to the historical critical method, but an acceptance that
some revision in our understanding of the tradition is required if we, unlike our ancestors, have now, through no particular merit of our own,
become aware of new facts. I have mentioned the *ba'al teshuvah* movement in a previous chapter. In modern parlance, with a pun on the word
teshuvah (which can mean both 'repentance' and 'answer') the *ba'al
teshuvah* is now often said to be 'one who accepts the answers' traditionally given by defenders of the tradition. Against the *ba'al teshuvah* ('the
one who accepts the answer') is the 'one who reverts to the question',
that is, the *ba'al teshuvah* who finds the answers inadequate. In a sense,
this has been my spiritual adventure. In relation to my parents' home, I
was a *ba'al teshuvah* of a sort when I entered the yeshiva, but became a
questioner once I had studied Jewish history at university level. But the
new questioning was not of the basic issues of religious faith, but rather
of the way I had hitherto mistakenly understood the faith to have come
about.

Even in my yeshiva days, questions of background and disposition
came into the picture. For instance, students at the yeshiva did not shave
with a razor—that is forbidden by Jewish law—but they did not usually
sport beards. (We used scissors or an electric shaver or a foul-smelling

depilatory.) But none of us, for all the admiration some of us may have had for hasidism, would have dreamed of growing the hasidic type of long beard and earlocks, or of wearing the wide black hat and long coat worn by the hasidim instead of a trilby and short jacket. When one of the more enthusiastic boys started to grow a beard and copy other hasidic ways, he was seen as an odd-bod even by Rabbi Dubov, himself a staunch hasid.

I have always tried to avoid counterfeit postures in religious matters, like pretending to be hasidic or ultra-Orthodox when I am neither, not as an exercise in piety but simply because it would be phoney for me and I would be fooling myself. As Rabbi Isser Zalman, a famous *rosh yeshivah*, once said, he avoids a certain course not out of *frumkeit* ('piety') but because such a course is *krumkeit* ('twisted' or 'crooked'). It is, of course, possible to fool oneself that one is being true to oneself, and I have no doubt often been guilty of this more subtle form of self-delusion, but 'to thine own self be true' remains the only course towards which one should strive in the religious, as in the moral, sphere.

Is this book, then, no more than an exercise in self-defence, no more than an attempt at self-justification, of little interest to those who do not share my predilections? It would be, were it not for the fact that others have trodden and are treading the same road. It is to these that the book is chiefly addressed. The *musar* teachers used to declare when preaching to others, 'I am preaching to myself, but have no objection to others overhearing what I say', or 'I am not referring to anyone in particular, but if anyone thinks I mean him I do mean him'. My experience as a rabbi in Orthodox or, at least, in traditional communities, has convinced me that many congregants find themselves at home in such communities because they love traditional Judaism, with all its problems, without being bothered too much, if they are at all, by theological issues. The question is not whether traditional Judaism is true in any absolutist sense. It is true for them. What I have been trying to do, inadequately no doubt, is to invite such worthy people to share in the quest for greater authenticity, in which what is true for me can approximate to what is really true or, if it is not too pretentious, to search for a tenable philosophy of traditional Judaism that can satisfy the mind as well as the heart.

I have to confess that my immersion in theological topics for over forty years, especially when the aim is to try to formulate my own position, has been a risky undertaking. After all, from one point of view, theology —a constant dwelling on how much one can say about God and about His Revelation—tends to engender a kind of know-all attitude at the worst and an unwholesome concentration on the particularism of a people and the individual at the best. Inevitably, thoughts on Judaism and the role of the Jewish people tend to crowd out the wider views regarding God's over-arching providence. Paradoxically, even when discussing the notion of self-annihilation, attention is drawn to the self that is annihilated. There is no way out for anyone who takes theology seriously except to have a sense of proportion or, better, a sense of the ridiculous. He has to remind himself constantly of the comical aspects of the whole exercise. I do not pretend that my efforts have been without presumption, but can only excuse my arrogance by saying that it goes with the theological job; a job, incidentally, to which I was never appointed. I simply grew into it. And, to be honest, there were also political implications in the whole 'Jacobs Affair'.

There is another point I have to make here. Although I have argued, against the genetic fallacy, that origins are not important and that it is what religious institutions came to be that matters, I do not believe that such an attitude justifies *everything* that has come down to us in the Jewish tradition. Once one acknowledges that all Jewish institutions have had a history, which we can now trace to a large extent, one is entitled—I would say duty-bound—to be selective in determining which practices are binding, because of their value for Jewish religious life today, and which have little or no value. The philosophy of revelation through the people cannot be made to justify every practice seen by Orthodoxy as the 'word of God', since, according to this way of looking at things, the 'word of God' has itself been modified and suffered dynamic change through teachers in all ages applying, consciously or unconsciously, the idea of value, as I have tried to show in my book *A Tree of Life*. I have always tried to speak of a quest, since there are whole areas in which complete certainty is not to be had, once one has abandoned fundamentalism but retained a sense of loyalty to the full tradition. How far can one go in adjusting the tradition to modernity? How should one go about effecting a correct balance between the results of scholarly investigation and religious commitment? If it be granted that, on our understanding, God has revealed His will *through* the Jewish people and not only *to* them, what is the role of modern Jews in the process? Which kind of change is helpful to our religious strivings and which destructive, and what are the criteria by means of which the distinction is made? Is the tradition fair to women and, if it is not, how should greater justice be achieved? These and many similar questions still await their solution, and it is the kind of solution that can only be found if a sufficient number of traditional Jews are prepared to affirm that we have a questing tradition and that the search for Torah is itself Torah.

Obviously, my whole approach has been strongly influenced by the Conservative movement in the USA. I would like here to elaborate a little on how I found myself becoming increasingly attracted to this movement. Once I had been introduced to the critical historical method by my teacher, Dr Siegfried Stein at University College, I began to read Zechariah Frankel, a thinker who, Dr Stein suggested, could serve as a guide for contemporary Jews, loyal to the tradition, but non-fundamentalist in outlook. I entertained at one time the notion of writing my doctoral dissertation on Frankel, and read a good deal by him and on him, supplemented, especially, by the writings of Solomon Schechter and Mordecai Kaplan. It was my friend Wolfe Kelman, at that time serving as a temporary replacement for the rabbi at the Reform Synagogue in Upper Berkeley Street, who introduced me to the Conservative movement. Wolfe provided me with a wealth of literature on the movement and eventually urged me to become a member of the Rabbinical Assembly of America, which I did. To this day, I do not know whether Wolfe arranged this, but much was made of the fact that I was the thousandth member of this body. Although my synagogue, the New London, was, and still is, an Orthodox synagogue (in the older Anglo-Jewish sense in which the term is used), it was so close to Conservative Judaism that it became affiliated to the body of Conservative congregations known as the World Council of Synagogues. When, as an arm of Conservative Judaism, the Masorti movement was established in Israel, a similar Masorti movement was started here, which today has several affiliated synagogues.

And yet, for all my acknowledgement of the influence of Conservative Judaism on my thinking, and indeed, on my whole life as a Jew, I admit to a certain unease with attempts at modelling Masorti in the UK on the American style. For one thing, Conservative Judaism in the USA arose in reaction to radical Reform in that great country and was, at first, identified with Orthodoxy of a moderate kind. In fact, at one stage in the development of 'American' Orthodoxy, there was serious talk of a merger between the Jewish Theological Seminary and the Isaac Elhanan Seminary for the training of Orthodox ministers. In the UK, on the other hand, there was, at first, no need to conserve Judaism since Orthodoxy, again of a moderate kind, was the norm. It can perhaps be put in this way: in nineteenth-century America, if you wanted to be 'American' you had to be a Reform Jew, whereas to be an 'English' Jew at that time you had to be Orthodox.

To this day there is much talk in the USA of American Judaism. The problem there of adaptation to Western mores concerns, in reality, American mores. While admiring the tremendous contributions to Jewish life and thought made by residents of that highly influential community, neither all the problems nor all the solutions over there are necessarily suitable for Anglo-Jewry. Many of us in this country would not think so much in terms of Anglo-Jewry but of a universal Jewry and Judaism as a whole, albeit seen from an Anglo-Jewish perspective. There is the further point that if one speaks of a *quest* it is hardly suitable to abandon the search for authenticity by adopting positions that have already hardened and have thus been given by others, no matter how eminent. In the language of tradition, each person has his or her portion in the Torah. I believe that a degree of eclecticism is required in which the good, seen to some extent in a personal way, is adopted from all the movements in Jewish life, provided that this does not result in contradiction; to avoid such contradiction is precisely the purpose of the quest. Many of us see both the strength and weakness of Orthodoxy in its certainties in all matters, and the strength and weakness of Reform in its openness in all matters. You cannot have complete openness without anarchy, as you cannot have complete certainty without fundamentalism.

I conclude this book with an anecdote told of Professor Ernst Simon which summarizes the stance I and many similar-minded Jews have adopted. Professor Simon, an observant but questing Jew, used to frequent a rudimentary Conservative synagogue in Jerusalem. Rabbi J. B. Soloveitchik, the leader of Modern Orthodoxy in the USA, asked Professor Simon why he preferred this type of synagogue to an Orthodox or Reform congregation. In the version I heard, Simon replied, 'First, I cannot claim to be Orthodox since I do not keep all the *dinim* [laws].

Secondly, I do not think one should keep all the *dinim*. But thirdly, while I can *daven* [pray] with the Orthodox I cannot talk to them, and while I can talk to the Reform I cannot *daven* with them. I need a congregation in which I can both talk to the other members and *daven* with them.' Exactly.

Glossary

aharonim 'Later ones': halakhic authorities who lived after the *Shulḥan arukh* (q.v.) was composed.

amora An authority cited in the Gemara (which, with the Mishnah (q.v.), forms the Talmud).

Ba'al Shem Tov 'Master of the Good Name', Israel ben Eliezer (*c.*1700–60), founder of the hasidic movement.

baraita (Aramaic; pl. *beraitot*) 'Outside'; statement of a *tanna* (q.v.) not found in the Mishnah (q.v.).

bat kol Heavenly voice, a divine communication.

beit din Court of Jewish law.

Beth Din See *beit din*.

daven (Yiddish) To pray.

dayan Judge in a *beit din* (q.v.).

dinim Halakhic rulings, concerning both civil and religious matters.

frum (Yiddish) Pious, scrupulous in observance of halakhah. See also *meshugga frum*.

gaon 'Excellency', title of the heads of the great colleges in Babylonia down to the eleventh century; later, title of any distinguished rabbi and talmudist.

Habad The Lubavitch hasidic movement; the term is an acronym of the three Hebrew words *ḥokhmah* (wisdom), *binah* (discernment), and *da'at* (intellect or knowledge), that express the Lubavitch philosophy.

halakhah Jewish law.

ḥamets Food containing fermented dough, forbidden on Passover.

Haskalah 'Enlightenment'; the movement which arose in the nineteenth century advocating the adoption of Western learning and culture.

ḥavruta 'Associate'; study partner in a yeshiva.

ḥazan Cantor.

ḥidushim Sometimes referred to as novellae, these are new ideas, and particularly new halakhic applications, derived from studying sacred texts; the exposition of such ideas lies at the heart of halakhic creativity.

imitatio dei (Latin) 'Imitation of God'.

Karaites Adherents of Karaism, a schismatic movement in Judaism (from the ninth century CE) which rejected rabbinic authority.

kasher 'Fit' to be eaten in accordance with the dietary laws (in popular usage, 'kosher').

kashrut Abstract noun meaning 'the concept of that which is kosher'.

kol be'ishah ervah 'The voice of a woman constitutes lewdness' for a man while he is engaged in prayer.

kolel An institution in which graduates of a yeshiva continue their talmudic study after marriage.

maskilim Followers of the Haskalah (q.v.).

Masoretic text Standard Hebrew text of the Bible.

melakhah 'Work' forbidden on the sabbath.

meshugga frum 'Madly *frum*'; term used in Anglo-Jewry to denote excessive piety.

Midrash (adj. **midrashic**) Body of rabbinic literature from the mishnaic and talmudic periods, containing homiletical expositions of biblical texts, sermons, and halakhic analyses of biblical texts; also the (continuing) activity of so treating biblical texts.

Midrash hagadol 'Great Midrash', a thirteenth-century compilation of early rabbinic texts on the Pentateuch.

mikveh (pl. *mikva'ot*) Ritual bath, used primarily by married women in order to purify themselves after menstruation, and in which proselytes immerse themselves on conversion to Judaism.

Mishnah First and most authoritative codification of halakhah (q.v.) found in the Oral Torah, dating from the early third century CE.

mitnagedim 'Opponents' of the hasidic movement in the eighteenth and nineteenth centuries.

mitsvah (pl. *mitsvot*) Religious precepts or commandments.

muktsah Items such as money, tools, and electrical equipment that should not be handled on the sabbath.

musar 'Instruction'; self-scrutiny with the aim of character improvement, hence the nineteenth-century Lithuanian *musar* movement.

nevelah 'Carcass'; an animal that has not been killed by *shehitah* (q.v.).

Peshitta Early Syriac translation of the Bible.

pilpul Talmudic dialectics; sometimes used to denote excessive casuistry.

Pirkei avot 'Ethics of the Fathers'; title of a tractate in the Mishnah (q.v.).

posek (pl. *posekim*) One who renders decisions in Jewish law.

Rabbanites Opponents of the Karaites (q.v.), faithful to the rabbinic tradition.

rebbe (Yiddish) Title of a hasidic master, used to distinguish him from a traditional rabbi.

rosh yeshivah (pl. *rashei yeshivah*) Principal of a yeshiva.

Sadducees First-century movement in Judaism which, among other things, denied retribution after death and rejected the authority of contemporary (pharasaic) rabbis.

semikhah Rabbinic ordination.

sheheḥeyanu (lit. 'Who has kept us alive'); a reference to the benediction recited when something new is done, whether in the absolute sense (e.g. wearing new clothes) or in the cyclical sense (e.g. celebrating a religious festival anew each year, eating a new fruit at the start of its season).

sheḥitah The traditional Jewish method of killing animals for food.

shiurim Lectures given in a yeshiva or elsewhere on traditional Jewish sources or topics.

shtetl (Yiddish) Small town in eastern Europe.

shtiebel (Yiddish) 'Little room'; in practice, a little room functioning as a small synagogue for prayer and study, usually in a private house.

Shulḥan arukh The authoritative code of Jewish law compiled by Joseph Karo in the sixteenth century, with glosses by Moses Isserles (1525/30–1572).

Sifra Halakhic Midrash (q.v.) on Leviticus.

Sifre Halakhic Midrash (q.v.) on Numbers and Deuteronomy.

talmid ḥakham Talmudic scholar.

tanna (pl. *tannaim*) An authority cited in the Mishnah (q.v.).

Targum 'Translation'; Aramaic translation of Pentateuch.

terefah Food forbidden by the dietary laws.

Tosefta 'Addition'; collection of tannaitic *beraitot* (q.v.), arranged according to the order of the Mishnah.

tsadik (pl. *tsadikim*) Righteous person; leader of a hasidic group.

yarmulke Skullcap worn by Jewish men when praying or studying, and at all times by the more pious among them.

zuz A small coin.

Bibliography

ABRAHAM BEN ZE'EV NAHUM BORNSTEIN OF SOCHACZEW, *Eglei tal* [Pietrikow, 1905] (New York, 1968).

AHAD HA'AM (Asher Ginzberg), *Essays, Letters, Memoirs*, trans. and ed. L. Simon (Oxford, 1946).

ALON, GEDALYAHU, 'The Lithuanian Yeshivot', trans. Sid Z. Leiman, in Judah Goldin (ed.), *The Jewish Expression* (New Haven, Conn., 1976), 452–68.

ALTMANN, ALEXANDER, *Essays in Jewish Intellectual History* (Hanover, NH, 1981).

BETTAN, ISRAEL, *Studies in Jewish Preaching: Middle Ages* (Cincinnati, Oh., 1939).

BLEICH, J. DAVID, *Contemporary Halakhic Problems*, 4 vols. (New York, 1977–95).

—— *With Perfect Faith* (New York, 1983).

BLOCH, JOSEPH LEIB, *Shiurei da'at*, 3 vols. (Tel Aviv, 1953).

BLUM, RAPHAEL, *Birkot shamayim* (New York, 1971).

BONFIL, ROBERT, *Rabbis and Jewish Communities in Renaissance Italy* (London, 1993).

BUCKSBAUM, J. (ed.), *Sefer hazikaron for Rabbi Y. Abramsky* (Jerusalem, 1978).

CARMELL, ARYEH, and DOMB, CYRIL (eds.), *Challenge: Torah Views on Science and its Problems* (Jerusalem, 1978).

CASSUTO, UMBERTO, *The Documentary Hypothesis*, trans. Israel Abrahams (Jerusalem, 1941).

—— *A Commentary on the Book of Genesis*, trans. Israel Abrahams (Jerusalem, 1944).

—— *A Commentary on the Book of Exodus*, trans. Israel Abrahams (Jerusalem, 1951).

COHEN, A., *The Teachings of Maimonides* (London, 1947).

—— *Everyman's Talmud* (London, 1949).

COHON, SAMUEL S., *Jewish Theology* (Assen, 1971).

The Condition of Jewish Belief: A Symposium Compiled by the Editors of 'Commentary' Magazine (repr. Northvale, NJ, 1989).

CORDOVERO, MOSES, *The Palm Tree of Deborah* [*Tomer devorah*], trans. Louis Jacobs (London, 1960).

—— *Elimah rabati* (Brody, 1881).

CRAIG, WILLIAM LANE, and SMITH, QUENTIN, *Theism, Atheism and Big Bang Cosmology* (Oxford, 1995).

DESSLER, E. E., *Mikhtav me'eliyahu,* ed. Aryeh Carmel, 4 vols. (Jerusalem, 1983).

DINUR, BENZION, 'Wissenschaft des Judentums', *Encyclopaedia Judaica* (Jerusalem, 1972), xvi. 570–84.

DOV BAER OF MEZHIRECH, *Magid devarav leya'akov,* ed. Rivka Schatz-Uffenheimer (Jerusalem, 1976).

DRESNER, SAMUEL H., *The Zaddik* (New York, 1960).

DROSNIN, M., *The Bible Code* (London, 1997).

EICHENSTEIN, TSEVI HIRSCH, *Hakdamah vederekh le'ets haḥayim* [Lemberg, c.1832]; repr. with commentary by Tsevi Elimelekh of Dynów as *Sur mera va'aseh tov* [Lemberg, 1840] (Munkacz, 1901); trans. and annotated by Louis Jacobs as *Turn Aside from Evil and Do Good: An Introduction and a Way to the Tree of Life* (London, 1995).

ELIADE, MIRCEA (ed.), *The Encyclopaedia of Religion,* 16 vols. (New York, 1987).

ELIMELEKH OF LYZHANSK, *No'am elimelekh* [Lemberg, 1788]; ed. G. Nigal, 2 vols. (Jerusalem, 1978).

EPSTEIN, ISADORE, *The Faith of Judaism* (London, 1956).

EPSTEIN, KALONYMUS KALMAN, *Maor vashemesh* (Tel Aviv, 1965).

FEINSTEIN, MOSHE, *Igerot moshe: Oraḥ ḥayim, Yoreh de'ah* (Benei Berak, 1981).

FINKELMAN, SHIMON, and SCHERMAN, NOSSAN, *Reb Moshe: The Life and Ideals of HaGaon Rabbi Moshe Feinstein* (Brooklyn, NY, 1986).

—— and WEISS, YOSEF, *The Manchester Rosh Yeshivah: The Life and Ideals of HaGaon Rabbi Yehudah Zev Segal* (Brooklyn, NY, 1997).

FISHMAN, TALIA, 'Shaking the Pillars: 'Voice of a Fool', an Early Modern Jewish Critique of Rabbinic Culture* (Stanford, Ca., 1977).

FLEW, ANTONY, *God and Philosophy* (London, 1966).

FORTA, ARYE, 'Progressive Orthodoxy: A Direction for the Future', *Le'ela,* 44 (Oct. 1997), 33–8.

FRANKEL, ZECHARIAH, *Darkhei hamishnah,* ed. I. Nussbaum (Tel Aviv, 1923).

FRIEDLANDER, M., *The Jewish Religion* (London, 1900).

FRIEDMAN, RICHARD ELLIOT, *Who Wrote the Bible?* (San Francisco, Ca., 1989).

GERZ, M., 'The Old Man of Slabodka', in Lucy Dawidowicz (ed.), *The Golden Tradition: Jewish Life and Thought in Eastern Europe* (London, 1967), 179–85.

GILLMAN, NEIL, *The Death of Death* (Woodstock, Vt., 1997).

GINZBERG, LOUIS, *Students, Scholars and Saints* (Philadelphia, Pa., 1928).

GOLDMAN, ROBERT N., *Einstein's God: Albert Einstein's Quest as a Scientist and as a Jew to Replace a Forsaken God* (Northvale, NJ, 1997).

GOODBLATT, DAVID, *Rabbinic Instruction in Sassanian Babylon* (Leiden, 1975).

GRADE, CHAIM, 'My Quarrel with Hersh Rassayner', trans. Milton Himmelfarb, in Irving Howe and Eliezer Greenberg (eds.), *A Treasury of Yiddish Stories* (London, 1956), 579–609.

GROSS, S. K., *Shevet hakehati* (Jerusalem, 1967).

HABERMAN, JOSHUA O., *The God I Believe In* (New York, 1994).

HANOKH OF ALEKSANDROW, *Ḥashavah letovah* [Pietrikow, 1929] (repr. Jerusalem, 1992).

HARRIS, MICHAEL, 'An Inventory of Modern Orthodox Beliefs', *Le'ela*, 43 (Apr. 1997), 20–2.

——, FORTA, ARYE, and NEWMAN, ARYEH, 'Modern Orthodoxy: The Debate Continues', *Le'ela*, 45 (Apr. 1998), 33–7.

HASMAN, JUDAH LAIB, *Or yahel* (Jerusalem, 1938).

HAYIM IBN ATAR, *Or haḥayim* [Venice, 1741]; 2 vols. (Jerusalem, n. d.).

HEILMAN, SAMUEL C., *Defenders of the Faith: Inside Ultra-Orthodox Jewry* (New York, 1992).

HELLER, YOM TOV LIPMANN, *Tosafot yom tov*, on the Mishnah (Warsaw, 1882).

HELMREICH, WILLIAM B., *The World of the Yeshiva: An Intimate Portrait of Orthodox Jewry* (New York, 1982).

HERTZ, J. H., *The Pentateuch and Haftorahs* (London, 1950).

HIRSCH, EMIL G., 'Asceticism', *Jewish Encyclopaedia* (New York, 1901), ii. 165–9.

HIRSCH, SAMSON RAPHAEL, *The Collected Writings*, 5 vols. (New York, 1988).

HOROVITZ, DAVID, 'Busting the Bible Code Breakers', *The Jerusalem Report*, 4 Sept. 1997, pp. 14–18.

HOROWITZ, ISAIAH BEN ABRAHAM HALEVI, *Shenei luḥot haberit* [Amsterdam, 1648]; 2 vols. (Jerusalem, 1963).

HURWITZ, PINHAS ELIAH, *Ta'am etso*, commentary on Ricchi's *Mishnat ḥasidim* (Jerusalem, 1982).

HUSIK, ISAAC, *A History of Mediaeval Jewish Philosophy* (Philadelphia, Pa., 1958).

HUXLEY, JULIAN, *Religion without Revelation* (London, 1957).

IBN EZRA, ABRAHAM, Commentary on the Pentateuch.

ISSERLES, MOSES, *Torat ha'olah* (Königsberg, 1854).

JACOB JOSEPH OF POLONNOYE, *Toledot ya'akov yosef* [Koretz, 1780] (repr. Jerusalem, 1966).

JACOBS, LOUIS, *We Have Reason to Believe* (London, 1957; 4th edn., London, 1995).

—— *Montefiore and Loewe on the Rabbis* (London, 1962).

—— *Principles of the Jewish Faith* (London, 1964; new edn., Northvale, NJ, 1988).

—— *Faith* (London, 1968).

—— *A Jewish Theology* (London, 1973).

—— 'The Relationship between Religion and Ethics', in Gene Outka and John P. Reeder (eds.), *Religion and Morality: A Collection of Essays* (Garden City, NY, 1973), 155–72.

—— *Theology in the Responsa* (London, 1973).

—— *Hasidic Thought* (New York, 1976).

—— 'Eating as an Act of Worship in Hasidic Thought', in S. Stein and R. Loewe (eds.), *Studies in Jewish Religious and Intellectual History Presented to Alexander Altmann on the Occasion of his Seventieth Birthday* (Birmingham, Ala., 1979), 157–66.

—— *A Tree of Life* (Oxford, 1984; rev. edn. forthcoming).

—— *Helping with Inquiries* (London, 1989).

—— *The Jewish Religion: A Companion* (Oxford, 1995).

—— *Jewish Mystical Testimonies* (new edn., New York, 1996).

JOSEPH, MORRIS, *Judaism as Life and Creed* (London, 1903).

JUDAH HEHASID, *Perushei hatorah*, ed. I. S. Lange (Jerusalem, 1975).

KADUSHIN, MAX, *The Rabbinic Mind* (New York, 1965).

KATZ, DOV, *Pulemos hamusar*, 4 vols. (Jerusalem, 1958).

—— *Tenuat hamusar*, 5 vols. (Tel Aviv, 1958).

KAUFMANN, YEHEZKEL, *The Religion of Israel*, trans. and abr. Moshe Greenberg (London, 1961).

KELLER, CHAIM DOV, 'Modern Orthodoxy: An Analysis and a Response', in Reuben P. Bulka (ed.), *Dimensions of Orthodox Judaism* (New York, 1983), 253–71.

KERSHEN, ANNE J., and ROMAIN, JONATHAN, *Tradition and Change: A History of Reform Judaism in Britain 1840–1995* (London, 1995).

KOHLER, KAUFMANN, *Jewish Theology* (new edn., New York, 1968).

KOOK, ABRAHAM ISAAC, *Orot hakodesh*, 2 vols. (Jerusalem, 1938).

Kovets zikaron for Rabbi Y. Abramsky (Benei Berak, 1977).

KROCHMAL, NAHMAN, *Moreh nevukhei hazeman* (Lemberg, 1851).

LAMM, NORMAN, *Torah Umadda: The Encounter of Religious Learning and Worldy Knowledge in the Jewish Tradition* (Northvale, NJ, 1990).

—— and WURZBURGER, WALTER S. (eds.), *A Treasury of Tradition* (New York, 1967).

LANDAU, DAVID, *Piety and Power: The World of Jewish Fundamentalism* (London, 1993).

LANDAU, EZEKIEL, *Noda biyehudah* (Jerusalem, 1969).

LEIBOWITZ, NEHAMA, *Studies in the Book of Genesis* (Jerusalem, 1972).

LERNER, BEREL DOV, '*Omphalos* Revisited', *Jewish Bible Quarterly*, 23 (1995), 162–7.

LEVANON, A. Z., 'The Yoke of the Kingdom of Heaven' (Heb.), in D. Weinberger (ed.), *Hasaba mislabodka* (Brooklyn, NY, 1987), 65–8.

LEVI, AMNON, *Haharedim* (Jerusalem, 1988).

LEVI, YEHUDAH, *Sha'arei talmud torah*, 2nd edn. (Jerusalem, 1982).

LEVI YITSHAK OF BERDITCHEV, *Kedushat levi* (Jerusalem, 1964).

LEVINE, EPHRAIM, *The History of the New West End Synagogue 1879–1929* (London, 1929).

LEVINGER, JACOB S., *Concepts of Judaism* (Jerusalem, 1974).

Leviticus rabbah, ed. M. Margulies (Jerusalem, 1972).

LEWIN, B. M., *Otsar hageonim: Gittin* (Jerusalem, 1941).

LIPSHÜTZ, ISRAEL, *Tiferet yisrael*, commentary on the Mishnah (Hanover, 1830–51).

LUZZATTO, MOSES HAYIM, *Mesilat yesharim* [Amsterdam, 1740]; with English trans. by Mordecai M. Kaplan as *The Path of the Upright* (Philadelphia, Pa., 1936).

MAHLER, RAPHAEL, *A History of Modern Jewry 1780–1815* (London, 1971).

MAIMONIDES, MOSES, *Mishneh torah* (*Yad hahazakah*) (Warsaw, 1882).

—— *Sefer hamitsvot* (Warsaw, 1883).

—— *The Guide of the Perplexed*, trans. M. Friedlander (London, 1881); trans. Shelomo Pines (Chicago, Ill., 1963); trans. J. Kapah (Heb.) (Jerusalem, 1971).

MASHASH, JOSEPH, *Mayim hayim*, 2 vols. (Jerusalem, 1985).

MATTHEWS, W. E., *The Purpose of God* (London, 1935).

Mekhilta, ed. I. H. Weiss (Vienna, 1865).

Midrash hagadol: Leviticus, ed. A. Steinsaltz (Jerusalem, 1975).

MILLER, AVIGDOR, *Rejoice O Youth!* (New York, 1962).

MODENA, LEON DA, *Kol sakhal,* ed. I. S. Reggio (Gorizia, 1852).

MONTEFIORE, C. G., and LOEWE, H., *A Rabbinic Anthology* (London, 1938; new edn., with a preface by Raphael Loewe, New York, 1974).

MOORE, GEORGE FOOT, *Judaism,* 3 vols. (Cambridge, Mass., 1958).

MOSHE HAYIM EPHRAIM OF SUDYLKOW, *Degel mahaneh efrayim* [Koretz, 1810] (Jerusalem, 1963).

NADLER, ALLAN, *The Faith of the Mithnagdim* (Baltimore, Md., 1997).

NAHMAN OF BRATSLAV, *Likutei moharan* (Warsaw, 1808–11).

NAMPORT KEY, *A Lay of the Battle of New West End* (London, 1892).

NEUSNER, JACOB, *The Rabbinic Traditions about the Pharisees Before 70* (Leiden, 1971).

New West End Synagogue, *Report on the Sabbath Readings of the Scriptures in a Triennial Cycle* (London, 1913).

PADGETT, ALAN G. (ed.), *Reason and the Christian Religion: Essays in Honour of Richard Swinburne* (Oxford, 1994).

PELI, PINHAS, 'Asceticism', *Encyclopadia Judaica* (Jerusalem, 1972), iii. 677–80.

PERL, JOSEPH, *Megaleh temirin* (Vienna, 1819).

PLATO, *Laws,* ed. R. G. Bury (Cambridge, Mass., 1926).

PLAUT, W. GUNTHER, *The Growth of Reform Judaism* (New York, 1965).

RABBINOVICZ, RAPHAEL, *Dikdukei soferim* (Brooklyn, NY, 1875).

RICCHI, IMMANUEL HAI, *Mishnat hasidim* [Cracow, 1889] (Jerusalem, 1982).

ROSENBLUM, YONASON, *Reb Yaakov: The Life and Times of HaGaon Rabbi Yaakov Kemenetsky* (Brooklyn, NY, 1993).

ROSSI, AZARIAH DEI, *Meor einayim,* ed. D. Cassel (Warsaw, 1899).

ROTH, CECIL, *The Jews of Italy* (Philadelphia, Pa., 1946).

ROTH, LEON, *The Guide for the Perplexed: Moses Maimonides* (London, 1948).

SA'ADYA GAON, *Sefer ha'emunot vehade'ot,* trans. S. Rosenblatt as *Beliefs and Opinions* (New Haven, Conn., 1948).

SARACHEK, JOSEPH, *Faith and Reason: The Conflict over the Rationalism of Maimonides* (New York, 1935).

SCHECHTER, SOLOMON, *Aspects of Rabbinic Theology* (New York, 1961).

SCHOLEM, GERSHOM, *Major Trends in Jewish Mysticism,* 3rd edn. (London, 1955).

Sefer hazikaron for Rabbi I. Weiss (Jerusalem, 1990).

SEGAL, M. H., *The Pentateuch* (Jerusalem, 1967).

SHAW, STEVEN, 'Orthodox Reactions to the Challenge of Biblical Criticism', *Tradition*, 10 (Spring 1969), 61–85.

SHELOMO ZALMAN OF KOPUTS, *Magen avot* (Berditchev, 1902).

SHKOP, SIMEON, *Sha'arei yosher* (Warsaw, 1928).

SHNEUR ZALMAN OF LYADY, *Likutei amarim: Tanya* (Vilna, 1930).

Sifra, ed. I. H. Weiss (Vienna, 1862).

Sifre, ed. L. Finkelstein (New York, 1969).

SILVER, ABBA HILLEL, *Where Judaism Differed* (New York, 1956).

SINGER, SIMEON, *Authorised Daily Prayer Book* (London, 1890, and subsequent editions).

SOLOMON, NORMAN, *The Analytical Movement: Hayyim Soloveitchik and his Circle* (Atlanta, Ga., 1993).

SOLOVEITCHIK, J. B., *Ish hahalakhah* (Jerusalem, 1979); trans. Lawrence Kaplan as *Halakhic Man* (Philadelphia, Pa., 1983).

SORESKY, AARON, *Marbitsei torah umusar* (Brooklyn, NY, 1977).

SPINOZA, BENEDICT, *Tractatus Theologico-politicus* (Hamburg, 1670).

SPITZ, LEWIS S., 'Humanism', in Mircea Eliade (ed.), *Encyclopaedia of Religion* (New York, 1987), vi. 513.

STEINBERG, MILTON, *Anatomy of Faith* (New York, 1980).

STERN, NATHAN, *The Jewish Historico-Critical School of the Nineteenth Century* (New York, 1910).

SUFRIN, A. E., 'Asceticism, Jewish', in James Hastings (ed.), *Encyclopaedia of Religion and Ethics* (Edinburgh, 1908), ii. 97–9.

SWINBURNE, RICHARD, *The Existence of God* (Oxford, 1979).

TISHBY, ISAIAH, *The Wisdom of the Zohar*, 3 vols. (Oxford, 1989).

TRANI, MOSES DI, Commentary on *Perek shirah*, *Beit elohim* [Venice, 1576] (Warsaw, 1872).

TSEVI ELIMELEKH OF DYNÓW, *Derekh pikudeikha* [Lemberg, 1851] (Jerusalem, n.d.).

URBACH, EPHRAIM, *Ḥazal* (Jerusalem, 1969); trans. as *The Sages: Their Concepts and Beliefs* (Jerusalem, 1979).

VIDAS, ELIJAH DE, *Reshit ḥokhmah* [Amsterdam, 1708] (Jerusalem, 1984).

VITAL, HAYIM, *Mevo she'arim*, ed. J. L. Ashlag (Tel Aviv, 1961).

WARDI, CHAIM, 'Pico della Mirandola, Giovanni', *Encyclopaedia Judaica* (Jerusalem, 1972), xiii. 500–1.

WEINGREEN, J., *Introduction to the Critical Study of the Text of the Hebrew Bible* (Oxford, 1982).

WEISS, J. G., 'The Question of Religious Problems in the Doctrine of R. Nahman of Bratslav' (Heb.), in the Schocken Festschrift, *Alei ayin: Minḥat devarim leshelomo salman shoken* (Jerusalem, 1948–52), 245–91.

WERTHEIMER, JACK (ed.), *Tradition Renewed: A History of the Jewish Theological Seminary of America* (New York, 1997).

WINSTON, DAVID, *Philo of Alexandria* (London, 1981).

WITZUM, DORON, and RIPS, ELIYAHU, *Hameimad hanosaf* ('The Additional Dimension') (Jerusalem, 1989).

WOSNER, S., *Shevet halevi*, 2nd edn., 6 vols. (vols. i–v, New York, 1981–4; vol. vi, Benei Berak, 1986).

YELLIN, DAVID, and ABRAHAMS, ISRAEL, *Maimonides* (London, 1935).

YOM TOV ISHBILI (Ritba), *Ḥidushei haritba* on *Eruvin*, ed. M. Goldstein (Jerusalem, 1980).

ZEVIN, S. J., *Sefarim vesoferim*, 3 vols. (Tel Aviv, 1959).

ZLOTOWITZ, MEIR (ed.), *The ArtScroll Commentary to the Book of Esther* (New York, 1977).

—— *The ArtScroll Commentary to the Book of Jonah* (New York, 1978).

ZOHAR, *see* Tishby, Isaiah.

Index

of rational precepts, reason for 109–10
see also Torah: evolution of; Torah:
fundamentalist view of origin; *Torah min hashamayim*
Ricchi, Immanuel Hai 210
Rips, Eliyahu 89–90
Ritba 73
ritual, reform of 7–9
Rosh Hashanah 124
sounding *shofar* on 124
Rossi, Azariah dei 32, 71, 210–11
Rubenstein, Richard 176
Ruth, as prototype of righteous proselyte 46

S

Sa'adya Gaon 108–10
on Creation 207
sabbath 126–9
kindling lights on 125, 127
prohibitions of rabbinic origin 126–7
references to in Pentateuch 126
Sacks, Chief Rabbi Jonathan 3, 17
sacrifices, prohibition on offering outside the Temple 44–5
Sadducees 41, 43
sages, the, see *ḥazal*
Salanter, R. Israel 134, 139–40
Samuel (3rd-cent. Babylonian teacher) 72, 212, 215
Sanhedrin 117
Schechter, Solomon 13, 168, 230, 238, 241
Schiller-Szinessy, Rabbi S. M. 166
Schneersohn, R. Menahem Mendel 203
Scholem, Gershom 187
Schor, R. Yitshak 222–3
Schwab, R. Simeon 138
science and belief 94–105
see also faith and reason
Scripture, interpretation of, see biblical criticism *and under individual books*
secular Judaism 174–84
Seer of Lublin 220
Segal, M. H. 86–7
Segal, R. Moshe Yitshak 159
Segal, R. Yehudah Zev 157

Septuagint 38
Alexandrian, influence of Greek philosophical background 42
sexual intercourse:
no benediction for 221
doctrine that pleasure for husband is disgraceful 220
hasidic view of purpose of 220
impossible without the 'evil inclination' 221
purpose of in rabbinic thought 219–20
Shammai, House of, *see* Hillel: House of
Shapira, R. Meir 145
Shavuot 121, 123–4, 192
Shaw, Steven 103–4
Shekhinah 186
Shema 201–2
fundamentalist and non-fundamentalist reasons for reciting 129–31
Shkop, R. Simeon 117–18, 136, 151–2
Silver, Abba Hillel 169, 215–18
Simeon bar Yohai, Rabbi 189, 191
Simhat Torah 123
Simon, Ernst 242–3
Singer, R. Simeon 6–7, 15
Society for the Study of Jewish Theology 11
Sofer, R. Moses 142–3
Solomon ibn Gabirol 206
Solomon, King 35, 60
authorship of Ecclesiastes, *see* Ecclesiastes, authorship of
Solomon, Norman 137
Soloveitchik, R. Hayim 134, 136, 140, 206
Soloveitchik, R. Joseph B. 206, 242
Song of Songs 21
Spektor, R. Yitshak Elhanan 140
Spielmann, Isidore 7
Spinoza, Baruch 35–6
explanation of Ibn Ezra 37–8
State of Israel:
attitudes to 148–9
and messianic process 148–9
secular Judaism in 179
Stein, Siegfried 187, 241